Arab background series

Editor: N. A. Ziadeh, Emeritus Professor of History,
American University of Beirut

What is Islam?

Second edition

W. Montgomery Watt

Longman London and New York
Librairie du Liban

LONGMAN GROUP LTD
London and New York

Associated companies, branches and representatives throughout the world

LIBRAIRIE DU LIBAN

First published 1968, Second edition 1979

ISBN 0 582 78302 X

Watt, William Montgomery
What is Islam?—2nd ed.—
(Arab background series).
1. Islam
I. Title II. Series
297 BP50

ISBN 0-582-78302-X

*Printed in Great Britain by Butler and Tanner Ltd.
Frome and London*

Contents

Editor's Preface

The Arab World has, for some time, been attracting the attention of a growing public throughout the world. The strategic position of the Arab countries, the oil they produce, their sudden emancipation and emergence as independent states, their revolutions and *coups d'etat*, have been the special concern of statesmen, politicians, businessmen, scholars and journalists, and of equal interest to the general public.

An appreciation of the present-day problems of Arab countries and of their immediate neighbours demands a certain knowledge of their geographical and social background; and a knowledge of the main trends of their history—political, cultural and religious—is essential for an understanding of current issues. Arabs had existed long before the advent of Islam in the seventh century AD, but it was with Islam that they became a world power. Arab civilization, which resulted from the contacts the Arabs had with other peoples and cultures, especially after the creation of this world power, and which reached its height in the ninth, tenth and eleventh centuries, was, for a few centuries that followed, the guiding light of a large part of the world. Its rôle cannot, thus, be ignored.

The Arab Background Series provides the English-speaking, educated reader with a series of books which attempt to clarify the historical past of the Arabs and to analyse their present problems. The contributors to the series, who come from many parts of the world, are all specialists in their own fields. This variety of approach and attitude creates for the English-speaking reader a unique picture of the Arab World.

N. A. ZIADEH

Foreword

I should like in the first place to thank the editor of the series and the publishers for inviting me to write this general book on Islam for the Arab Background Series. At the same time I may call the attention of readers to the fact that certain aspects of Islamic life, notably jurisprudence and mysticism, have been dealt with briefly, since they are to be treated more fully in other volumes of the series. I trust, however, that the contribution of these aspects to the whole has been sufficiently indicated. The translations of the Qur'ān are normally those of Professor A. J. Arberry from *The Koran Interpreted* (London, Allen and Unwin, 1955), and I should like to thank Messrs Allen and Unwin for permission to use them. I have also to thank Mr Alford T. Welch and Miss Helen A. Pratt for compiling the Index of Topics and that of Proper Names and Arabic Words respectively.

The University,
Edinburgh,
December, 1967

W. MONTGOMERY WATT

Acknowledgements

We are grateful to the following for permission to reproduce copyright material:

George Allen & Unwin Ltd and Macmillan Co. for extracts from *The Koran Interpreted* by A. J. Arberry, Copyright 1955 by Allen & Unwin Ltd; Oxford University Press for extracts from *On Heroes, Hero Worship and the Heroic in History* by Thomas Carlyle; Uppsala University for extracts from *Studies In Arabian Fatalism* by Helmer Ringgren.

Introduction
The nature of the inquiry

On Friday, 8 May 1840, Thomas Carlyle delivered a public lecture in Edinburgh on Muḥammad and Islam. It was the second of a series 'On Heroes, Hero-worship and the Heroic in History', and had the particular title 'The Hero as Prophet'. Carlyle had no special qualifications as Arabist or Islamist for lecturing on this subject, and yet the lecture has an important place in the development of Islamic studies in Europe, since here for the first time in a prominent way was it asserted that Muḥammad was sincere and the religion of Islam basically true. Carlyle frankly admits that he has chosen Muḥammad as the prophet 'we are freest to speak of', and by this he doubtless means that he can attempt to reconstruct in imagination the inner experience of Muḥammad without being limited by considerations of theological propriety, as would have been the case had he chosen a biblical prophet. We in turn may admit that for much of the lecture Muḥammad is simply a tag on which to hang Carlyle's own thoughts about human life. We may smile at some of his grandiloquence:

> Ah no: this deep-hearted Son of the Wilderness, with his beaming black eyes and open social deep soul, had other thoughts in him than ambition. A silent great soul; he was one of those who cannot *but* be in earnest; whom Nature herself has appointed to be sincere.[1]

Yet just because of the nature of his aims Carlyle had boldly to face the great difficulty confronting any European, indeed any occidental student of Muḥammad and Islam.

The difficulty is that we are the heirs of a deep-seated prejudice which goes back to the 'war propaganda' of medieval times. This is now coming to be widely recognized, and recent studies have indicated the steps in the formation of the European image of Islam and the motives underlying the selection of points for special emphasis.[2] From about the eighth century A.D. Christian Europe began to be conscious of Islam as her great enemy, threatening her in both the military and the spiritual sphere. In deadly fear Christendom had to bolster confidence by placing the enemy in the most unfavourable light possible, consistent with some genuine basis in fact. The image created in the twelfth and thirteenth centuries continued to dominate European thinking about Islam, and even in the second half of the twentieth century has some vestigial influence. According to this image Islam was a perversion of Christian truth, even an idolatrous religion; it was a religion of violence, spread by the sword; it was a religion without asceticism, gaining adherents by pandering to their sexual appetites both in this world and in the world to come. Muḥammad was a deliberate propagator of false doctrines, thinking only of increasing his own power. In 1697 an English ecclesiastic in a scholarly work referred to him as 'a wicked impostor' and 'the old lecher'.[3] Nearly a century later Edward Gibbon in the *Decline and Fall* summed up his opinion of Muḥammad's character in the words that he 'indulged the appetites of a man and abused the claims of a prophet'.

Carlyle was aware of the strength of this image and inveighed against it.

> Our current hypothesis about Mahomet, that he was a scheming Imposter, a Falsehood incarnate, that his religion is a mere mass of quackery and fatuity, begins really to be now untenable to anyone. The lies, which well-meaning zeal has heaped round this man, are disgraceful to ourselves only.[4]

He insisted that such conceptions ultimately made nonsense of the world view of those who held them.

> The word this man spoke has been the life-guidance now of a hundred-and-eighty millions of men these twelve-hundred years. . . . Are we to suppose that it was a miserable piece of spiritual legerdemain, this which so many creatures of the Almighty have lived by and died by? I, for my part, cannot form any such supposition. . . . One would be entirely at a loss what to think of this world at all, if quackery so grew and were sanctioned here.

It would be tedious to add further quotations in this vein, or to insist further on the points made. Yet we should not allow ourselves to forget that we are not yet wholly freed from the entail of the past, so that, in order to understand the being of Islam, it is well for us to follow Carlyle's plan in studying Muḥammad: 'I mean to say all the good of him I justly can; it is the way to get at his secret.'

Prejudice is only one of the difficulties to be met by the European or American student of Islam. As soon as he begins to describe Islam as 'the religion of the Qur'ān' or 'the religion of the six hundred million Muslims of today', he introduces a category which does not fit, the category of 'religion'. For what does 'religion' now mean to the occidental? At best, for the ordinary man, it means a way of spending an hour or so on Sundays in practices which give him some support and strength in dealing with the problems of daily life, and which encourages him to be friendly towards other persons and to maintain the standards of sexual propriety; it has little or nothing to do with commerce or economics or politics or industrial relationships. At worst it fosters an attitude of complacency in the more prosperous individuals and breeds smugness. The European may even look on religion as an opiate developed by exploiters of the common people in order to keep them in subjection. How different from the connotations to the Muslim of the verse (3.19/17): 'the true religion with God is Islam'! The word translated 'religion' is *dīn*, which in Arabic commonly refers to a whole way of life. It is not a private matter for individuals, touching only the periphery of their lives, but something which is both private and public, something which permeates the whole fabric of society in a way of which men are conscious. It is—all in one—theological dogma, forms of worship, political theory, and a detailed code of conduct, including even matters which the European would classify as hygiene or etiquette. If this is how the Muslim sees the *dīn* of Islam, how is it to be described to the European?

The difficulty just considered merges into another. The views of both the ordinary Muslim and the ordinary Christian on the nature of religion (or *dīn*) differ from the scientific observer's conception of the function of religion in society. There is of course no agreement among the scientific observers and theorists—the sociologists. There are those who would claim to hold on scientific grounds that religion is always an opiate, rendering men complacent about social injustice. This appears, however, to be a generalization based on a limited range of data taken from recent European history. Most of those who have studied religion on a wider scale have allowed it a positive function, even if they do not go so far as Emile Durkheim who considered that 'religious ideas are collective ideas which represent collective realities'.[5] There appears to be something exceptional about the place of religion in the contemporary occident. It certainly has often the appearance of being peripheral, and may really be so. Because of this there is necessarily an element of prejudice in the ordinary occidental man's conception of religion, whether he is religious or irreligious. To counter this prejudice, and to try to find a common approach for occidental and Muslim, this book will adopt the methodological standpoint of sociology, though not the doctrines of any sociological school.

The precise view of religion towards which this book moves is close to that of Durkheim. Religion is held to have an important function in the life of society; it may be said to enable a society to become aware of itself and of its own deepest nature. Religion does this by providing a basic plan into which are integrated all the activities of the society, economic, social, intellectual. In the higher religions this basic plan is expressed in a system of ideas or a world view, which may be contained in lengthy scriptures (such as the Bible or Qur'ān). The religious world view, however, though it should be in accordance with the current scientific world view, is not of the same type, since it is inseparably linked with religious practice in such a way that it is often difficult to say which is primary—that is, whether a practice is based on a previously known world view or whether a previously approved practice is subsequently justified by the assertion that the world has such a character.

For the centre or core of a world view I shall use the word 'vision'; the advantages of this usage will be explained in Chapter 1. In general it will be found that the Islamic vision permeates and 'informs' the whole life of society and of individuals in the Islamic world. This does not mean that the vision or religious belief absolutely determines the whole of life, for there are various aspects which have a relative autonomy; but it exercises a certain control or pressure on the whole. Such a conception of the function of religion is closer to the Muslim conception of *dīn* than to the usual occidental conception; but it places more emphasis on the central core.[6]

Yet another difficulty in answering the question arises from the existential nature of the question. Much of the book will be historical, yet it is not primarily a historical study. It is addressed to the question, What *is* Islam?, and Islam is a contemporary fact. Moreover, just as you cannot say what a baby—another contemporary fact—is without taking into account what it is capable of becoming, you cannot say what Islam is without considering its potentialities. Whatever our view of the place of religion in modern life, whether we think it peripheral, harmful or central, our personal attitudes are likely to be upset by the fact of Islam. It is a commonplace that we are moving into a condition of what some have called 'inter-religion'; by that they mean a world in which the adherents of the various great religions are mingling with one another on an unprecedented scale. Because our world has become 'one world' in certain external ways, there are pressures making for the dominance of a single religion, and several religions may be said to be striving for the position of the 'one religion'. Islam is one of the contestants, a serious rival of Christianity and humanism. By the year 2000 most of Africa is likely to be under its sway, and it is growing in South-east Asia. When it threatens our conception of our 'religion' in the world (whether that 'religion' be Christianity, humanism, Marxism or some other), and so threatens our conception of ourselves, how shall we be able to judge it objectively and assess its potentialities?

Perhaps Thomas Carlyle was not a bad guide after all, though he used his imagination lavishly. He was trying to find in the particularities of Islam that which is common to all men. He saw Muḥammad and his followers wrestling with the universal destiny of man, the need to realize something of value in our transient lives, and to do so in a world of suffering, pain, injustice, frustration, as well as of joy and achievement. The word *islām* is properly a verbal noun meaning 'the surrendering of oneself' (*sc.* to God), and Carlyle expands this in his own way.

> . . . and then also '*Islam*', That we must *submit* to God. That our whole strength lies in resigned submission to Him, whatsoever He do to us. For this world, and for the other!

He quotes a saying of Goethe, 'if this is *Islam*, do we not all live in *Islam*?' Then he further expands:

> It has ever been held the highest wisdom for a man not merely to submit to Necessity,—Necessity will make him submit,—but to know and believe well that the stern thing which Necessity had ordered was the wisest, the best, the thing wanted there. To cease his frantic pretension of scanning this great God's-World in his small fraction of a brain; to know that it had verily, though deep beyond his soundings, a Just Law, that the soul of it was Good. . . . A man is right and invincible, virtuous and on the road towards sure conquest, precisely while he joins himself

to the great deep Law of the World, in spite of all superficial laws, temporary appearances, profit-and-loss calculations; he is victorious while he cooperates with that great central Law, not victorious otherwise:—and surely his first chance of cooperating with it, or getting into the course of it, is to know with his whole soul that it *is*: that it is good, and alone good! This is the soul of Islam; it is properly the soul of Christianity. . . . Christianity also commands us, before all, to be resigned to God.[7]

Since we occidentals tend to emphasize the aspect of inner experience in religion, we are more likely to appreciate Islam if we began where Carlyle began. We shall then see Islam as expressing a vision of the world and of life not very different from that of Christianity and Judaism. The differences will be chiefly due to a different social background and different categories and connotations of language. We shall be able to look on Islam as a religion from which we have something to learn (as Carlyle assuredly learnt). From this we shall be able to go on to appreciate Islam as being more than a 'religious' factor in the narrow occidental sense. We shall see it as a mighty force in world affairs, which, because it was despised by French politicians, had a large share in bringing to nought one hundred and thirty years of French effort and travail in Algeria. As we look to the future we shall know that, precisely because of the inner aspect which Carlyle emphasized, Islam is capable of making important contributions—how important we cannot estimate yet—to a just and stable ordering of the 'one world'.

Part 1

The vision which came to Muḥammad

Chapter 1

The nature of the vision

1. The heart of a religion

In the nineteenth century it was commonly assumed that to discover what a thing *is* you look at its earliest, original form. This was convenient in a period of rapid change, when radical adjustments had to be made and many old forms abandoned; a custom or rite of which reformers disapproved could easily be ridiculed by asserting that it was *really* just a piece of primitive savage life. It is now realized, we hope, that this is like saying Shakespeare is really just a baby because he was once a baby. Shakespeare is not just a baby grown up, and the great world religions of today are not just primitive savagery in a more sophisticated dress. If we would know what religions are we must look at them in their highest manifestations.

If we are asked what the difference is between Buddhism, Hinduism, Islam and Christianity, we may point to their official set of dogmatic beliefs. Yet this seems to be somewhat superficial, and we feel there is some more fundamental or essential difference. The difference is deeper than these verbal formulations, something at the very heart of the religion. It is this heart or central core of a religion that I mean to indicate when I use the word 'vision'. A religion's vision is its way of looking at the world and dealing with the world; it is its basic answer to the question, 'What is life and how is it to be lived?' The theoretical and practical sides of both question and answer are inseparable, for they are complementary one to the other. Perhaps in speaking of vision we tend to think chiefly of the theoretical aspect, and this is not misleading, provided we remember that theory is not separate from practice. My answer to the question 'What is life?' is not a proper answer unless I am living it as well as thinking it.

The vision of any religion, say the Buddhist vision, is not to be identified with its theological or philosophical formulations. These are indeed an expression of the vision, but the vision itself is both simpler and deeper. The vision is not exhausted by the formulations any more than a landscape, or a painting of a landscape, is exhausted by a description in words. The formulations are certainly an indication of the distinctive character of the vision, but they are made or selected in a special way with a view to the edification of the community. The sociologist or student of the history of religion can often indicate more briefly what is distinctive in a vision; and this is often advantageous for his purposes. Thus it could be said that Islam looks on this world as absolutely controlled by a power which though strict and stern is good and favourable towards men, so that when a man submits to this power his life is satisfactory; moreover the satisfactory character which it is possible for a human life to have somehow transcends space and time. For some purposes the historian of religion might find this sufficient, though for other purposes he would require a fuller description and possibly one with a different emphasis.[1]

There is no necessary contradiction between brief descriptions of this kind and the official intellectual formulations of belief. Both are true, but true 'diagrammatically'. This conception of the 'diagrammatic' character of religious ideas may be explained briefly, since I have expounded it elsewhere.[2] It has long been recognized that in religious contexts it is often necessary to understand words in a metaphorical or analogical sense. Unfortunately in recent times this has come to have a certain connotation of unreality, in that what is only metaphorically true is felt to be not quite true. To avoid this connotation I suggest the term 'diagrammatic'. If we consider a map or diagram, we know that the object represented is not shown as it really is. A map of a town or country is never a replica of it. Yet, within the limits of scale, colouring, etc., the map shows certain features or aspects of the town or country with absolute truth. A map is constructed for certain limited purposes, say, to show the roads from town to town. It fulfils this function perfectly (assuming it is a good map) so long as we observe the conventions, and do not, for example, expect that a road marked red on the map will actually have a red surface. We may think of a map as a special kind of complex diagram, or a diagram as a very simple map.

Many religious ideas are diagrammatic in this way. They indicate by a kind of convention certain features of the universe and of human life, and they do so in order to enable men to live well.

This function the ideas fulfil perfectly so long as men observe the conventions. Part of the convention is to understand that a phrase like 'the hand of God' or 'the face of God' does not imply a body with bones, flesh, blood and other features of human bodies. Another part of the convention is to understand that the function of such ideas is limited. Taken in the proper way they enable men to live well; but it is not part of their purpose to satisfy man's curiosity to have a fuller theoretical knowledge of the universe. Muslim theologians were aware of this problem, and many of them insisted that anthropomorphic terms applied to God were to be taken *bi-lā kayf* ('without how'), that is, without specifying the precise manner (literally, metaphorically, etc.) in which they were to be taken. We might put this in another way and say that a man may make adequate practical responses to the set of ideas of which the phrase 'the hand of God' is a part, although he is unable to express this set of ideas in other language. What appear to be alternative expressions—for example, the scholar's brief description of a religion and the official formulation of its beliefs—are not exact equivalents, but are diagrams constructed on different principles and for different purposes, though both are expressions of the same vision.

Implicit in what has just been said is the distinction between the vision or way of looking at the universe and the verbal or intellectual expression of this vision. It further follows from this distinction that it is possible to have an intellectual knowledge of the expressions of the vision in words and ideas without fully sharing in the vision, that is, without looking at the world in this way. Of those who fully share the vision one might say that they 'enter into' it, or that they 'make it their own', or that they appreciate the values contained in it. All these are ways of insisting that a religious vision is more than intellectual knowledge, and requires to be accepted as a basis for living. This may also serve to explain how a vision may fade; it would seem to be possible for most of the adherents of a religion to become content with a purely intellectual apprehension of its ideas without 'entering into' the vision.

Since a vision is a way both of looking at the world and of dealing with it, it also follows that a vision is always something that has to be lived out. This means that it has to be 'embodied' in the life both of individuals and of society as a whole, since man is a social animal. Some of the quotations from Thomas Carlyle may have suggested that embodiment in the life of the individual is the primary thing and that embodiment in the life of society is secondary and a consequence. This is not wholly so, however, and the individualistic emphasis comes chiefly from the nineteenth century. One of the earliest *sūras* of the Qur'ān (106) calls on the tribe of Quraysh which inhabited Mecca to thank God for their prosperity. Where the vision fades, it may be that men have to begin again from the grass roots of an individualistic experience; but this will not be widely applicable unless it applies in the first place to the individual in the context of his society; and then it is certain in the long run to lead to social embodiment.

This conception of vision enables us to give a neat definition of the purpose of worship, namely, as the revival or renewal of vision. This is in accordance with Durkheim's statements that 'the real function of religion . . . is to make us act, to aid us to live', and that worship in its external form 'is a collection of the means by which this [*sc.* the faith] is created and recreated periodically'.[3]

2. The vision in its dependence

During the nineteenth century scholars became very keen on questions of literary or historical dependence, and more generally on tracing the ancestry of ideas and practices. This vogue doubtless had something to do with the prominence attained by Darwin's evolutionary theories, and the widespread belief that if you could point to the source or origin of anything you knew what it really was. This scholarly procedure was sometimes abused and made the basis of a depreciatory judgment on what the scholar disliked. Thus it was sometimes stated or implied that the Qur'ān was a poor selection of ideas from the Bible, and that Arabic philosophy was an unworthy stepchild of Greek. Such judgments were naturally objected to by Muslims. They are moreover a misunderstanding or misrepresentation of what has been discovered. To learn about the literary ancestry of, say, *Hamlet*, and the sources from which Shakespeare derived the bare bones of the story, is interesting and leads to insights of various kinds; but it does not show us wherein the greatness of *Hamlet* lies. In other words, studies of sources and origins satisfy our intellectual curiosity and show us something of the mechanisms which play a subordinate part in literary creativity, but the essential creative work of genius eludes such studies. Let us, then, taking the Qur'ān as a fresh irruption into man's intellectual world, try to restate its relation to previous thought.

The Islamic vision (which is contained in the Qur'ān) came to one of the citizens of Mecca about the year A.D. 610 and was shared by him with some of his fellow-citizens. Now we know something about the intellectual outlook of the Meccans at this time, partly from things said or implied in the Qur'ān, partly from pre-Islamic Arabic poetry, and partly from the stories about Muḥammad and his Companions. There are difficulties about all these sources of information. The Qur'ān is contemporary evidence, but is sometimes difficult to interpret; it is sometimes difficult to know if the pre-Islamic poetry is genuine, though much of it certainly is; and the stories about Muḥammad often reflect the outlook of the first and second Islamic centuries. Despite these difficulties our conception of the intellectual outlook of Mecca about 610 is sound in its general outline. This outlook had as its core the view of the world developed by the Arabs as a result of their experiences as nomads in the desert. To this was added a body of Jewish, Christian and Persian ideas, which had come to the Meccans in various ways. There were Jewish settlements in several districts of Arabia, such as Medina and Khaybar. Christian influences came to them by many channels: some Meccans had made trade journeys to Syria and had been in touch with officials and probably also monks; the Yemen had been under an Ethiopian Christian government for about half of the sixth century, and Meccan traders had been there and perhaps also to Ethiopia; and Christianity was spreading among several nomadic tribes. Arabia was in touch with Persia through the Lakhmid rulers of al-Ḥīra (on the frontier between the desert and the cultivated area of Iraq) and had derived much from its material and intellectual culture.

As a result of these various influences the world view of the Meccans was something of an amalgam. Though there were still many shrines of pagan deities in Arabia, and these were frequented by the common people, the Meccans, like other leading men in Arabia, did not seriously believe in such deities. Abū-Sufyān is said to have taken images of the goddesses al-Lāt and al-'Uzzā into battle against the Muslims at Uḥud, but this was doubtless to raise the morale of the common people. The Meccans knew that Christians and Jews worshipped a single supreme deity, God (*al-lāh*, 'the god' in Arabic), and some of them were attracted by monotheism. In the early seventh century, however, to become a Christian or Jew had political implications. Christianity had a close connection with the Byzantine and Ethiopian empires, while Judaism had a looser connection with the Persian. In order to keep their trade between Persian Yemen and Byzantine Syria the Meccans were virtually forced to remain neutral (though under constant pressure to adhere to one side or the other). It is therefore not surprising that few Meccans became Christians. Those who were most dissatisfied with the existing religious vacuum are said to have been looking for a pure monotheism, presumably one without political strings attached. The attitude of many is best described as 'vague monotheism' in the sense that, while they were inclined to believe in a supreme deity, they had no corresponding cult practices and did not consider their belief incompatible with some acknowledgment of the beings represented by idols.

In the Mecca of about 610 there was also a deep-seated social malaise, which is to be traced above all to the change from a nomadic to a mercantile economy. The ancestors of the Meccan merchants had been nomads only a generation or two back, for it seems to have been only in the second half of the sixth century that the trade of Mecca grew to sufficient proportions to support a large population. One of the consequences of mercantile success was that the entrepreneurs became conceited and individualistic. They came to think that wealth and the power it gave conferred on them control over practically all events. At the same time their sense of solidarity with their clan was seriously weakened; many of them were clan chiefs, but they began to neglect the traditional duty of clan chiefs to look after the poor and unfortunate. Mecca in 610 was very prosperous. The standard of living for all was rising, but at the same time the gap between rich and poor was increasing. Among those who were deeply dissatisfied were many of the sons and younger brothers of the richest men. Muḥammad's clan of Hāshim, which had once been in the forefront of Meccan enterprise under his grandfather 'Abd-al-Muṭṭalib, seems relatively to have lost ground in the three decades before 610; and Muḥammad himself as a posthumous child had an inferior position in his family until his talents gained the favour of a wealthy woman, Khadīja, who became his first wife.

This, in broad outline, was the world into which the Islamic vision came.[4] The message of the Qur'ān was a message for men who had an intellectual outlook of this kind and were facing these social tensions. It follows that the message had to be formulated in terms of this intellectual outlook if they were to understand it, and also had to be relevant to the social situation in which they found themselves. From this standpoint the biblical materials in the Qur'ān can be seen in a new light. They are not part of the fresh irruption which is the Islamic vision, but part of the milieu in which this vision is to be embodied. If the Qur'ān may be regarded as the solution of a spiritual problem, then the biblical materials in it are part of the problem, not of the solution. Or perhaps it would be more accurate to say that, in so far as the Meccans were trying to solve their problems by a 'vague monotheism', these biblical materials are part of that not too successful attempt at solution. The same might be said of certain Arabic materials in the Qur'ān such as the stories of the prophets Hūd and Ṣāliḥ; the theological interpretation given to these stories may well be at least in part pre-Islamic.

Current occidental studies of literary ancestry and dependence are in fact studies of the precise manner in which something novel is continuous with the past. In all mundane phenomena there is inevitably an element of continuity, even where there is also prominent discontinuity. The fact that we are, possibly for good reasons, chiefly interested in the new irruption or element of discontinuity is no reason for denying or neglecting the element of continuity. It is not so much the Qur'ān itself as a certain trend in later Muslim scholarship which exaggerates the discontinuity.

3. The vision in its originality and novelty

We are provisionally considering the Islamic vision as a fresh irruption from beyond human consciousness into the intellectual world of man. Yet according to the Qur'ān itself, although its scriptures in their totality may be described as an irruption, the essential message is not a novelty.

> We have revealed to thee as We revealed
> to Noah, and the Prophets after him,
> and We revealed to Abraham, Ishmael,
> Isaac, Jacob and the Tribes,
> Jesus and Job, Jonah and Aaron
> and Solomon, and We gave to David
> Psalms,
> and Messengers We have already told thee of
> before, and Messengers We have not told thee of. . . . (4.163/164f.)

This is usually taken to mean an essential similarity in the messages, though not complete identity. The nature of the similarity is further illustrated by those *sūras* where there is a collection of passages about previous prophets.[5] In general there is a pattern repeated throughout the stories, with variations only in secondary details. As an example the stories of Noah and 'Ād in *sūra* 7 may be taken.

> And We sent Noah to his people;
> and he said, 'O my people, serve God!
> You have no god other than He;
> truly, I fear for you the chastisement
> of a dreadful day.'
> Said the Council of his people, 'We see thee
> in manifest error.'
> Said he, 'My people, there is no error
> in me; but I am a Messenger from
> the Lord of all Being.
> I deliver to you the Messages
> of my Lord, and I advise you
> sincerely; for I know from God
> that you know not.' . . . (59/57–62/60)
>
> And Ad to their brother Hood;
> he said, 'O my people, serve God!
> You have no god other than He;
> will you not be godfearing?'
> Said the Council of the unbelievers
> of his people, 'We see thee
> and we think that thou art
> one of the liars.'
> Said he, My people, there is no folly
> in me; but I am a Messenger from
> the Lord of all Being.
> I deliver to you the Messages
> of my Lord; I am your adviser
> sincere, faithful. . . . (65/63–68/66)

The only similarity in the message here is the assertion of the existence of God, though there are similarities in the attitude of the prophet's people to him, in their fate and in his final vindication. This is the view commonly found in the Qur'ān about the relation of the Qur'ān to previous messages, namely, that there is an identity in essentials but not in detail. Another way of expressing the relation is to say that the Qur'ān is a confirmation (*taṣdīq*) of the previous messages (e.g. 10.37/38). Thus the Qur'ān is both a fresh irruption and at the same time a repetition in essentials of an older message.

This way of looking at the matter is difficult for the modern occidental, even when he admits the basic identity of the Jewish, Christian and Islamic visions. The difficulty arises from the occidental awareness of historicity—of historical connections and the nature of historical evidence. Since he regards Judaism, Christianity and Islam as all stemming from the experience of Abraham, it is convenient to speak of the three visions as forms of a single Abrahamic vision. Moreover there is considerable historical continuity between Judaism and Christianity, despite the fresh irruption of Jesus; and the occidental tends to hold that there is at least a slight measure of continuity between the two older forms of the Abrahamic vision and the youngest. There were Jews and Christians in Arabia in Muḥammad's time; indeed Khadīja's cousin, Waraqa ibn-Nawfal, who lived in Mecca, is said to have been a Christian. We must further suppose that the Jewish and Christian visions had not completely faded in the Arabian environment, but that Waraqa and others like him had 'entered into' them to some small extent. An interesting question is whether Muḥammad himself had to any significant degree 'entered into' these visions. If, as seems likely on general grounds, he had done so, this would not prevent the distinctive Qur'ānic teaching from being a fresh irruption, any more than Jesus's appreciation of contemporary Jewish religion reduced his originality.[6] Something like this was suggested in the previous section when remnants of previous 'solutions' were said to be part of the milieu in which the new Qur'ānic solution had to be embodied. Another way of putting it would be to regard the Islamic vision as 'taking into itself' something of the older visions.

Whatever we may say about the forms of the single Abrahamic vision and their relation to one another, it is the particularity of the Islamic vision which is important; and this means the adaptation of the Abrahamic vision to the thought world of the Meccans and the social problems of their town. Details of the Meccan and Arabian reference of the Qur'ānic teaching will be mentioned throughout the next few chapters, and need be only briefly mentioned here. Thus the assertion of God's existence with its implication of man's dependence on him corrects the pride and undue self-reliance of the Meccan tycoons. The doctrine of the Last Day constitutes a sanction exerting pressure on these same men when their individualism made them neglect the duty of providing for unfortunate kinsmen. The insistence on the functions of the prophet made a stable political order possible in Medina. In general it might be held that the values of Islam come from its combining the insights gained as nomads with the insights of the Abrahamic vision.

Ultimately we cannot isolate the vision from its embodiment in history. Any attempt to express the vision briefly may be diagrammatically true, but the briefer the expression (and the simpler the diagram) the more is omitted of the life-giving qualities of the vision. To have a full and rich appreciation of the Islamic vision one must, if one is not a Muslim, have a wide familiarity with the historical embodiment, and know how multitudes of our fellow men found inspiration and guidance in the Islamic vision as they wrestled with the deep problems of living common to all of us.

4. The source of the vision

The discussions of the previous sections have brought us near the heart of the difficulty about the Qur'ān. How can an occidental who believes in God but is not a Muslim attach some meaning to the doctrine that the Qur'ān is the revealed Speech of God? By speaking of 'the Islamic vision' I have tried to soften the difficulty, and to exclude the former crude European view that Muḥammad deliberately preached ideas he did not himself believe in order to gain political power and sensual gratification. I have also provisionally used the phrase 'fresh irruption' in order to present various aspects of the problem before attempting a solution.

We may begin by considering the actual process by which Muḥammad received the Qur'ān. About the external aspects there can be little dispute. From the time when he considered himself called to be a prophet passages presented themselves to Muḥammad at frequent intervals (with the exception of one longer interval near the beginning). The passages varied in length, some being no more than a dozen or two words. It seems that Muḥammad himself began to collect the passages together in *sūras*, but the final arrangement was made by a committee of scholars during the reign of the caliph 'Uthmān (644–56). It also seems likely that from time to time Muḥammad received revised versions of certain passages; some verses were certainly said to be abrogated. Despite the care with which the 'Uthmānic recension was made, variant readings continued to exist or made their appearance, until about 900 seven sets of these were accepted as equally canonical.

For the internal aspect of the process of receiving the passages or 'revelations' which were collected to form the Qur'ān as we have it, the following passages are important:

> It belongs not to any mortal that
> God should speak to him, except
> by revelation, or from behind
> a veil,
> or that He should send a messenger
> and he reveal whatsoever He will
> by His leave. . . . (42.51/50–1)

> Truly it is the revelation of
> the Lord of all Being,
> brought down by the Faithful Spirit
> upon thy heart, that thou mayest be
> one of the warners. . . . (26.192–4)

The 'manners' (*kayfiyyāt*) of revelation indicated here—(? direct) revelation (*waḥy*), from behind a veil, and by sending a messenger (who may be angel of Spirit)—are expanded in the Traditions (or collections of anecdotes about Muḥammad); and later scholars made lists of from five to ten different 'manners'. Thus Muḥammad is reported to have said: 'Sometimes it comes to me like the reverberation of a bell, and that is the hardest on me; then it leaves me and I have understood what he (? God) said; sometimes the angel takes the form of a man for me and I understand what he says.' His favourite wife 'Ā'isha also recounted how, when the revelation came down on him on a very cold day, his forehead ran with perspiration.[7] This experience, however, was presumably exceptional, and the most usual 'manners' were doubtless those mentioned in the Qur'ān. References to the Spirit, to angels, and latterly to Gabriel (e.g. 2.97/91) are probably to be understood as an explanation rather than a description; that is to say, Muḥammad did not have any vision of an angel, but simply found the words in his heart somehow, and eventually came to regard this as occurring by the operation of Gabriel.

One of the words used for revelation is *waḥy*, and this came to be the most usual in the doctrinal discussions of later centuries. Richard Bell carefully examined the uses of this word in the

Qur'ān, non-technical as well as technical, and on this basis tried to say something more precise about the inner form of Muḥammad's experience.[8] While his account may be roughly correct, it is not convincing in detail; he places too much weight on the word *waḥy*, and neglects another word used more frequently, *nazzala* or *anzala*. It is safest to conclude that no detailed reconstruction of Muḥammad's inner experience can be more than conjectural, but it appears to be certain that he considered himself able to distinguish between revelation and the product of his own consciousness.

The precise manner of the revelation, however, is less important than what may be called its cosmological character. Thomas Carlyle has various attempts to express this:

A messenger he, sent from the Infinite Unknown with tidings for us. . . . Direct from the Inner Fact of things;—he lives, and has to live, in daily communion with that. . . . It is from the heart of the world that he comes; he is portion of the primal reality of things.

The man's words were not false, nor his workings here below; no Inanity and Simulacrum; a fiery mass of Life cast-up from the great bosom of Nature herself.

The Word of such a man is a Voice direct from Nature's own heart.[9]

The latest English translator of the Qur'ān has given a testimony which may be quoted in this context.

This task [*sc.* the translation] was undertaken, not lightly, and carried to its conclusion at a time of great personal distress, through which it comforted and sustained the writer in a manner for which he will always be grateful. He therefore acknowledges his gratitude to whatever power or Power inspired the man and the Prophet who first recited these scriptures.[10]

The very imprecision of these expressions is a mark of the difficulty of the problem.

If we start by thinking of Muḥammad's reception of the Qur'ān as analogous to the activity of genius by which Shakespeare wrote *Hamlet*, we immediately see there is a difference. *Hamlet* may indeed be said to contain a vision of life; but it does not include a set of ideas that are capable of becoming the basic ideas of the world view of millions of men. This is one of the facts about the Qur'ān of which we must not lose sight. Muḥammad's central ideas, his vision, have proved adequate to guide the lives of millions; and, while most of the millions may have been at or below average, countless thousands have made (so far as we can tell) a very good job of this business of living which is common to them and to us. It is the particularity, too, of the Islamic vision which has achieved this, and it would be unrealistic to say that the achievement is due to the common Abrahamic element.

The problem for the occidental is thus seen to be one of finding how to express several truths at once without becoming involved in contradiction. We have to allow a large measure of truth to the Islamic vision, not merely for what it has achieved in the lives of Muslims, but also for what we ourselves may learn from it. At the same time we cannot fully accept the standard Islamic view that the Qur'ān is wholly true and the criterion of all other truth; for in the strictly historical field we cannot hold that the Qur'ān may override the usual canons of historical evidence. The solution of this problem would appear to be most likely of attainment through some expansion of the diagrammatic conception of truth. Other points have to be taken into consideration, however, in finding a consistent formulation of those mentioned, so that the whole operation properly belongs to the province of theology and cannot usefully be discussed further here.

Finally a personal word may be in order. Critics of my books on Muḥammad have accused me of not stating my views clearly. Presumably they meant that I did not state a view obviously concordant with their own, or else one they could easily denounce as false. I may have fought shy of a decision, but the matter is difficult when one is writing for a great variety of readers who will understand the key concepts in many different ways. May I put my position as follows? I am not a Muslim in the usual sense, though I hope I am a *muslim* as 'one surrendered to God'; but I believe that embedded in the Qur'ān and other expressions of the Islamic vision are vast stores of divine truth from which I and other occidentals have still much to learn.

Chapter 2

Man dependent and limited

1. The pre-Islamic experience of man's dependence

In an interesting section of *A Study of History* (iii. 7–22) Arnold Toynbee has spoken of nomadism as a *tour de force* in response to the challenge of recurring and increasing desiccation. At an earlier stage, when the herds of wild animals decrease, the hunter leaves the steppe and becomes a cultivator in the oases, and while in this stage learns to tame and domesticate certain animals.

> And now, when the rhythmic process of desiccation, in its next onset, has made life still more difficult in the oases, and more difficult on the Steppe *a fortiori*, the patriarchs of the Nomadic Civilization audaciously return to the Steppe in order to wring out of it, now, no mere subsidiary supply but their entire livelihood—and this under climatic conditions under which the hunter and cultivator alike would find life on the Steppe quite impossible. The Nomad grapples with the arid Steppe in the strength of his new-found pastoral art; but, in order to practise this art successfully under these exceedingly exacting conditions, he has to develop a special skill; and, in order to exercise this skill, he has also to develop special moral and intellectual powers (12 f.).

These conclusions are based mainly on studies of nomadism in Central Asia, but they appear to be true in a general way of Arabia. Many of the Arab tribes of Muḥammad's time had memories of how their ancestors of a century earlier had abandoned an agricultural life in the Yemen and taken to the desert. The chief difference from Central Asia seems to be that in the mountainous area of south Arabia there was a large rainfall and an elaborate system of irrigation, so that it was not an oasis culture in the main. The decline of agriculture, too, may not have been due to a change of climate; traditionally, it was caused by the breakdown of the irrigation system (symbolized by 'the dam of Ma'rib'); and this in turn may have been the result of a lower level of general prosperity brought about by a decline in the commerce on which that prosperity rested.

Something is known about the manner of life and the outlook of the nomadic Arabs from the old Arabic poetry and the stories of desert life contained in the commentaries on this poetry. In general, life was extremely hard, and there were numerous failures, partial or complete. A group of nomads might become too small to support itself and would either disappear or come under the protection of a stronger group into which it might eventually be absorbed. To maintain a tribe successfully in the desert was only possible where there was a high level of human excellence and no serious run of ill-luck. Arnold Toynbee emphasizes this moral factor.

> . . . the Nomad patriarch cannot wrest victory out of this annual economic campaign without exercising—and exacting from the human beings and animals under his patriarchal authority—those virtues of forethought and self-control and physical and moral endurance which a military commander exercises, and exacts from his troops, when Man is at war with Man and not with Physical Nature.
>
> Thus the material *tour de force* of Nomadism demands, from those who take the responsibility on their shoulders, a rigorously high standard of character and behaviour. They must combine the pastoral with the military virtues. They must know, by sure intuition, when to be benevolent and when to be severe; when to be prudent and when to be prompt in action (14).

It might perhaps be added that this deliberate return to the harsh conditions of the desert is probably made only by those who already have certain qualities of character, such as a love of freedom.

While much of what was valuable in the nomadic Arab outlook has been taken into the central core of Islam and there transformed, there would also appear to be matters which have been given an Islamic dress without any fundamental change. Thus there is a belief, put into Muḥammad's mouth in different forms, that four things are decided for a human being while he is still an embryo in the womb. According to one version Anas ibn-Mālik reported of the Prophet that he said, 'God has entrusted an angel with the womb. . . . When God wills to complete the forming of it [the embryo], the angel says, "O Lord, male or female? wretched or happy? what is its food (*rizq*)? what is its term-of-life (*ajal*)?" These points are written down while it is in the body of its mother.'[1] Although the existing form of this story necessarily belongs to the Islamic period, there is some justification for taking it as an indication of the ways in which a nomadic Arab felt his life to be limited. Of the four points mentioned the first is the most dubious, since there are apparently no references in poetry to the uncertainty of the sex of a child. There is in the Qur'ān, however, considerable attention paid to the growth of the embryo in the womb; and if this represents a wide contemporary interest in the matter, the uncertainty of the sex might also have been noticed. The second and fourth points may be fully documented from poetry, and the third is present by implication, though not mentioned explicitly. A verse of the poet 'Alqama, for example, is translated thus:

And he who is destined to be fed with booty wins it on the day of plundering whithersoever he goes; and he who is withheld from it [*sc.* by Fate] gets nothing.[2]

The angel's question 'wretched or happy?' must in pre-Islamic times have referred to the general character of a man's destiny in this life. In the desert this, like the date of his death and even his food, clearly depended on forces beyond his control. So much might depend on a chance encounter in the middle of the desert. If a man had been an hour earlier or later at a particular point, or if his route had lain a mile or two to right or left, a catastrophic meeting might never have happened. Muhalhil, the brother of a great chief who had been murdered, ran into a young man called Bujayr in the open desert, learnt that he was a distant relative of the killer of his brother, and despite the remonstrances of his companions killed the young man; this initiated a disastrous war between the two important tribes of Bakr and Taghlib.[3] Such events are completely beyond human control, since, on the available information, the most careful planning and calculations can neither make them happen nor prevent them.

The nomad of the desert is confronted by the same incalculability in his quest for food. Where he lives from the proceeds of robbery, the chance encounter may play a large part. Such a remark as the following (from a theistic frame of reference) is not uncommon: 'As 'Urwa lay in wait, God bestowed on him a man travelling alone with his wife and camels; 'Urwa killed him and took the camels and the woman for himself.'[4] Even where the nomad lives solely from pasturing his camels his dominant experience in Arabia is not that of the regularity of nature but of its capricious irregularity. In the season of spring (*rabīʿ*) the nomads move to the tracts where luscious vegetation grows for a short time after the rains. This is part of the *tour de force* of nomadism, for the human beings gain all their requirements of liquid from the camels' milk, since the camels, though there are no wells, find sufficient herbage to provide liquid for themselves and their masters. Usually this is a happy time for all. It may happen, however, that in a particular year no rain falls in a certain valley, though twenty miles away on every side there is plenty; and those who frequent that valley must find their sustenance—if indeed they can find any—in some other way.

One of the most notable features of the pre-Islamic outlook, as reflected in the poetry, is that all these misfortunes are ascribed to an impersonal force, Time or Fate. Several Arabic words are used to express this. A common one is *dahr*, which properly means 'time' simply, though it is often used specially of 'time as determinant of events'; but the ordinary word for 'time' (*zamān*) is also found, and also phrases like 'the days' and 'the nights'. Several points are illustrated by the following verses:

O daughter of the good! verily, we are the bond-slaves of the changes of the days and the nights.

Time (*ad-dahr*) has made an onset and taken me as his object; and aforetime he was wont to cast his snares upon others like me. . . .

There is no marvel in what thou seest: but cause for wonder there is how fated ends (*ājāl*) overtake all on every side.[5]

There are also a number of words which appear to mean 'fate' rather than 'time', such as *maniyya*. The pagan view of the influence of Time (*dahr*) is described in the Qur'ān (45.24/23):

> They say,
> 'There is nothing but our present life;
> we die, and we live, and nothing but
> Time destroys us.'

This is in full accord with what is found in poetry. It is possible that this conception of time as the determiner of events is derived from the Persian conception of *zurvān*; but, even if this is the case, it is clear that the conception corresponded to a deep experience of the Arabs, and they may well have modified the ideas that came to them from outside in order to express what they themselves felt.

There is no evidence for any serious worship of Time or Fate among the Arabs. There is indeed a female deity called Manāt, whose name is related to *maniyya* and means something like 'fate'. Her worship, however, was nothing like so widespread as the references in the poems would require; moreover, her name is compounded with words meaning 'good fortune' and 'increase' (Sa'd-Manāt, Zayd-Manāt)[6] and may originally have meant 'providence' rather than 'fate'. In general the nomadic Arabs by Muḥammad's time had little respect for the idols and the cults connected with them. This was doubtless because idols and cults had originally belonged to an agricultural society, and were largely irrelevant to a nomadic one. One well-known story is that of the poet Imru'-al-Qays who consulted an idol (which gave answers by means of arrows) on whether to set out to avenge his father. When he received (some versions say, repeatedly) a negative answer, he broke the arrows and flung them in the face of the idol with the words, 'If it had been *your* father, you would have given a different answer.'[7] A somewhat similar story was told of the deity Sa'd (a sacred rock). A nomad brought his camels to graze near it to acquire its *baraka* (virtue, mana), but when they smelt the blood of animals sacrificed on it they fled in all directions. With an imprecation the nomad went in search of his camels, and on finding them made up verses ending: 'Is Sa'd aught but a rock . . . which neither misleads nor guides aright?'[8] While there was certainly a continuing belief in these primitive deities among many people, it is also clear from the stories that there was growing scepticism.

The effective religion of the nomads, in so far as they had not become Christians, is to be described rather as 'tribal humanism'.[9] By this is to be understood that what gives value and significance to a man's life is human excellence, manifested in the performance of deeds of nobility and generosity and the other virtues admired by the Arabs; but it was further held that the ability to do such deeds depended on coming from a good tribal stock. As it has been well expressed,

> all the virtues which enter into the Arabian conception of Honour were regarded not as personal qualities inherent or acquired, but as hereditary possessions which a man derived from his ancestors, and held in trust that he might transmit them untarnished to his descendants.[10]

This conception of the honour of the tribe was the centre round which the lives of these Arabs were organized, just as 'boastings' (*mafākhir*) about the nobility and excellence of the tribe were at the heart of many of the poems. The public recitation of the poems had thus a religious cult function, namely, to renew and keep alive men's belief in the honour of their tribe. For each individual the aim in life was to uphold and enhance the honour of the tribe within the narrow limits set for him by Time. His attitude to tribal honour, however, was not monolatrous. He might take part in cults at various shrines, and do so sincerely; but usually he seems to have expected from the deity a limited temporal favour, such as right guidance about a perplexing decision, or a measure of *baraka* (blessing) for a particular activity. In this way the pagan cults remained peripheral, while 'tribal humanism' was at the centre.

Finally, it should be noticed that belief in fate, as an acknowledgement that in certain respects strict limits, not known beforehand, are set to human life, can be a source of spiritual strength. Indeed some such belief is a necessity if men are to make a success of life in the desert. He who thinks by careful planning to avoid the disastrous possibilities he can conceive is bound to fail because of the anxiety engendered precisely by this planning and carefulness for the morrow. So the poets insist that planning to escape suffering and calamity is useless:

> He who (in flight) seeks refuge from the fearfulness of war
> is held back by his destined term.
> Not so! Death is there and swords are drawn
> before he slips away.[11]

Once this fact about human life in the desert has been fully accepted there comes a freedom of the spirit, because of which a man is likely to adopt the best possible course in an emergency.

> Go your way, walking without getting angry,
> until it becomes clear what the Allotter allotted to you.[12]

One of the things that makes this acceptance of unforeseeable fate, together with a carefree attitude, possible for the Arab is his belief that, whatever happens to the individual, the tribal stock is permanent.

> As though the Fates beating against us met
> a black mountain, cleaving the topmost clouds,
> strong and mighty above the changes of things,
> which no shock of Time (*dahr*) can soften or shake.[13]

Such, then, were the ways in which the nomadic Arabs acknowledged and dealt with the dependent and limited character of human life.

2. The continuance of pre-Islamic attitudes in the Qur'ān

In the previous section a Tradition about four things decided for every human being while an embryo in the womb was used as a clue to the pre-Islamic outlook. The four things were the sex of the child, its happiness or misery, its food and its term-of-life; and it was assumed that the mention of these matters in a Tradition was a continuation of the pre-Islamic outlook into Islamic times. In this book the occidental view is accepted, according to which the material in the Traditions does not necessarily come from Muḥammad himself; but in the particular matters mentioned there is much Qur'ānic evidence, even if the overall attitude of the Qur'ān is somewhat different.[14]

The conception of a predetermined term-of-life (*ajal*) is frequent in the Qur'ān.

> It is He who created you of
> clay, then determined a term
> and a term is stated with Him. . . . (6.2)

In another passage there is a reference to the danger of being diverted from God by possessions and children, and of finding, as one's term approaches, that further time is needed to set one's affairs in order. Such a person is imagined praying for deferment, but is given the stern reply: 'God will never defer any soul when its term comes' (63.11). Not only do human beings have a fixed term-of-life, but so also does every community or nation (*umma*), and 'when their term comes they shall not put it back by a single hour nor put it forward' (7.34/32). Even the sun and moon have each a term (35.13/14). The chief difference between the Qur'ānic and the pre-Islamic conceptions of the term-of-life is that the Qur'ānic is clearly said to be determined by God, whereas for the pre-Islamic poets it is simply a brute fact of life that each man has a term fixed for him somehow. The practical effect of this difference is slight. God observes the term which he has fixed and does not defer death; Time brings death to a man at his appointed term.

There is similarly a slightly more anthropomorphic tinge about the Qur'ānic conception of God as the bringer of death. In reply to the argument of the pagans that it is only time which destroys them, Muḥammad is told to say:

> God gives you life, then makes you die,
> then He shall gather you to the Day
> of Resurrection (45.26/25)

Several other verses speak of God as the giver of life and death, frequently adding also that he brings man to life again at the resurrection (e.g. 15.23). Not only death but also misfortune comes to man from God, or at least it is only by his permission that affliction befalls a man (64.11). In general the Qur'ān depicts human life as limited and uncertain in much the same way as the pagan poets:

> The likeness of this present life is as water that
> We send down out of heaven,
> and the plants of the earth mingle with it
> whereof men and cattle eat,
> till, when the earth has taken on its glitter
> and has decked itself fair,
> and its inhabitants think they have power over it,
> Our command comes upon it
> by night or day, and We make it stubble, as though
> yesterday it flourished not. (10.24/25)

There is perhaps a reference to the irregularity of rainfall in Arabia in such phrases as God's 'preferring some to others in provision (*rizq*)' (16.71/73). Even the description in the Traditions of how God's decisions are written down by an angel is to be found in the Qur'ān, at least to the extent that there is mention of a 'book' or something written.

> No affliction befalls in the earth
> or in yourselves, but it is in a
> Book, before We create it . . . (57.22)

> No female bears or brings forth, save with His knowledge;
> and none is given long life who is given long life
> neither is any diminished in his life, but it is in a Book. (35.11/12)

The latter quotation may be taken to include the predetermination of the sex of the child. In both these quotations it is clear that the reference is to something written down beforehand, but it is not always possible to distinguish in Qur'ānic passages between a 'book' of this type and the 'book' in which a man's deeds are recorded, as he does them, by an angel.

God's provision (*rizq*) for men is frequently mentioned explicitly in the Qur'ān, and also frequently implied. One instance may suffice:

> God is He that created you, then He provided for you,
> then He shall make you dead, then He shall give you life. (30.40/39)

Thus the 'provision' is all that is necessary to keep man alive, but the primary reference is to food and drink. This Qur'ānic emphasis on provision is in accordance with the Tradition about the four things predetermined for a man while he is an embryo, except that the provision is seldom said to be predetermined; instead it is spoken of (as in the verse quoted) as being given by God at the time at which the man receives it. There is no necessary contradiction here, of course, since God may act in accordance with what he has predetermined; the difference is one of emphasis. In either case, however, there is a contrast with the pre-Islamic attitude, where Time is regarded as causing the absence of food as much as its presence. In the Qur'ān God's provision is always a sign of his goodness and bounty, though he may be spoken of as stinting it (89.16). Indeed the very use of the word *rizq* in the sense of provision seems to be a mark of the new Qur'ānic attitude.[15]

In view of the quotation from 'Alqama above (p. 24) about those who were destined to be fed with plunder, one wonders whether God's provision for men in the Qur'ān can be taken to include plunder and booty. At a later date Muslims of the Mu'tazilite sect insisted that, since God is just, what a man gained by stealing could not be regarded as 'God's provision', but this may not have been Muḥammad's own outlook; and in any case plunder and booty were not normally regarded as wrongful gain. Such a phrase as 'journeying in the land seeking the bounty of God' (73.20), even though Muslims and occidentals now understand it of commerce, might originally have been applied to journeys from which the seeking of plunder was not excluded. The Mu'tazilite commentator az-Zamakhsharī (d. 1144), speaking of the word here translated 'journeying', says it may apply to journeys 'for commerce and other things'.[16] So it seems likely that plunder and booty were thought of as God's provision.

Where so much in the Qur'ān is very close to the pagan conception of Time, one is bound to ask whether God was not simply identified with Time. In support of an affirmative answer to this question one may quote the Tradition according to which Muḥammad reported that God said: 'The son of man insults me in blaming Time; I am Time; in my hands is the Command; I cause the alternation of day and night.'[17] There were certainly Muslim scholars, however, who objected to this identification and who tried to avoid it by a slight change of vowelling; by reading *ad-dahra* instead of *ad-dahru* the objectionable phrase could be taken to mean not 'I am Time' but 'I am for time', that is, 'I am eternal'.[18] Study of the Qur'ān as a whole makes it clear that the latter point of view is sound, even if to us the method of defending it appears to be dubious. There are important differences between the conception of God and the pagan conception of Time. They may be summed up in the assertions that God is good and that God will judge all men. The first of these points will be examined in the next section, and the other in the following chapter.

3. The 'signs' of God's power and goodness

It has been noticed by scholars[19] of the Qur'ān that there are many passages in it which recount 'signs' (*āyāt*) of God's power and beneficence. In what appear to be the earlier passages it is often one particular sign which is mentioned, but there are other passages where the more important signs are all mentioned together. A short passage of this kind is:

> It is God who created the heavens and the earth,
> and sent down out of heaven water
> wherewith He brought forth fruits to be your sustenance.
> And He subjected to you the ships
> to run upon the sea at His commandment;
> and He subjected to you the rivers
> and He subjected to you the sun and moon
> constant upon their courses,
> and He subjected to you the night and the day,
> and gave you of all you asked Him. (14.32–4/37)

The following longer passage conveys the general tone better:

> He created the heavens and the earth in truth . . .
> He created man of a sperm-drop . . . And the cattle –
> He created them for you; in them is warmth, and uses
> various, and of them you eat . . .

and they bear your loads unto a land that you
never would reach, excepting with great distress . . .
And horses, and mules, and asses, for you to ride,
and as an adornment; and He creates what you know not . . .

It is He who sends down to you out of heaven water
    of which you have to drink,
and of which trees, for you to pasture your herds,
    and thereby He brings forth
for you crops, and olives, and palms, and vines,
    and all manner of fruit . . .
And He subjected to you the night and day, and
the sun and moon; and the stars are subjected
    by His command.
Surely in that are signs for a people who understand . . .
It is He who subjected to you the sea, that you
    may eat of it
fresh flesh, and bring forth out of it ornaments
    for you to wear;
and thou mayest see the ships cleaving through it . . .
And He cast on the earth firm mountains, lest it
    shake with you,
and rivers and ways; so haply you will be guided;
and waymarks; and by the stars they are guided. (16.3–16)

These passages may be regarded as summaries of a considerable volume of material; and thus it will be useful to look at the chief points more in detail. In this way we shall come to appreciate better the picture of the world held by the early Muslims. The order of the second passage may be taken as a guide.

First of all there is the creation of the heavens and the earth. The views of older peoples on these matters are taken over. God is regarded as having created the heaven and the earth and what is in them in six days; but what happened on each day is not specified, except that in one passage it is stated that in the first two days the heavens and the earth received their form, while the remaining four days were devoted to the creation of their contents (41.9/8–12/11; 32.4/3). Similarly the view that there are seven heavens is accepted (41.12/11; 78.12). On both points, however, the Qur'ān and the Arabs seem to be taking over standard beliefs merely, without any feeling that there is something in these beliefs of vital importance. They seem to be more concerned with present realities than with what happened in the distant past, and do not look upon the past as giving insight into the nature of the present. Some of the other assertions about the heavens and the earth are based on observation of the present and give the impression of having been much more meaningful. The heaven is regarded as a kind of roof over the earth (21.32/33); and the earth is spread out as a carpet is in a tent (91.6). It is cause for wonder that the roof stays up without anything to support it; only God is able to do this (13.2; cf. 22.65/64). The phrase is puzzling about the mountains being placed on the earth to prevent it shaking or moving; one would naturally think of the swaying of tent-poles, or perhaps the placing of goods on a carpet to prevent it being blown about. There may be a change of picture, however, since one traditional interpretation of the phrase is that the mountains anchor the earth, as it were, and so keep it from moving, that is from heaving and tossing on the sea (21.31/32).[20] In all this the chief point of importance for men as they go about their lives is that the heavens and the earth have been given to them as a suitable environment for their lives, but that their suitability is ultimately due to the vast power of God.

Next comes the creation of man himself. Once again the Qur'ān includes the biblical account, yet lays little emphasis on it. Mankind has all developed from one person, or rather one pair, by natural descent; but the first pair were created from clay (6.98; 7.189; 32.7/6–9/8). The first man is usually nameless, however, and is not called Adam, and Adam is not usually spoken of as the first man; on the other hand, there is nothing to contradict the identification of Adam with the first man. The chief centre of interest, however, is the normal process of human reproduction. Man is created from a drop of liquid. This then becomes an embryo or 'blood-clot' (96.2) in the womb of the mother, and passes through various stages which are given Arabic names, but for which the English renderings, 'clot', 'tissue', 'bones', 'flesh' (23.12–14), have hardly the right connotations. Besides this physiological process there has to be growth in respect of human characteristics such as hearing, sight and understanding (16.78/80; 23.78/80). All this is described as something which deserves to be met with the highest degree of awe and wonder on man's part. It is a process which takes place without any conscious cooperation on man's part. Though he knows the stages of the embryo in the womb, he does not know everything about it—for example, its sex; but God knows 'what every female bears, and the wombs' shrinking and swelling' (13.8/9). The process of birth happens, of course, within a social context, since men have been given spouses to produce sons and helpers, to share their homes, and to be bound to them in mutual help and love (16.72/74; 30.21/20).

In some contexts the development of human life is looked at differently, namely as part of the cyclical process of growth and decay in nature. Man is created weak and helpless, then grows into the full strength of manhood, yet at the end of life comes again to grey hairs and weakness (30.54/53). In general all these processes, those of decay as well as those of growth, are regarded as good, because human life is good. Man is rightly filled with wonder when he contemplates them, and at the same time he ought to realize that they are all beyond his conscious power, and that strict limits are set to his conscious control of events.

The place of animals in the nomadic picture of the world is one appropriate to the outlook of nomads. The animals referred to are chiefly domesticated animals. Often the generic term 'cattle' is used, and this appears to apply chiefly to camels, even when not specifically stated, since they are said to carry heavy loads to distant lands (16.7). They are also used for riding and for food, though from pre-Islamic materials we get the impression that it was only occasionally that the Arabs ate the meat of camels; their staple food was milk and milk products such as cheese. Milk is several times mentioned or alluded to in the Qur'ān, and the fact that it comes from the camel's belly, where there is also much filth, is also cause for wonder (16.66/68). Another marvel is the growth of all animals from 'water' (24.45/44), by which is presumably meant seed. Birds are mentioned because of the wonder of flight, especially of that moment when the wings of the bird are close to its side, and there is apparently nothing to support it; in such a case the bird is said to be held up by God (67.19).

It is not surprising that in a largely desert land the most frequent references to God's 'signs' are to the coming of rain and the growth of vegetation. The Qur'ān is addressed to men whose fathers for generations, living in a parched land, had scanned the horizon for clouds, and noticed every change of wind that seemed to bode the coming of clouds and life-giving moisture. Sometimes a wind will bring towering masses of clouds, 'mountains'. There may be a reference to the fortuitous and capricious character of Arabian weather in the clouds that bring hail to one tribe and not to another (24.43). When the water has come down from the clouds, the dead earth is revived (25.48/50 f., etc.). Sometimes it is pointed out that this is a sign of God's power to raise men from the dead (e.g. 30.50/49), but at other times the parallel is passed over in silence. After the earth has been brought to life again it produces crops of various kinds—pasture for the 'cattle', and date-palms, vines, olives and other fruits (23.18–20, etc.).

All this is extremely interesting from the standpoint of comparative religion. It is a transformation of the agriculturalist's conception of the forces of nature, which adapts it to the experience of the nomad. The forces of nature were not worshipped for themselves, as was done in agricultural communities, but were thought of as under the control of God. Yet, just as among peasants the annual revival of nature is seen as being in some respects a foreshowing of the resurrection, God's revival of nature shows his power to revive men. The whole is looked at somewhat sadly, however, with the nomad's sense of the vanity and uncertainty of his life in this world. Just as man comes in old age to weakness again, so crops are reduced to stubble or blacking wrack carried down by the torrent (87.5). Indeed this cycle of growth and decay is a picture of life as a whole:

> The likeness of this present life is as water that
> We send down out of heaven,
> and the plants of the earth mingle with it
> whereof men and cattle eat,
> till, when the earth has taken on its glitter
> and has decked itself fair,
> and its inhabitants think they have power over it,
> Our command comes upon it
> by night or day, and We make it stubble, as though
> yesterday it flourished not. (10.24/25)

Astronomical phenomena also contribute to making the world a suitable place for human life. The Arab seems to have been fascinated by the alternation of night and day; and the Qur'ān points out how the night is suitable for rest and the day for activity (78.10 f.). Life would be very difficult for men if the whole of time were day or the whole of it night (28.71–3). Again, the phases of the moon conveniently mark the longer periods of time (10.5), while the sun's shadow (in a sundial or similar instrument) may be used for the division of the day.

While we happily refer to the camel as the ship of the desert, we do not readily think of ships as the camels of the oceans. It is interesting that this same coupling should be made in the Qur'ān, and that in a book for a land-travelling people there should be so many descriptions of the sea and its storms. Doubtless, though the Meccans were originally a people of the land, they did not hesitate to take to the sea in their pursuit of commerce; mostly, no doubt, it was the crossing of the Red Sea to Ethiopia, where they had trade contacts. Their connection with the sea, too, seems to have been as passengers rather than as seamen or sea captains. So the Arabs are told that God has appointed for them such ships and cattle as they ride, so that, when they are seated on their backs, they may remember God's favour to them (43.12/11 f.). One passage in particular describes the landsman's terrifying experience of a storm at sea:

> It is He who conveys you
> on the land and the sea;
> and when you are in the ship—
> and the ships run with them
> with a fair breeze,
> and they rejoice in it,
> there comes upon them a strong wind,
> and waves come on them from every side,
> and they think they are encompassed;
> they call upon God,
> making their religion His sincerely:
> 'If Thou deliverest us from these, surely
> we shall be among the thankful.'
> Nevertheless when He has delivered them
> behold, they are insolent. (10.22/23 f.)[21]

Finally, there are a few passages which attribute to God the prosperity of the Meccans. One such—which, it is interesting to note, follows on a mention of the ingratitude of those who have safely completed a voyage by sea—speaks of 'a sanctuary secure' (29.67) as one of God's blessings to them. This no doubt refers to the fact that the territory round Mecca constituted a sacred area, within which blood feuds were in abeyance, so that all sorts of people could come safely to the markets or fairs. A short but very interesting *sūra* (106) calls on the people of Mecca to worship the 'Lord of this House' (the Ka'ba), that is, God, because he has enabled them to send out the winter and summer caravan, has fed them against hunger, and secured them from fear. To God is also attributed the transformation of Muḥammad himself from being an orphan, erring and needy to being a man who had a home and was guided and provided for (93.6–8). What is here ascribed to God reminds one to a certain extent of the inscrutable operations of Time as conceived by the pagan poets; but there is the striking difference that God is here regarded as being good and showing favour to men.

Such, then, is the picture of the world which we obtain by studying the passages which speak about 'signs'. It is, above all, a world which is eminently suitable for the development of human life. Moreover this suitability is something which has been given to it by the operation of mighty forces; it is not something which man could have done for himself. The men who ride on ships and camels are to say, when they are seated on them, 'Glory be to Him who has subjected this to us, when we ourselves were not equal to it' (43.13/12). These points are made quite clearly, and have a certain justification. Yet in them there is something which to modern man is curious and unexpected. All the emphasis is on the activity of God. Modern man tends to be impressed rather by human skill and ingenuity in making use of the sun and moon for the reckoning of time, in domesticating camels and other animals, and in constructing ships capable of surviving in stormy seas. For the Qur'ān, however, the use of the human intellect is nothing. The great wonder is that, before man began to busy himself in the various ways mentioned, the world had already been made (by God) a suitable place for these activities.

Before any further discussion of this matter it will be well to look at Qur'ānic passages of a slightly different character, which ascribe to God what is usually ascribed to man.

4. The limits to human control

So insistent is the Qur'ān on man's dependence on forces mightier than himself, that even acts which are everywhere normally ascribed to man are taken from him. In the year 624 some three hundred Muslims from Medina defeated two or three times their number of Meccan pagans, and killed many of them, including several leaders. Referring to this the Qur'ān says:

> You did not slay them, but God slew them;
> and when thou threwest, it was not
> thyself that threw, but God threw . . . (8.17)

At first sight this is extremely puzzling. On reflection one can see that death comes about through the properties of the metal of which the weapon is made, and through the inter-relatedness of various physiological processes. Similarly in the throwing (by which is probably meant the shooting of arrows),[22] the operation of natural forces by which the arrow is able to pass through the air must be ascribed to God, and possibly also the success of the bowman in aiming exactly in the right direction. Even so, this Qur'ānic passage is puzzling. It could also, of course, be taken in a slightly different way, since the particular movements might be regarded as the work of the man, but the fact that these lead to a certain overall result might be due to the operation of God.

The same idea occurs in a passage mentioning various 'signs' as an argument for the truth of the resurrection.

> Have you considered the seed you spill?
> Do you yourselves create it, or are We
> the Creators? . . .
> Have you considered the soil you till?
> Do you yourselves sow it, or are We
> the Sowers? . . .
> Have you considered the water you drink?
> Did you send it down from the clouds, or
> did We send it? . . .
> Have you considered the fire you kindle?
> Did you make its timber to grow, or
> did We make it? (56.58–72/71)

In the case of the human seed, the water and the fire, man's activity is dependent on the regular action of the natural forces; but sowing appears to be different, since the human activity of casting seed upon the ground is apparently ascribed to God. Perhaps 'sowing' is to be understood as the whole complex operation resulting in the germination of the seeds, and there is clearly a sense in which this is not due to man's actions.

It is certainly a Qur'ānic idea, however, that God's activity is able to override human activity and to produce results the opposite of those the men in question expected. When the pagan Meccans were 'devising' against Muḥammad, and planning to stop his preaching or to kill him or to expel him, their plans came to nothing; instead they had the humiliating defeat at Badr. 'The unbelievers . . . were devising, and God was devising; and God is the best of devisers' (8.30). The same words are also used in a description of the attempts of the opponents of Jesus to frustrate his work (3.54/47). This is in line with the deep assurance expressed in the Qur'ān that God will eventually make his Messengers successful and will discomfit their opponents (e.g. 14.42/43–47/48). If at this point a modern man begins to ask questions about the relation of God's activity to man's activity, there is some difficulty in finding an answer. We might say that there is no suggestion that man's activity is 'obliterated' by miraculous interventions contrary to the course of nature; but the Arabs of the early seventh century had little feeling of regularity in nature, since they had had so much experience of nature's irregularities. An example may make this clearer. The Qur'ān makes it plain that the Muslim victory at Badr was due to God; but it is also plain that the Muslims did not sit down as spectators while unseen hands caused the pagan Meccans to fall dead. On the contrary the Muslims had to fight hard, with all the courage and skill they possessed. The pagans were frustrated by the activity of God, yet not as a *deus ex machina*, but through the courage and skill of men. The overriding power of God is seen, not in each detail, but in the final or overall result.

From the standpoint here attained we may look at a number of topics appearing frequently in the Qur'ān, such as God's guidance of men and his leading them astray or abandoning them. In many passages it appears that God's activity of guiding or abandoning has nothing to do with the merits of the man concerned.

> Whomsoever God desires to guide,
> He expands his breast to Islam;
> whomsoever He desires to lead astray,
> He makes his breast narrow, tight . . . (6.125)

> If God helps you, none can overcome you;
> but if He forsakes you, who then can help you
> after Him? (3.160/154)

> . . . And but for
> the bounty of God to you, and His mercy,
> you would surely have followed Satan.
> except a few. (4.83/85)

> . . . When they swerved,
> God caused their hearts to swerve;
> and God guides never the people
> of the ungodly. (61.5)

At the same time there are other passages which seem to assert that God's guidance or abandonment of a man is somehow the consequence of what the man has previously done.

. . . Thereby [*sc.* by similitudes] He leads
many astray, and thereby He guides
many; and thereby He leads none astray
save the ungodly
such as break the covenant of God
after its solemn binding, and such as cut
what God has commanded should be joined,
and such as do corruption in the land . . . (2.26/24 f.)

God guides not the people of the evildoers. (3.86/80)

And We wronged them not [*sc.* those who were punished],
but they wronged themselves . . . (11.101/103)

Those that believe not in the signs of God
God will not guide . . . (16.104/106)

As for him who gives and is godfearing
and confirms the reward most fair,
We shall surely ease him to the Easing.
But as for him who is a miser, and self-sufficient,
and cries lies to the reward most fair,
We shall surely ease him to the Hardship;
his wealth shall not avail him when he perishes. (93.5–11)

Yet other passages may be found which assert in the strongest terms God's absolute control over even man's inner attitudes.

It [*sc.* the Qur'an] is naught but a Reminder
unto all beings,
for whosoever of you would go straight;
but will you shall not, unless God wills,
the Lord of all Being. (81.27–29)

And if thy Lord had willed, whoever
is in the earth would have believed,
all of them, altogether . . .
It is not for any soul to believe
save by the leave of God. (10.99 f.)

As for the unbelievers, alike it is to them
whether thou hast warned them, or hast not warned them,
they do not believe.
God has set a seal on their hearts and on their hearing,
and on their eyes is a covering. (2.6/5 f.)

We are now faced with the problem of how to resolve the apparent contradiction between the absolute, autocratic sovereignty of God and the suggestion that some consideration is paid to human merit. It is clear that all such passages express primarily a bold conception of God's absolute omnipotence. Whatever happens on earth happens according to his will or at least with his permission. Such a conception has an obvious appeal for pagan Arabs who have been accustomed to see their lives absolutely controlled by Time. The corollary of this conception is that whatever man plans and purposes is bound to be unsuccessful unless it is what God has willed and permitted. Just how this frustration of human plans comes about is not stated. The Arabs were not interested in this point. Part of their experience in the desert was that any human plans may easily be upset, and that what upsets them is usually a concatenation of circumstances and events, which there is neither time nor opportunity to investigate. Does a man's prior activity contribute to his present unhappy state? It may or it may not. We do not know, and usually it does not much matter. All we know is that God is supreme, and that human plans are *always* liable to failure. This has proved the case even in the experience of Europeans. 'Man proposes, and God disposes.' 'The best laid schemes o' mice and men gang aft agley.' Or, in modern terms, the costliest space probes easily go off course.

This conclusion perhaps gives us a clue to the further problem of how to reconcile God's omnipotence, manifested in his present activity, with the idea that various matters are predetermined or 'written in a book'. The pagan Arabs had believed that certain matters were predetermined. It was easy for believers in God to accept this belief, while holding that it was God who had predetermined the points in question. From this it was easy to go on to the view that God's present activity was somehow or other in accordance with what he had predetermined, and that, in any case, he had foreknowledge of all events. The Arabs were chiefly concerned with practical life and its presuppositions, and did not ask out of curiosity exactly why things were as they were. This latter question is a mark of Greek inquisitiveness, the attitude which has largely formed our modern scientific outlook, and which has an important place in human life. Yet for the sheer business of living the ideas on which the Arabs concentrated are more important. At some point man, however clever he is, has to learn simply to trust the forces which mould his life, to trust them in their inscrutability.

5. The unity of the forces determining human life

Belief in God as unique and such that no other being shares in his essential attributes may be said to be assumed in the earliest passages of the Qur'ān but it does not receive any special emphasis. This is in strong contrast to the insistence of later passages of the Qur'ān that God is one and unique, and that apart from him there is no deity. In this connection we must pay attention to the story of the 'satanic verses'. This story must be true in essentials, since no Muslim would have dared to invent it about Muḥammad; and indeed there is confirmation of it in the Qur'ān. The story is that on one occasion—perhaps about the year 615, or seven years before the Hijra to Medina—Muḥammad was sitting in the Ka'ba wondering what he could find to say which would persuade the leading men of Mecca to accept his religion. At this moment he began to receive a revelation: 'Have you considered Al-Lāt and Al-'Uzza, and Manāt, the third, the other?' These verses are still found in the Qur'ān (53.19 f.), but immediately after them, and instead of the verses which now stand in the Qur'ān, Satan introduced certain false verses: 'these are the high-soaring ones, whose intercession is to be hoped for'.[23] Muḥammad at once announced this revelation, and the permission for prayers to these deities led all the men in the Ka'ba to join with Muḥammad in his worship. Later, however, Muḥammad realized that these verses could not be correct, and the true continuation of the passage was revealed to him.

The following verse, which may not have been revealed until several years afterwards, is usually taken to refer to this incident, and is the justification for speaking of 'satanic verses':

> We sent not ever any Messenger
> or Prophet before thee, but that Satan
> cast into his fancy, when he was fancying;
> but God annuls what Satan casts, then
> God confirms His signs (verses) . . . (22.52/51)

If we may assume that for a time—whether long or short does not matter—Muḥammad did not find anything amiss in the verses later rejected, then we are bound to infer that he and his contemporaries did not find any obvious incompatibility between intercessions to the goddesses and worship of one supreme God. To appreciate this point it is necessary to look a little further at Arab beliefs about the world of deities and spirits.

First of all, there are the angels. These are frequently mentioned in the Qur'ān, the Arabic word being *malā'ika* (singular *mal'ak*). An important function is the bearing of messages for God, especially the bringing of revelations to men. In some of the earlier passages it is 'the angels with the spirit' who bring God's messages (e.g. 16.2), and the usual interpretation (which would seem to be correct) is that 'the spirit' here is simply an angel. In 26.192–5 it is said to be 'the faithful spirit' (*ar-rūḥ al-amīn*) which has brought down the revelation upon Muḥammad's heart; and in 2.97/91 almost the same words are used of Gabriel. Thus, despite variant expressions in the earlier passages, the Qur'ān may be said to hold consistently that the angel Gabriel is the agent of revelation. Besides acting as messengers, however, angels have many other functions. There are those who bear up his throne on the Last Day (69.17), and those which in his nearer presence worship him (7.206/205). Thousands of angels fought along with the Muslims at Badr (8.9–12; 3.124/120 f.). There are angels which watch over men and record their deeds (82.10–12; etc.). An angel of death calls a man to God (32.11); and there are angels which guard Hell (74.30). Finally, there are fallen angels: Hārūt and Mārūt who taught magic in Babel (2.102/96), and Iblīs (the name being probably a corruption of the Greek *diabolos*), also called apparently *ash-shayṭān* or '*the* demon'.[24]

Most of these beliefs about angels closely resemble Jewish beliefs, and probably came originally from a Jewish or Christian milieu. The form of the Arabic word for 'angel' tends to confirm this, since it is close to the Hebrew and even closer to the Ethiopic.[25] Occidental scholars are now inclined to think, however, that these beliefs about angels were present in Arabia, at least in part, before the time of Muḥammad. The older Arabic belief was in spirits called *jinn* (singular *jinnī*, anglicized as 'genie'), and there seems to have been some assimilation and confusion between the two sets of beliefs; e.g. in one Qur'ānic verse (18.50/48) Iblīs is spoken of as one of the Jinn. The Jinn are beings created by God, but of flame and not, like men, of clay (55.15/14); but on the other hand Jinn are like men in that they are created in order to serve and worship God (51.56). Like men they may be either good or bad. Messengers from God were sent to the Jinn as they were to men (6.130); and indeed some of them heard the Qur'ān from Muḥammad and believed (46.29/28; 72.1, etc.). Believers among the Jinn are referred to as Muslims and, it is implied, go to Paradise, while the unbelievers go to Hell (72.14 f.). Different classes of Jinn are known in pre-Islamic lore,[26] but of these only the *'ifrīt* is mentioned in the Qur'ān (27.39). The *shayāṭīn* (satans, demons or devils) seem mostly to be distinct from the Jinn, since they are nearly always purely evil, though some were apparently made to work for Solomon (38.37/36), who was also said to have Jinn subject to him (27.17). Iblīs was, of course, the outstanding *shayṭān.*[27]

In the present study it is not necessary to go further into the details of pre-Islamic beliefs, since what has been said is sufficient to enable us to understand what the Qur'ān says about the pagan deities. As already pointed out, by about the year 600 belief in these was of a vestigial character. The idea of a supreme God, however, seems to have been widely accepted; and it is a likely inference from the call to 'worship the Lord of this House' in *sūra* 106 that, even before Muḥammad began to receive revelations, there were people in Mecca who thought of the chief deity of the Ka'ba as the supreme God. Such people, however, may not yet have been monotheists in the strict sense. From the Qur'ān it appears that they held two beliefs about the pagan deities. Firstly, they held that these beings interceded with the supreme God on behalf of their worshippers.

> They serve, apart from God, what hurts them not
> neither profits them, and they say,
> 'These are our intercessors with God.' (10.18/19)

The 'satanic verses' ostensibly give permission for intercession of this kind; but in general the Qur'ān strenuously opposes the practice (30.13/12; 39.38/39, 43/44; cf. 6.94; 39.3/4). Secondly, these people seem to have held that the pagan deities were daughters of the supreme God (*banāt Allāh*), probably also at the same time conceiving of them as angels or Jinn (16.56/58–59/61; 43.17/16–19/18; 37.149–58; 6.100). The phrase 'daughters of God' should not be taken in the personal sense given to it in Greek mythology, but as being an Arabic way of expressing an abstract conception, and therefore meaning no more than 'beings sharing in the divine character'. The Qur'ān, however, takes it fairly literally, and uses against the conception the argument that, since in Arabia daughters are much less wanted than sons, it would be an unfair division to let God have only daughters while human beings have sons (53.21 f.; etc.)

Apart from the denial of these two assertions, the Qur'ān

makes various statements about the pagan deities. In the passage replacing the 'satanic verses' it is said (53.23) that these three are 'nothing but names' given by men. This might sound a way of saying they are imaginary, but that is not the usual conception of the Qur'ān. So perhaps the words should be understood as an assertion that the connotation of the names was false, though they denoted something real. In other passages the deities are certainly spoken of as real beings, created by God, but themselves unable to create anything, and so powerless to help those who mistakenly worship them, indeed rather bearing witness against their worshippers before God. The Qur'ān is prepared to accept the view that they are Jinn, but rejects the common Meccan view that they are angels (34.40/39 f.). At one point they are said to be dead and unaware of the date of their being raised from the dead (16.21). Like other created beings they will be brought before God for judgment on the Last Day and will be sent to Hell (21.98).

The repudiation of the 'satanic verses' was tantamount to insistence on a strict monotheism and the rejection of any compromises with paganism such as acknowledging a supreme deity while permitting intercession to inferior deities regarded as angels or Jinn. From this time onwards Islam was characterized by a vigorous assertion that there is no deity but God. This had the immediate practical consequence that Arab tribes, on becoming Muslims, had to destroy their idols. Throughout the centuries this has continued to be a distinctive mark of Islam. Why was the oneness of God in this sense so much emphasized? What was its deeper meaning for the Arab of the seventh century?

First of all certain more superficial considerations must be dealt with. The 'satanic verses' were probably not understood by Muḥammad's contemporaries as sanctioning all intercession to pagan deities, but only as sanctioning intercessions at three important shrines—to al-Lāt at aṭ-Ṭā'if, to al-'Uzzā at Nakhla (near Mecca) and to Manāt at Qudayd (between Mecca and Medina). It is possible that in the period before the amending revelation came Muḥammad and the Muslims had begun to realize that to tolerate intercessions at these places would lead to confusion. It was likely, too, that intercessions at other shrines would have to be permitted also. Perhaps the root of the difficulty was that the unique character of the revelation to Muḥammad was threatened. Certainly the Muslims must have felt that something of great value to them was in danger of being lost. At the same time the results of the compromise may, in some way we do not understand, have proved unsatisfactory. Such considerations may have prepared the Muslims for the change.

Deeper considerations were probably also involved. The pre-Islamic Arabs had been inclined to ascribe everything to Time, and thus to assert a unity in the forces controlling human life, even if they considered that Time brought misfortune more often than good fortune. This conception of Time doubtless contributed something to the belief in a supreme deity held by some of the pre-Islamic Arabs. In so far as the Qur'ān asserted the goodness of that which controls human life, it was also necessary to insist that it was one. Any second comparable power might have an operation which was contrary to that of the first and bad for human beings. Thus, although in the earliest passages of the Qur'ān there is no insistence on the truth that there is no deity but God, this may be said to be implicit in the assertion of the goodness or benevolence of the powers controlling human life. God can only be fully trusted because he is absolutely supreme. These deeper considerations were presumably supported by the desire to be like the Christians, Jews and Zoroastrians. The Arabs of Mecca were familiar with the peoples of Syria and Iraq and with their vastly superior culture (in certain respects), and they realized that these peoples mostly believed in God who was one. In this way admiration for superior culture made the acceptance of monotheism easier.

The points at which there is open conflict between two movements, such as Islam and paganism, are not necessarily the basic issues between them. They are more likely to be points at which one side thinks it has got a good argument, and which the other side considers important bastions, not to be lightly abandoned, or areas where the defence is stronger than the attack. The tendency of the Arabs to ascribe every event to Time conceived as unitary, the example of the great empires of the Byzantines, Persians and Abyssinians, and various considerations of a general nature, encouraged the Muslims to stand fast against the pagans on this point of the unity or oneness of God, so that it became the first article of their *shahāda* or confession of faith—'there is no deity but God'.

Note on the word '*Allah*'. It became common in European languages in the latter part of the nineteenth century and earlier part of the twentieth to speak of 'Allah' rather than of 'God' when referring to Islam. This usage rests on confusion of thought and is to be avoided. The particular confusion is between the being denoted by a word and the cluster of ideas associated with a word in a given context. Admittedly the average Muslim's cluster of ideas is different from the average Christian's, but the correct way to express this is not by saying that the being denoted is different—unless one supposes that the being is nothing more than a cluster of ideas! Especially because of the influence of Judaism and Christianity on the Arabian environment, Muslims must in intention be worshipping and speaking about the same being as Christians, even if some of their assertions about this being differ. It is mistaken loyalty to Christianity to suppose that its cause is helped by refusing to Muslims the right to use the word 'God'. After all there are Christian Arabs, Orthodox, Catholic and Protestant, and their only word for God is *Allāh* (which, like the Greek *ho theos*, means simply 'the god').

Chapter 3

The perspective of transcendence

1. The dimension of transcendence

In the previous chapter human life (according to the Qur'ānic conception) has been depicted as dependent on a superior power, and as limited by various factors ultimately controlled by this power. The power is essentially good—'merciful and compassionate'—so that an optimistic view is possible of the potentialities of human life. This might be described as seeing human life in the perspective of dependence and limitation. In the present chapter we go on to see it in another perspective, that of transcendence. The power on which human life is dependent transcends space and time, and therefore human life occurs in a context of such transcendence. Here, even more than in speaking about the existence of God, we have to use language diagrammatically. Among the ideas most used to express the perspective of transcendence are those of the world to come or other world, the judgment by God of his creatures, and the assignment of some to Paradise and others to Hell. Christian theologians and scholars of comparative religion like to speak of 'eschatology' and the chapter might have been called 'the eschatological perspective'; but 'transcendence', though vague, will convey more to a wider audience. Let us therefore turn to look at this background of eternity against which the Qur'ān sees human life.

The beliefs about this background may be said to be summed up in the doctrine of the Last Day. According to this doctrine men are restored to life again after death; they are then brought before God to be judged in respect of their deeds during this present life. The judgment consists in assigning some to spend eternity in Paradise or Heaven as a reward of their good deeds, and others to spend eternity being tortured in Hell as a punishment for their bad deeds. This is the bare outline of the doctrine. On certain points there is much more detail in the Qur'ān; and there was considerable further elaboration by Muslims of later times. The various points may be considered separately.

It should be noticed first of all that the Qur'ān takes a monistic conception of man as distinct from the dualistic conception common in certain circles in the occident, partly as a result of Greek influence. According to the dualistic conception man consists of two things, soul and body, of which the former is the more important; in extreme forms of the view the soul is the true man, and the body an unfortunate temporary addition—'the body is the tomb of the soul'. For the monistic view, on the other hand, while it may recognize some distinction between body and soul or body and spirit, the body is an essential part of the man. This latter view is the common Semitic view, found in the Old Testament and in sayings of Jesus, for example, about entering the life to come with a hand cut off or an eye plucked out. It is the monistic view which is taken in the Qur'ān. Resurrection implies a revival or rather new creation of the body. In particular the use of the word *nafs* must be noted carefully. It may be translated 'soul', but this is in the sense of 'person' or 'self'.[1] This continues to be the meaning in Arabic writings in the main stream of Islamic thought. When Greek philosophical works were translated into Arabic, however, *nafs* was used to translate the Greek *psychē* with a dualistic or approximately dualistic sense. This leads to difficulties in the precise understanding of texts, but it remains true that a Muslim writer's conception of man is monistic unless he has come heavily under the influence of Greek thought through the influence of philosophers writing in Arabic.

The monistic conception of man affects Islamic ideas about what happens at death and afterwards. When his time has come, a man is summoned by the angel of death (32.11). Sometimes it seems to be implied that he is immediately taken into God's presence and judged. Thus those who have fallen in battle, fighting for the cause of God, are said to be already alive in God's presence (3.169/163 f.). This is probably, however, to be regarded as exceptional. In many of the descriptions of the Last Day (e.g. 84.4; 99.2) it is implied that the dead will then be removed from the tombs; and from that it follows that up to this point they have been in the tombs, and not in Paradise or Hell or any intermediate state. Later Islamic theology accepted a belief in 'the punishment of the tomb', and alleged that it was referred to in certain Qur'ānic verses; while the verses may be compatible with such a belief, they certainly do not make it necessary.[2] On the other hand, those who are to be punished are described as supposing that they had not been in the graves more than an hour (10.45/46; 46.35), and this seems to imply that in the grave they are without consciousness. One verse (23.100/102) speaks of some men 'having a barrier behind them' until they are raised up; this barrier or *barzakh* is often interpreted as a kind of purgatory, but all that the text necessarily implies is an interval between death and resurrection. The conclusion is that, while there is a measure of consistency in these pictures of what happens after death, there are slight variations in the ideas of the Qur'ān, presumably due to variations in the ideas of those addressed.

The Day of Judgment (*yawm ad-dīn*) or the Last Day, which has several other names in the Qur'ān, is the day when men and Jinn are assembled and brought before God to be judged. The coming of 'the Hour' is heralded by a shout or a thunderclap or a blast (or two) on the trumpet (36.53; 80.33; 69.13; 78.18; 39.68: two blasts).[3] Various fearsome things happen. The earth is violently shaken, the mountains crumble away and become like 'plucked wool-tufts' (101.5/4), the seas boil up, the sun is darkened, the stars fall and the sky is stripped off like the skin of a dead camel (81.1–14; etc.). Eventually God appears surrounded by the angels in ranks (89.22/23). The unbelievers and the beings they have worshipped are all trying to avert punishment from themselves, each quite unscrupulously at the expense of his fellows (43.67; 32.20–33/32; etc.). Most of those to be judged can do no more than listen in silence to the pronouncing of the sentence upon them, since only those to whom God has given permission may speak formally (78.38). Certain favoured servants of God are given the right to intercede on behalf of others (20.109/108; etc.), and by this is probably to be understood the right of prophets to intercede on behalf of their communities. Certainly later Islam made much of Muḥammad's power of intercession.

The judgment is based on the records of men's good and bad deeds kept in 'books' by recording angels. These are weighed on a balance (*mīzān*), presumably the good deeds against the bad deeds.

> Then he whose deeds weigh heavy in the Balance
> shall inherit a pleasing life,
> but he whose deeds weigh light in the Balance
> shall plunge in the womb of the Pit. (101.6/5–9/6)

In one place it seems to be implied that the mark of the difference between reward and punishment is that those rewarded are given their books in their right hands whereas those who are punished are given their books behind their backs (84.7–12). The kinds of deeds which lead to punishment will be considered more fully in the next section. Later Muslims came to believe that after this both rewarded and condemned had to walk across a path or bridge (*ṣirāṭ*) stretched over Hell; the ridge of the *ṣirāṭ* was fine as a hair and the wicked fell into Hell.[4]

Paradise or Heaven, the reward of the pious, is usually referred to as 'the Garden' (*al-janna*) in the Qur'ān. In the descriptions of it there are many features that point the contrast to the harsh life of the desert.

> So God has guarded them from the evil of
> that day, and has procured them radiancy
> and gladness,
> and recompensed them for their patience
> with a Garden, and silk;
> therein they shall recline upon couches,
> therein they shall see neither sun nor
> bitter cold;
> near them shall be its shades, and its clusters hung
> meekly down,
> and there shall be passed around them vessels of
> silver and goblets of crystal,
> crystal of silver that they have measured
> very exactly.
> And therein they shall be given to drink a cup whose
> mixture is ginger,
> therein a fountain whose name is called Salsabīl.
> Immortal youths shall go about them;
> when thou seest them, thou supposest them
> scattered pearls,
> when thou seest them, thou seest bliss
> and a great kingdom.
> Upon them shall be green garments of silk
> and brocade; they are adorned with
> bracelets of silver, and their Lord shall
> give them to drink a pure draught. (76.11–21)

As is well known—too much has been made of the point in the occident—among the delights of Paradise are to be 'wide-eyed houris as the likeness of hidden pearls' (56.22), also described as 'maidens with swelling breasts, like of age' (78.33).[5] Just how this is to be related to the future state of female Muslims is not clear. Are the maidens simply these transformed and rejuvenated? The Qur'ān certainly envisages the reward of Paradise for women as well as men. In view of the completely erroneous conception formerly current in the occident, and not yet completely buried, that Muslims hold that women have no souls, it will be well to quote the following verse:

> Surrendered (*muslim*) men and surrendered women,
> believing men and believing women,
> obedient men and obedient women,
> truthful men and truthful women,
> enduring men and enduring women,
> humble men and humble women,
> men and women who give in charity,
> men who fast and women who fast,
> men and women who guard their private parts,
> men and women who remember God oft—
> for them God has prepared a forgiveness
> and a mighty wage. (33.35)

Not merely do women enter Paradise as a reward for their merits, but husbands and wives enter together.

> 'Oh My servants, today no fear is on you, neither do you sorrow . . . Enter Paradise, you and your wives, walking with joy!' (43.68, 70)

It must further be insisted that the delights of Paradise are by no means merely material. For one thing there are different grades or levels there. Four distinct gardens are spoken of in one *sūra* (55.46, 62), and the statement in another passage (6.165) that God 'has raised some of you in rank above others', though it may originally have applied to this world, is usually interpreted of Paradise. Part of the joy of Paradise is that men will know that they are pleasing in God's sight (89.28). Social relationships will be perfect; 'therein they shall hear no idle talk, no cause of sin, only the saying "Peace, Peace!" ' (56.25/24 f.). Paradise is indeed 'the abode of peace' (10.25/26). The chief of its joys, moreover, is the vision of God. This is the almost unanimous view of later Muslims, and it seems to be implied by the words, 'upon that day faces shall be radiant, gazing upon their Lord' (75.22 f.). and also by the assertion that on that day the wicked 'shall be veiled from their Lord' (83.15). Thus the Qur'ānic pictures of Heaven contain aspects suitable to various levels of spiritual development.

Hell is first and foremost the Fire. God has laid up for the damned 'fetters, and a furnace, and food that chokes, and a painful punishment' (73.12 f.). They will be roasted in a flame which 'spares not, neither leaves alone, scorching the flesh' (74.28 f.); in this they will neither die nor live (20.74/76). Various other touches are added here and there; the damned will be given boiling water and pus to drink (38.57); they will have to eat the bitter fruit of the tree of Zaqqūm whose 'spathes are as the heads of Satans' (37.62/60–66/64). In various places there are verses that suggest that one of the features of Hell is the lack of social harmony and lack of peace (e.g. 38.60–64). In short it is a picture of the greatest torments that could be conceived by the Arab mind, and of these continuing for ever.

Such is the perspective of eternity—an eternity of reward or an eternity of punishment—within which human life is set by the Qur'ān.

2. The practical implications of the transcendent

These pictures of Heaven and Hell, we have said, are to be understood 'diagrammatically'. In other words, they were meant to help men to live truly in this world, and we shall appreciate them better if we consider how they affect the actual living of one's life. The key question to ask is: Which acts led to punishment and which to reward? To this the Qur'ān appears to give three answers. These are not contradictory, but rather vary the emphasis according to the varying needs of the hearers at different stages in the early life of the community of Muslims.

The first answer is to be found in those passages which, so far as we can tell, are the earliest of the whole Qur'ān. It perhaps belongs to the period at the beginning of Muḥammad's career when his preaching was getting some response from the Meccans but had not encountered any serious opposition. In these early passages men are called on to worship God and to believe in him and in what he reveals through his Messenger. Apart from that it is found that most of the acts which are praised or blamed are closely connected with a man's attitude to wealth. Hell-fire is said to call those 'who amassed and hoarded' (70.18), who did not urge men to the feeding of the poor (69.34), who treated orphans under their care badly and seized their inheritance, and in general loved wealth ardently (89.17/18–20/21), and consequently were niggardly (92.8). The pious, on the other hand, are those who are always ready to share with beggars and outcasts (51.19), and who are generous with their wealth (68.17).[6]

It is curious at first sight that there should be an emphasis of this kind in the earliest passages of the Qur'ān. Yet on reflection it can be seen to be linked with conditions in Mecca. It is an emphasis on those parts of the old morality of the nomads which were being neglected in a commercial town like Mecca. There is no mention of killing or inflicting physical injury, for the principle of the blood feud was still in full operation and took care of this aspect of social relations. Involvement in commerce, however, had developed an individualistic outlook among the chief participants; these were mostly also the leading men of the clans of Quraysh, and they tended to disregard the old obligations of the nomadic shaykh to the weaker members of his clan like widows and orphans. Money-making had become so important for such men that they were unscrupulous in helping themselves to other people's money where they could do so with impunity. For such persons the Qur'ānic doctrine of the Last Day provided a sanction inducing them to respect these traditional duties. Though they neglected the obligations, they were ready to make use of the privileges and advantages of the position of shaykh, such as the readiness of a family or clan to support one of their members, right or wrong, against all others. In this way they could overcome human or local opposition. About 590, for example, a Meccan merchant refused to pay a debt owed by him to a Yemeni in Mecca, and got the other leading merchants to support his action; it was probably aimed at stopping the Yemenis from organizing caravans between the Yemen and Mecca, so that only Meccans could do so and reap the profits. The Qur'ān repeatedly insists that on the Last Day a man will have to stand alone before God; neither his wealth nor the number of his sons will impress the judge and help his suit (26.88; 35.18/19; etc.). In this way the doctrine of the Last Day exerts pressure on a man (if he believes it) to fulfil his obligations to the poor and unfortunate of his family and clan.

The second answer to the question is that eternal punishment is for those who have disbelieved. Such persons may disbelieve God's signs, or the doctrines of the resurrection, the judgment and future reward and punishment; or they may disbelieve the revealed message and warning.[7] In the last resort these are different ways of describing rejection of God's Messenger and the Message, so that unbelief becomes identified with such rejection. If the first point is criticism of the moral condition of Mecca, the second reflects a later stage in the relations of Muḥammad to his fellow-townsmen, when many of them were rejecting him, but before he had begun to look upon his followers as a new community. In the stories of the previous prophets one has the impression that whole communities are involved in the rejection and consequent punishment. Thus Noah was helped by God against his opponents:

> and We helped him against the people
> who cried lies to Our signs; surely
> they were an evil people, so We drowned them
> all together. (21.77)

Similarly the Arabian tribe of Thamūd to whom the prophet Ṣāliḥ was sent hamstrung the camel of God and were all punished (91.15; 26.155 f.).

In all this one can see the reflection of what happened to Muḥammad at Mecca, especially his rejection by a large part of the community. Yet there is the important difference that Ṣāliḥ, for example, is depicted as rejected by the whole of his community, and Noah by the whole of it except a few members of his own family. This apparent neglect (in theory) of Muḥammad's faithful followers is significant. The only community they knew was the kinship group, that is, the clan or tribe; and they had not yet come to think of themselves as constituting a community of a new kind. Thus the Qur'ānic emphasis here is on the solidarity of a community in its opposition to God; and this was doubtless a phenomenon which had become evident among the pagan Meccans. One passage (7.38/36) speaks of communities (or 'nations') entering Hell as communities. Thus the second aspect of Qur'ānic teaching about the reasons for eternal punishment emphasizes opposition at communal level to God's Messenger and his Message, but the community is not spoken of as organized round a positive centre.

The third Qur'ānic answer to the question raised moves on to a positive account of the condemned community; it is condemned for 'associating other gods with God'. From this it would seem possible to infer—what is indeed likely on other grounds—that as opposition in Mecca to Muḥammad continued it turned to base itself more and more on the old gods and goddesses. A certain revival of the old religion would seem to have come about; this would be in accordance with the rule that in times of stress men turn to more primitive forms of experience. The Qur'ān consequently emphasizes the heinousness of worshipping 'associate-gods'. At the same time it implies the existence of another community—a new community—of those who believe in God. The conflict has thus become one between Muḥammad's religion and paganism, and this is necessarily a communal affair—the pagan community against Muḥammad's community. Judaism and Christianity presented a complicating factor, but so long as he was at Mecca Muḥammad had no real practical problems with the older religions. In accordance with Qur'ānic teaching he could regard them as allies—other branches of his own religion. Thus the Qur'ānic condemnation of the *mushrikīn* (polytheists, 'associators') to Hell is essentially something communal, though in later times Muslim mystics could regard *shirk* ('associating'), understood as failing to be single-minded in the service of God, as a great individualistic sin, in that it was contrary to the integration of the personality round a single object of worship.

Let us turn now from these Qur'ānic reasons for condemnation to Hell to look in a more general way at their implications. We may begin with the assertion (from a modern standpoint) that the quality of life and character which leads to Heaven has transcendent value, while that which leads to Hell lacks this. A popular word nowadays for transcendent value is 'significance' or 'meaningfulness'. Thus we may regard the Qur'ān as asserting that generosity and care for the unfortunate has significance in the individual life; and that the whole life of communities, provided they have a proper theistic basis, is significant. Here is a sphere in which it is necessary to hold on firmly to two truths, although intellectually it is difficult or impossible to harmonize them. We must hold that individual conduct is capable of manifesting transcendent value (that is to say, when it is 'upright'); and we must also hold that the lives of members of a truly based and oriented community have transcendent value. The intellectual difficulty makes its appearance when we have to define the position of such members of a truly oriented community as commit numerous acts of sin. At a later period some Muslims—the Khārijites—insisted that even a single act of serious sin led to a man's exclusion from the community;

but this view produced impossible political situations. On the other hand, to say (as some early scholars did) that, if a man is a member of the community of Muslims, sin does not matter, is to belittle the importance of conduct. Later Muslims tended to harmonize the opposites and to retain the truth in both by asserting that no member of the community of Muslims (provided he did not by *shirk* or polytheism lose his membership) would be eternally in Hell, but that sins would be punished, either on earth or by a temporary residence in Hell. This is to abandon the individualistic interpretation of the weighing of men's deeds as commonly understood. Yet the continuing feeling that men were still responsible for their deeds and liable to punishment led to the development of the conception of Muḥammad's intercession on behalf of sinful members of his community. In this way the main body of Muslim thought held to both truths—the importance of individual conduct and the importance of being a member of a rightly oriented community.

The primary reference of the last phrase, of course, is to the Islamic community, because of its belief in God, his Messengers and the Messages they brought. For most Sunnites their community was one in which a man found deliverance from Hell or salvation (*firqa nājiya*). It was divinely founded through the sending of Messengers, culminating in Muḥammad, and was constituted by the divinely given or revealed way of life (*sharī'a*). The Sunnite Muslim thus could feel that the community promoted his welfare in the fullest and most ultimate sense. This was comparable to the way in which in pre-Islamic times many Arabs had felt that all that was valuable and significant in their lives came from the tribe, since it was the nobility of his tribal and family stock that enabled a man to perform noble deeds. It is worth noting in passing that this stock which gave life its significance was pictured as a strong, high mountain which persisted unmoved through the vicissitudes of time, thus linking significance with something not unlike eternity.

> As though the Fates beating against us met
> a black mountain, cleaving the topmost clouds,
> strong and mighty above the changes of things,
> which no shock of Time (*dahr*) can soften or shake.[8]

Thus we see that, even before the preaching of monotheism, some Arabs were aware of values that somehow transcended time.

A pessimistic attitude to this-worldly affairs was certainly never far from the Arab of the desert. There are passages in the Qur'ān which assure the hearers that the life of Paradise is better and more enduring than this transitory 'nearer life' (*al-ḥayā ad-dunyā*).[9]

> This present life is naught but a diversion
> and a sport; surely the Last Abode is Life,
> did they but know. (29.64)

All we know of the Arabs of this period, however, makes it clear that they were not world-forsakers; especially in the later years of Muḥammad's life they were men conscious of their power to control this-worldly affairs. Once the great Arab expansion had begun such a consciousness was bound to grow. Thus, despite the outward form of these statements, they cannot have been understood as inculcating a world-forsaking attitude. They are rather connected with the choice between two sets of values. What Muḥammad's Meccan opponents were striving for was valuable only when measured by this-worldly standards; 'wealth and sons are the adornment of the present world' (18.46/44). The Qur'ān, on the other hand, though still going along with the old Arab view that there is no security or permanency in temporal life, insists that there is an enduring quality in noble deeds, acts of generosity, and above all in the sacrifice of life in the cause of God; in other words, in these forms of conduct there is transcendent value. Yet these are not forms of conduct which imply a contracting out of this-worldly life; rather they lead men into the thick of it. The attitude to life they express is positive.

It might seem that there is a contradiction between this aspect of Qur'ānic teaching and the sensual pictures of Paradise and Hell. The appearance of contradiction is due to a misunderstanding of the precise bearing of the Qur'ānic statements about the inferiority of this present world. They are not a condemnation of what the occidental would understand by 'this-worldly pleasures'. The Arab is less concerned than the occidental with 'things', even such things as pleasures; he is more concerned with persons. In particular the 'adornment of this present world' seems to have been taken to be primarily power to control other persons; this is the point of wealth and sons. Moreover the rich men of Mecca had come to regard such power as the be-all and end-all of life, and as being almost eternal. The Muslims were not averse to having power, but they were aware of its limited character and of its being subject to the overriding power of God. Even while wielding power they had a measure of detachment from it. The attitude to the pleasures of food and sex was probably similar. In the desert the Arabs had necessarily developed a measure of detachment from these things, otherwise life in the desert would have been unbearable. The Muslims enjoyed such pleasures when they had the opportunity; the pleasures were not in any way condemned except when they infringed social norms. Since in Paradise there can be no possibility of infringing social norms, there is no reason why sensual pleasures should not be enjoyed. Indeed, because of the monistic Arab conception of man, which refuses to think of him as a disembodied mind, the satisfactions of Paradise can hardly be expressed except in bodily terms.

To sum up the thoughts of this chapter, we may say that the Qur'ān presents human life as a sphere in which transcendent values may be realized. To achieve such a realization, however, a man must be a member of a 'rightly-guided' community. This is the *sine qua non* of all true achievement in life. Within the life of the community a man makes his individual contribution in acts of upright, generous and noble conduct. The Qur'ān thus turns the pessimistic outlook of the Arabs into optimism, but only for the believers. For the unbelievers the pessimism remains.

> Know that the present life is but a
> sport and a diversion, an adornment
> and a cause for boasting among you,
> and a rivalry in wealth and children.
> It is as a rain whose vegetation
> pleases the unbelievers; then it
> withers, and thou seest it turning
> yellow, then it becomes broken orts. (57.20/19)

The annual cycle of vegetation, however, can also be looked at in another way (as has been noticed in the previous chapter). The rain sent by God revives the dead earth and causes the plants to spring up. It is thus a sign of resurrection. So the pagan cycle of death coming to life and returning to death is transformed. It now becomes life going down to death and then being restored to life. Through the accounts of God's signs something of the optimism of the nature religions has been given to the sons of the desert.

Chapter 4

The religious leader and his community

1. Pre-Islamic religious leadership

In pre-Islamic times in Arabia, as throughout the Middle East in Islamic times, there was much less distinction between the religious and the secular than is currently made in the occident. There was a distinction, however, between natural powers and supernatural agencies, and certain human beings were believed to be helped by supernatural agencies, notably by the Jinn. Among the names given to a person of this kind were *kāhin* and *shā'ir*. The latter is the common word for 'poet' in Arabic, but its basic meaning is 'knower'. By the time of Muḥammad it was perhaps true that the *shā'ir* was merely the man who 'knew' the traditions of his tribe about the noble achievements of their ancestors; but the older meaning seems to have been one who possessed a deep supernatural or magical knowledge, not accessible to other human beings.[1] Even in older times the poet was expected to have full knowledge of his tribe's traditions, but he used these in a supernatural or magical way in the poetic contests which often preceded warfare. Because of his special 'knowledge' the *shā'ir* in early times was often, perhaps usually, the person who decided where and when the tribe was to camp and when it was to move on; he was thus its leader (*qā'id*).[2]

With the position and office of the *shā'ir* was linked a belief in the efficacy of verbal formulas, when pronounced by the proper person, in the proper circumstances and in the proper form. This was a very old belief common to various Semitic peoples. There are several instances in the Old Testament. Thus Isaac's blessing of Jacob is held to be effective, although he had really intended to bless Esau; and Balak, king of Moab, thought he could hire Balaam to curse the Israelites, his enemies.[3] In Arabia in the time immediately before Muḥammad the magical pronouncements of the *shā'ir* were normally made in a form of rhythmical prose known as *saj'*, in which the concluding words of the short sections or lines had an assonance or imperfect rhyme. The pronouncements of Balaam were somewhat similar. The *kāhin* or 'soothsayer' closely resembled the *shā'ir*, since he also used *saj'*, but differed from him in that he was for the most part linked with a particular shrine. Both *kāhin* and *shā'ir* were supposed to be influenced by Jinn or by one of the Jinn, and this was the basis of their supernatural or magical character.

The development of the early *shā'ir* into the poet of Islamic times can be guessed at, but the evidence is slight. One step was to give each section of the *saj'* the same metre, so that it became a line, and then to lengthen the lines. Another step was to replace the inexact assonances with strict rhymes. In this way the minatory or vilifying passages of *saj'* commonly pronounced before battles were transferred into the type of poem known as *hijā'* or 'satire', in which the defeats and ignoble deeds of the enemy were rehearsed. The contrasting type, deriving perhaps from the 'blessing' of one's own tribe, was the *fakhr* or 'boasting', which also had a military importance. Various metres of increasing complexity were developed. In short, before the advent of Islam Arabic poetry had attained the heights of the celebrated poems known as the *Mu'allaqāt*. Quite apart from actual combat, poetry had an important function in increasing the self-confidence of the tribe.

Nevertheless it would seem that by the time of the Qur'ān poets had fallen in some cases from this high esteem. The Meccans are represented as saying, 'Shall we leave our gods for a poet possessed (*shā'ir majnūn*)?' (37.36/35), and as asserting that Muḥammad has invented the Qur'ān and is a poet (21.5; cf. 52.30). The Qur'ān therefore insists that Muḥammad is not a *kāhin* or *shā'ir* (69.41 f.), that God has not taught him *shi'r* (36.69), that he is not possessed, *majnūn* (52.29), and that, on the contrary, the satans or demons descend on the liars and poets (26.221–6). While the last point may not represent any current views, it is clear from the others that the Meccans had a relatively low view of poets. Presumably they were still well thought of outside Mecca, but it would be natural to expect that in Mecca a decline in the status of poet would accompany the growth of individualism and the weakening of tribal solidarity. The impression is also given that for a man to be under the influence of Jinn was now regarded as a misfortune ('possession') rather than an advantage ('inspiration');

and that *majnūn*, which is strictly 'possessed by Jinn' was coming close to its modern meaning of 'mad'. Despite this change in the attitude to poets it is possible that something of the older attitude to 'the man who knows' was felt towards Muḥammad.

Another personage of whom we hear in the immediately pre-Islamic period, and whose function may have influenced the religious leadership exercised by Muḥammad, was the *ḥakam* or arbiter. In earlier days disputes might be taken to an appropriate shrine, where a *kāhin* would settle the matter by drawing lots with arrows or in some such way. It was conceivably as a result of the lessening regard for the *kāhin* and *sha'ir* that there appeared the apparently secularized office of arbiter. When disputants took cases to such a man for settlement, he relied not on Jinn but on his innate tact and his knowledge of tribal customs and political relationships. The arbiter had no executive power, but only a certain moral authority, and this was backed by the swearing of oaths and the giving of securities for the carrying out of his judgment.[4] The men of Medina, in inviting Muḥammad to go there, were almost certainly hoping that he would act as an arbiter between the bitterly hostile tribes of the Aws and the Khazraj.

2. The Qur'ānic conception of religious leadership

The conception of religious leadership in the Qur'ān is very different from that in pre-Islamic times, since it has its centre not in the *kāhin* or *shā'ir* but in the *nabī* or the *rasūl*, the prophet or the messenger. It would be surprising, however, if something of the old ideas had not crept into the new conception. Before any valid judgment can be passed on this point it is necessary to look in some detail at what is said about prophets and messengers.

The word first used to describe Muḥammad's activity is neither of these but *nadhīr* or 'warner'. In a very early passage he is commanded to 'rise and warn' (74.2). Now the word *andhara* or 'warn' means informing a person about something that is liable to injure or kill him, so as to put him on his guard against it. What kind of warning was Muḥammad to give to the people of Mecca? The chief alternatives seem to be warning of a temporal calamity and warning of the judgment of the Last Day. The latter certainly seems to have been present from a fairly early period, since it is presumably implied by such a phrase as 'to God is the return' (96.8).[5] Nevertheless, as has been remarked by various scholars, there are no graphic descriptions of Paradise and Hell in the earliest passages. The chief exception is 84.1–12, and what we find there is rather a description of the terrors of the Last Day; all that is said of the fate of the damned is that they shall 'roast at a Blaze'. It would seem, then, that from the first the warning given by Muḥammad must have included something about the Last Judgment. It seems also that this was described as a judgment on each individual as an individual, since it is frequently insisted that in this judgment—whatever may be the case before human judges—wealth and children do not help him, nor can his friends and kinsmen give him support (26.88; 82.19; 35.18/19).

Almost from the first the religious leader seems to have been regarded as combining this activity of 'warning' with one of 'reminding'. Muḥammad is commanded to 'remind (*dhakkir*) if the Reminder (*dhikrā*) profits' (87.9). The form *mudhakkir*, 'one reminding', occurs only once, but the root is frequent not only in this second verbal stem, but also in the first—*dhakara*, to remember—and fifth—*tadhakkara*, to accept and take to heart a reminder. The Arabic second verbal stem, however, seems to be wider than the English word 'remind', even if the latter is a convenient translation. It means more than recalling to men's minds what they have already known and have forgotten. It seems to mean rather bringing them to a full knowledge of that of which so far they have had only a dim awareness, and to which they have paid no special attention. In particular it means bringing men to realize that the supreme God, whose existence they vaguely acknowledge, is in fact the ultimately dominating power in their lives, so that they come to make this realization the basis of their conduct. Such a conception of the nature of 'reminding' fits in well with several of the earliest passages where there is no mention of 'warning'. Thus in the *sūra* entitled Quraysh (106) the people of Mecca are exhorted to worship God because he is the source of their prosperity and their relative security.

While the activities of reminding and warning continue to characterize the religious leader as portrayed in the Qur'ān, and exemplified at first almost exclusively by Muḥammad, they come to be complemented by the activity of the 'messenger' (*rasūl*), whom God has 'sent with a message' (*arsala*). The word *rasūl* is etymologically close to the English 'apostle', but the latter has become rather specialized, and so 'messenger' is a preferable translation. As this new facet of the conception of the religious leader is introduced, Muḥammad ceases to be the sole exemplar. The Qur'ān alludes to previous messengers, and sometimes gives briefly something of their stories. In view of its insistence on the similarities between the relationships of the different messengers to their community, we are justified in regarding these stories as illustrations of the main Qur'ānic conception of the relationship of messenger to community. In several *sūras* we find a string of such stories, one after the other. In each *sūra* the stories tend to have a common form—the same points are emphasized and the same lesson drawn. From *sūra* to *sūra*, however, there are variations, doubtless according to the particular circumstances of Muḥammad and his followers and to their changing needs.

The distinction between 'messenger' and 'prophet' (*nabī*) was much discussed by later Islamic theologians, but need be touched on only briefly here. It has been pointed out[6] that the Arabian figures, Hūd, Ṣāliḥ and Shu'ayb, are spoken of as messengers but are never referred to as prophets, and also that 'prophet' is restricted to biblical persons apart from its application to Muḥammad, though not to those called prophets in the Bible itself. Thus it would seem that a prophet is somehow connected with a written scripture, whereas a messenger may have conveyed merely an oral message. It may also be remarked here that, while in English Muḥammad is commonly 'prophet', his normal Arabic title, found in the Confession of Faith, is 'the messenger of God' (*rasūl Allāh*). These points hardly affect, however, the present discussion of the conception of the religious leader.

In stories of what appear to be the earliest type, the point emphasized is that a temporal calamity falls on communities whose conduct is evil. In one such (53.50/51–54/55) we read that

> . . . He destroyed Ad, the ancient,
> and Thamood, and He did not spare them,
> and the people of Noah before—certainly
> they did exceeding evil, and were insolent—
> and the Subverted City He also overthrew . . .

The point here appears to be that these communities are destroyed because of their wickedness. It is not suggested that they have rejected their messenger; presumably they are destroyed because they have failed to realize that their good fortune is from God. This links up with the activity of reminding.[7] Another rather similar passage is 51.38–46, where there is a slightly longer reference to Pharaoh, 'Ād, Thamūd and the people of Noah. With regard to 'Ād, only their destruction by a 'withering wind' is mentioned. The people of Noah are said to have been 'ungodly'. In the case of the other two, however, rejection of the messenger or the message is mentioned; Thamūd 'turned in disdain from the commandment', and Pharaoh turned his back on Moses and called him 'a sorcerer or man possessed'; in a later verse (52) these words are said to have been applied to all the previous messengers, and the implication is that Muḥammad also had been described in this way.[8]

The variety of emphasis which can be given to these stories of previous messengers is well illustrated by five *sūras*, in each of which there is a group of references to messengers; these references are longer than those previously considered. It is interesting that in these groups of stories a prominent place is taken by the Arabian non-biblical messengers. To the tribe of 'Ād was sent Hūd, and when they disbelieved him they were destroyed by a great wind. After this Ṣāliḥ was sent to the tribe of Thamūd, bringing with him as a sign from God a she-camel; they were commanded to share their water with this camel, but instead they killed her and were destroyed at the coming of 'the Cry'. Another essentially non-biblical story is that of how the prophet Shu'ayb was sent to Midian to warn them of punishment if they did not cease from dishonest practices; they disbelieved him and were destroyed by an earthquake. About the biblical stories all that need be said is that Lot is regarded as a prophet sent to the people of the Subverted Cities (or City); Abraham and Moses will be considered later. The following table (with the *sūras* arranged in reverse order as being nearer the chronological) will give some idea of the construction of these groups of stories about messengers:

54.9–42
people of Noah (9); 'Ād (4); Thamūd (10); people of Lot (8); Pharaoh (2);

29.14/13–40/39
Noah (2); Abraham (12); Lot (8); Shu'ayb (2); 'Ād, Thamūd (1); Pharaoh, etc. (2);

26.10/9–191
Moses (60); Abraham (36); Noah (18); Hūd (18); Ṣāliḥ (19); Lot (16); Shu'ayb (16);

11.25/27–96/98
Noah (25); Hūd (12); Ṣāliḥ (8); Abraham, Lot (13); Shu'ayb (14);

7.59/57–93/91
Noah (6); Hūd (8); Ṣāliḥ (7); Lot (5); Shu'ayb (9).

(In brackets after each name is the number of verses assigned to its story.)

It may be instructive to follow the story of Thamūd through these *sūras*, abbreviating it somewhat. In most of the stories of the group in *sūra* 54 the emphasis is on the rejection of the message and the frightfulness of the punishment; the section on Thamūd is fullest on the first point.

> Thamood cried lies to the warnings
> and said, 'What, shall we follow
> a mortal, one out of ourselves?
> Then indeed we should be in error
> and insanity!
> Has the Reminder been cast upon him
> alone among us? Nay, rather he is
> an impudent liar.' . . .
> How then were My chastisement and My warnings?
> We loosed against them one Cry,
> and they were as the wattles of a
> pen-builder. (54.23–32)

In *sūra* 29 there is less parallelism between the stories than in the others; the emphasis is on the punishment, but there is also mention of the rescue of Noah, Abraham and Lot. The fate of 'Ād and Thamūd is seen from the present condition of their homes: 'Satan decked out fair to them their works, and barred them from the way, though they saw clearly' (38/37). In *sūra* 26 while there is still some emphasis on disbelief and its punishment, there is a great expansion of the messenger's initial message

> Thamood cried lies to the Envoys
> when their brother Salih said to them,
> 'Will you not be godfearing?
> I am for you a faithful Messenger,
> so fear you God, and obey you me.
> I ask of you no wage for this;
> my wage falls only upon the
> Lord of all Being.

Will you be left secure in this here, among
gardens and fountains,
sown fields, and palms with slender spathes?
Will you still skilfully hew houses
out of the mountains?
So fear you God and obey you me,
and obey not the commandment
of the prodigal
who do corruption in the earth, and set
not things aright.'
They said, 'Thou art merely one of those
that are bewitched;
thou art not but a mortal, like us;
then produce a sign, if thou art
one of the truthful.'
He said, 'This is a she-camel.' . . .

But they hamstrung her, and in the morning
they were remorseful,
and the chastisement seized them. (26.141–58)

The next on our list, *sūra* 11, brings in several new points. There is more of a debate between the messenger and his people, and it comes round to the question of polytheism; the calamity is spoken of as the 'command' or 'affair' (*amr*) of God, and the deliverance of the messenger and those who believed is emphasized.

And to Thamood their brother Salih;
he said, 'Oh my people, serve God!
You have no god other than He.
It is He who produced you from the earth
and has given you to live therein;
so ask forgiveness of Him, then repent
to Him; surely my Lord is nigh, and
answers prayer.'
They said, 'Salih, thou hast hitherto
been a source of hope among us. What,
dost thou forbid us to serve that
our fathers served? Truly we are in
doubt, concerning what thou callest us
to, disquieting.'
He said, 'O my people, what think you?
If I stand upon a clear sign
from my Lord, and He has given me

mercy from Him, who shall help me
against God, if I rebel against Him?
You would do nothing for me, except
increase my loss.
O my people, this is the She-camel of
God, to be a sign for you . . .
But they hamstrung her, and he said,
'Take your joy in your habitation
three days—that is a promise not
to be belied.'
And when Our command came, We delivered
Salih and those who believed with him by a
mercy from Us, and from the degradation of that day . . .
And the evildoers were seized by the Cry,
and morning found them in their habitations
fallen prostrate
as if they never dwelt there: 'Surely
Thamood disbelieved in their Lord, so
away with Thamood.' (11.61/64–68/71)

The last group of passages, those in *sūra* 7, are not unlike those in *sūra* 11. In each case the deliverance of the messenger and his companions is emphasized. Slightly more prominence is given to those who believe in the message, especially in the stories of Ṣāliḥ and Shu'ayb; and in those two stories the messenger deliberately dissociates himself from the unbelievers.

And to Thamood their brother Salih;
he said, 'O my people, serve God!
You have no god other than He;
there has now come to you a clear sign
from your Lord—this is the She-camel
of God, to be a sign for you. Leave her
that she may eat in God's earth, and do not
touch her with evil, lest you be seized by
a painful chastisement.
And remember when He appointed you
successors after Ad, and lodged you
in the land, taking to yourselves castles
of its plains, and hewing its mountains
into houses. Remember God's bounties,
and do not mischief in the earth,
working corruption.'
Said the Council of those of his people
who waxed proud to those that were abased,

to those of them who believed, 'Do you know
that Salih is an Envoy from his Lord?'
They said, 'In the Message he has been sent with
we are believers.'
Said the ones who waxed proud, 'As for
us, we are unbelievers in the thing in
which you believe.'
So they hamstrung the She-camel
and turned in disdain from the commandment
of their Lord, saying, 'O Salih,
bring us that thou promisest us, if
thou art an Envoy.'
So the earthquake seized them, and
morning found them in their habitation
fallen prostrate.
So he turned his back on them, and said,
'O my people, I have delivered to you
the Message of my Lord, and advised you
sincerely; but you do not love
sincere advisers.' (7.73/71–79/77)[9]

The figure of Moses, though it appears in some of these groups, is in a different position, since there is much more material available about Moses. To some extent the Qur'ān teaches, through the additional material, lessons of the same sort as those taught by the stories common to all the messengers; thus the incident of Moses as an infant being set adrift in an ark shows God's care for those who believe in him. The point at which Moses differs most from other messengers is in his continuing to have a history as leader of a religious community after the punishment of those who rejected him. To begin with, the story of Moses and Pharaoh is just another of the 'punishment stories'; indeed in one version Moses is not mentioned.

The warnings came also to Pharaoh's folk.
They cried lies to Our signs, all of them,
so We seized them with the seizing of One
mighty, omnipotent. (54.41 f.)

Parallels can similarly be found to all the other emphases found in the messenger stories just examined. In particular the references noted in some to the body of believers who followed the messenger are continued and developed. In the case of prophets like Ṣāliḥ this body of believers was somewhat nebulous; but in the case of Moses there was actual story material.

The emphasis on the deliverance of the believers doubtless became important only towards the end of the Meccan period, when escape from Mecca was hoped for, or planned, or achieved. Caution must be shown in dealing with this point, since in several passages dealing with the escape from Egypt, the main emphasis is on the destruction of Pharaoh and his people.[10] More interest therefore attaches to descriptions of the situation of Moses and his people after their deliverance. They are said to be settled securely (10.87–93), and to dwell in the land after the drowning of Pharaoh (17.98/100 f.). In addressing his people after their deliverance Moses exhorts them to continue in gratitude (14.5–7); and the story of the golden calf (e.g. 7.138/134–160) illustrates the difficulties to be found after deliverance. All this does not amount to a great deal, and it may be that the paucity of references to later aspects of Moses' achievement is due to the fact that by the time such references would have been appropriate the Muslims were coming to think of the Jews as their enemies. The importance of another parallel—that between Moses as leader of a 'scriptural' community and Muḥammad—is to be seen in the references to Moses being given the 'book'.[11]

The Hijra to Medina was far from being the end of the development of the conception of the religious leader during Muḥammad's lifetime; but soon after the Hijra this development became a matter of practice rather than of theory, and so cannot easily be traced in the Qur'ān. The position of unchallenged leadership eventually attained by Muḥammad was gained by his tact, by the magnetism of his personality, and by the prestige accruing from his military successes. The Qur'ānic conception of the religious leader contributed a little to this development, but not much. The settlement of disputes within the community of believers seems to be the subject of the verse: 'every community has its Messenger; then, when their Messenger comes, justly the issue is decided between them, and they are not wronged' (10.47/48). The referring of disputes to Muḥammad is mentioned in the Constitution of Medina (§23; cf. §42);[12] but it may not have become normal to do so until several years after the Hijra. Indeed it is explicitly stated that, 'when they are called to God and His Messenger that he may judge between them a party of them are swerving aside' (24.48/47). This is probably just before the battle of Uḥud, since two verses later there is the phrase 'sickness in their hearts', which was applied at this period to 'Abd-Allāh ibn-Ubayy and those who thought like him. In the same passage the Muslims are also called on to 'obey God and the Messenger'. Yet a few verses were far from settling this question. In another passage (apparently about two years later before the Siege of Medina) we read:

> O believers, obey God, and obey the Messenger
> and those in authority among you. If you
> should quarrel on anything, refer it to God
> and the Messenger . . . (4.59/62)

After the failure of the Siege of Medina (the Khandaq), it was more difficult for Muslims not to obey Muḥammad. It was still more difficult after the expedition of al-Ḥudaybiya (with the Pledge of Good Pleasure), after the conquest of Mecca and after the victory of Ḥunayn. Yet the growth of the reality of Muḥammad's power is not matched by any change in the Qur'ānic theory. He is still simply God's Messenger to the believers of Yathrib and the surrounding regions, following God's commands where these point to specific actions, but otherwise deciding as he himself thinks best. There is a verse which expresses rather more strongly the duty of obeying him (possibly to be dated after al-Ḥudaybiya):

> It is not for any believer, man or
> woman, when God and His Messenger
> have decreed a matter, to have the choice
> in the affair. Whosoever disobeys
> God and His Messenger has gone astray
> into manifest error. (33.36)

There are also exhortations to the believers to lower their voices in Muḥammad's presence and not to raise them above his (49.2 f.), and to salute him (33.56); but these and similar demands for certain marks of respect are very little to ask for one who was effective ruler of a large part of Arabia. In a sense, we may say, the Qur'ānic conception of leadership already contained all the essential marks of the leader, and practical successes did not necessitate any further elaboration.

3. The community of the religious leader

It is worth considering briefly the nature of the community to which a messenger was sent. So far as we can tell, the Arabs of Muḥammad's time had no conception of a community, or body of people living a common life, other than the tribe. By 'tribe' is to be understood a group of people united by kinship, that is, descent from a common ancestor. After Muḥammad's time it was usually patrilineal descent that alone was taken into account; but previously there had been kinship groups descended from a common mother, like the Aws and the Khazraj of Medina, who, before they became the Anṣār, were collectively known as Banū Qayla from a common ancestress. The Arabs had a number of words for kinship groups of different sizes, but the commonest word in the Qur'ān is *qawm*, usually rendered 'tribe' or 'people'. Within the tribe subdivisions were recognized, and it is convenient in English to refer to these as sub-tribes or clans, though there may be no distinct Arabic equivalent for these terms. Apart from the Qur'ān the Arabs normally referred to any kinship group as 'the sons of N'. The ancestors of the clans of a tribe would often be the sons of the common ancestor of the whole tribe. The tribe and each subdivision had a chief or *sayyid*, who normally came from a particular family. There was no law of primogeniture, however, and the chief was mostly the best-qualified member of the chiefly family. He took certain decisions on behalf of the tribe, such as when to move camp and where to form a new camp; but in most respects he was only *primus inter pares*. All the adult males of the tribe expected to take part in tribal councils as (roughly) equals to the chief.

The tribe or clan could be extended to those who were not in fact kinsmen. An outsider could be included in it as a *ḥalīf* or confederate (after exchanging oaths of loyalty with a member of the tribe), as a *jār* or 'protected neighbour', or else as a *mawlā* or client. Tribes and clans could also become confederates of one another, and occasionally an outstanding man managed to build up a large confederacy. Modern scholars have suggested that some of the genealogies to be found in the books are fictitious, having been invented *post eventum* to strengthen an existing confederacy by giving it a basis in kinship. The Arabs had apparently no conception of a community other than the kinship group. In early stories about the Byzantine emperor he conducts himself very like the chief of a large tribe, except that he is a trifle more autocratic than an Arab chief would have dared to be. Religion cannot be said to have in any way constituted the basis of the Arab tribe, but most tribes had a definite custom of worshipping at certain shrines. A shrine was usually in the charge of a small kinship group, perhaps only a 'family', who saw to its maintenance on behalf of those who had the custom of worshipping there.

In comparatively early passages of the Qur'ān a *rasūl* or messenger is said to be sent to a *qawm*—'the people of Pharaoh' (44.17/16); 'the people of Noah' (71.2, 5). About the same time, or possibly a little later, appears another word about which there has been much discussion. This is *umma*, which is usually rendered 'community' or 'nation'. Modern scholars have tended to hold that the term has some religious reference. Thus it has been suggested that in the Qur'ān it normally means an ethnic, linguistic or religious community, regarded as having a place in God's purposes.[13] Now it must be admitted that in most of the Qur'ānic usages of *umma* there is a reference to God's sending of a messenger to it; but this in itself does not justify the suggestion just quoted. At one place (6.38) beasts and birds are said to be 'in an *umma*'. More serious is the fact that in the later Medinan passages of the Qur'ān the word *umma* is less and less used. Moreover, one of the contemporary documents in our hands, the Constitution of Medina (probably belonging to the early or middle part of Muḥammad's time there), speaks of all the people of Yathrib (including the Jewish confederates) as an *umma*, while the letters and treaties of Muḥammad preserved by Ibn-Sa'd (most of which are probably genuine) do not contain the word *umma*. Thus, whatever the precise connotation of *umma* in the Qur'ān, it was not normally used in the closing years of Muḥammad's life for the community and state he had founded.

This may be called negative evidence, since it means that the more Muḥammad's community came to have a religious basis, the less the word *umma* was used. There is also positive evidence that it often meant a natural community, that is, one without any religious basis. Indeed the Hebrew word *ummā*, which may have influenced the usage of the Arabic word,[14] means 'tribe' or 'people', just like the Arabic *qawm*. In many passages of the Qur'ān *umma* hardly seems to differ from *qawm*. The fact that every community (*umma*) is said to have had a warner or messenger sent to it by God (10.47/48; 16.36/38; 23.44/46; 35.24/22) might suggest that an *umma* had always a place in God's purposes; in a sense this is so, but it is a truism. It is also clear that in many cases, perhaps in most, an *umma* is not composed solely of those who believed in the messenger; on the contrary, in each community there are those who have disbelieved God's signs (27.83/88).[15] Moreover communities are thought of as coming *as communities* to be judged by God and in many cases to be punished (27.83/85; 45.28/27; 16.84/86; 28.75; 7.38/36). This emphasis on communalistic judgment, which is distinct from the judgment on individuals described in early passages, gives some further support to the view that an *umma* was a community with a natural basis (such as kinship) and not one with a religious basis.

It has also to be noted that Muḥammad's community and state could be *entirely* explained on traditional Arab lines. The Constitution of Medina depicts a federation of clans, which was recognizably a federation even for a pagan nomadic Arab. The religion of Islam certainly entered into the Constitution at several points, namely: (1) the primary parties to the agreement (as distinct from 'those who follow them and are attached to them') are 'believers and Muslims'; (2) the document is a 'writing of Muḥammad the Prophet'; (3) disputes are to be referred 'to God and to Muḥammad'; (4) Muḥammad is to give permission for warlike expeditions; and (5) there are one or two phrases such as 'the security of God' and 'fighting in the way of God'. These points, however, are not sufficient to make the Constitution a religious document. The primary parties have indeed a certain religious belief, and it is not surprising that there should be some references to their religious belief in the document; but their religious belief is as it were irrelevant to the essential character of the agreement. The Constitution is an agreement of the old pagan Arab type between groups of people who happen to have a certain religious belief.

This incidental or accidental character of the religious factor may be said to continue. As the federation grew, new tribes who became confederates of Muḥammad also became confederates of the groups already in his federation, and were thereby precluded from attacking them. Individuals who wanted to become Muslims, and who were not members of a federated tribe, had to become clients of Muḥammad himself (and his clan of Emigrants) or of one of the federated tribes. To begin with Muḥammad probably accepted as allies or confederates, without asking them to become Muslims, those who were already allies of his Medinan allies. When he became sufficiently strong, any tribe or clan wanting to become his confederates had to accept Islam. This was a matter of policy, which could conceivably have been altered, and not part of the essential nature of the community of Medina. For long after

Muḥammad's death—probably till after the fall of the Umayyad dynasty in 750—the Islamic state continued to be officially a federation of Arab tribes (all Muslim), with bodies of Jews and Christians attached to it as 'protected groups' (in much the same way as Jews had been attached to Arab clans in Medina). It was apparently soon after the coming of the 'Abbāsids in 750 that the Islamic state ceased to be officially a federation of this type; for the 'Abbāsids had considerable support from the Persian and other non-Arab Muslims who were no longer prepared to tolerate the suggestion of inferiority in the status of clients (*mawālī*) of Arab tribes.

Some further points about the relation of the Islamic polity to kinship groups may be mentioned. At the battle of Badr some of the Muslim emigrants were actually fighting against close kinsmen, and this might seem to be a breach of old custom. This is not necessarily so, however. Even according to Arab custom it was possible in certain circumstances for a tribe to disown one of its members, and to refuse to be responsible for his misdeeds; and it was also possible for a man to renounce his tribe. A renunciation of the latter type was indeed the essence of the *hijra* made by Muḥammad and those who went with him from Mecca to Medina; it was a severing of relationships, not a physical movement. Even for the Muslims of Medina, who had no external *hijra* to make, there were difficult questions of adjusting the demands of the new relationships to those of the old relationships. In one celebrated case a veteran clan chief of Medina (Sa'd ibn-Mu'ādh) decided that the Jewish clan of Qurayẓa, by disloyal intrigues against the *umma* during the siege of Medina, had forfeited the right to the protection of his own clan, who were their allies according to old Arab ideas. The offer of the son of 'Abd-Allāh ibn-Ubayy (for a time Muḥammad's chief opponent at Medina) to kill his father is perhaps only a young man's exuberant enthusiasm for Muḥammad and his cause; but it could be regarded as springing from the belief that disloyalty to the Islamic *umma* was a ground for regarding traditional ties as broken. ('Abd-Allāh ibn-Ubayy, though he and his supporters were known as *munāfiqūn* or 'hypocrites', was nominally a Muslim and a member of the *umma*.)

In the early days when things were difficult Muḥammad more than once had recourse to a practice of artificial 'brothering' (*mu'ākhā*) to increase the solidarity of his followers. The best-known instance was shortly after the Hijra when each Emigrant was given a Medinan 'brother'. After a time there seems to have been sufficient cohesion among the Muslims without this special arrangement. Again, towards the end of Muḥammad's life, when many groups of Arabs had entered the Islamic polity without deep religious conviction, and there had been instances of one group (*ṭā'ifa*) of Muslims fighting another, and one *qawm* satirizing another, the Qur'ān reminds the Muslims that they are all brothers (49.9–11). This may be said to indicate that kinship still continued to be a powerful factor, and that the Islamic polity was expected to have an effect in uniting men similar to that of kinship, but it does not show to what extent religion entered into the basis of the polity.

The Islamic polity's conception of its relation to the Jewish and Christian religious bodies will be considered in the next chapter, but a word may be said here about the application of the word *umma* to Jews and Christians. At one point the Qur'ān seems to suggest that those to whom Moses and Jesus were sent constituted one community, but later became divided into sects (singular, *ḥizb*) (23.52/54 f.). The general name for Jews and Christians came to be *Ahl al-Kitāb*, 'the people of the Book'. It then becomes possible for the Qur'ān, perhaps referring to Jews who were prepared to acknowledge Muḥammad as prophet, to speak of an *umma* from among the people of the Book in terms of approval (3.113/109; 5.66/70). Although the people of the Book would thus appear to be a corporate entity with a religious basis, the Qur'ān never refers to the body of Muslims as a community with a Book, even when the corpus of the revelations to Muḥammad is regarded as a Book. The adjective *ummī*, which is almost certainly intended to render the conception 'gentile' (roughly as held by the Jews), never appears to be connected with the noun *umma*.

If in the later years of Muḥammad's life the body of Muslims was not called *umma*, how was it referred to? At all periods the commonest term in the Qur'ān is 'believers' (*mu'minūn*) or 'those who have believed'; 'Muslims' (*muslimūn*) is much less frequent. For a time *ḥanīf* seems to have meant practically the same as *muslim*; but, although it occurs twice in the plural (22.31/32; 98.5/4), the plural never seems to have been used to designate the body of Muḥammad's followers, although in a variant reading (to 3.19/17, ascribed to Ibn-Mas'ūd) his religion is spoken of, not as Islam, but as the Ḥanīfiyya;[16] and we know that this name was common in early times. In treaties of Muḥammad's later years the body politic is referred to as the *jamā'a* or *jamā'at al-muslimīn* (whole body of Muslims), or again as *ḥizb Allāh* (the party of God), the latter phrase being taken from the Qur'ān (e.g. 58.22). These later names make it clear that by this time it was recognized that to be a full member of the complex body politic established by Muḥammad one had to be a Muslim, even though formally it was a federation of the old Arab type. As regards its formal character, then, there was nothing novel in the Islamic polity. Yet the novelty was present in embryo, and asserted itself gradually in succeeding decades. It consisted in the decision, presumably taken by Muḥammad before the meetings at al-'Aqaba prior to the Hijra, approved by his followers, and put into force as his strength permitted—the decision that only 'believers' were to be accepted as members of his body politic, that is, men who accepted his message and himself as messenger, and who performed certain outward acts—worship (*ṣalāt*) and the payment of tithes (*zakāt*).

Chapter 5

The historical perspective

1. The general historical perspective

The historical perspective of the Arabs of Muḥammad's time is one that is very strange to the modern occidental. The strangeness is in part concealed by the presence of a number of familiar landmarks—such names as Adam, Noah, Abraham, Moses and Jesus. To the occidental these names come from the Bible, which is arranged more or less chronologically, and he is therefore—if he has any education in these matters—aware of the chronological order. In this way the modern occidental fails to realize that there was no chronological order in these names as they came to the Arabs of Muḥammad's time. They were simply a number of persons who for a time had played a part on the stage of the world, and who for some reason or other were worthy to be remembered. The Arabs were not interested in the chronological order, and paid no attention to it, even when they knew it or could easily discover it.

To understand the historical perspective of the Arabs, then, we should realize that they were very interested in persons and the relations of persons, but not at all in a quasi-mathematical time, conceived as flowing regularly in a straight line. Their historical perspective was given by such things as genealogy, since the Arabs usually knew their ancestors for many generations back. The *sīra* or biography of Muḥammad by Ibn-Is'ḥāq (d. 768) commences with his genealogy back to Adam (the latter part being taken from the Bible), while the material about pre-Islamic Arabia and Mecca (occupying some seventy pages in the English translation) may be said to be arranged on a genealogical framework. This genealogical order gave little guidance on the relative dates of anecdotes connected with two different lines of descent, unless there happened to be some interaction between persons in the two lines. Among the best-remembered anecdotes were those connected with the 'days', that is, the 'battle-days' or notable battles, of the Arabs; these sometimes gave correlations between different genealogical lines, but at times there is vagueness and confusion.

There was also some chronological material in memories of the order in which tribes had occupied a certain locality or controlled a certain shrine. Thus it was remembered that the shrine at Mecca had long been in the hands of the tribe of Jurhum, then in that of Khuzā'a, then in that of Quraysh. With this fact is to be linked the awareness, implied in many parts of the Qur'ān, that whole communities may disappear and be replaced by others. Among the tribes that have completely vanished are 'Ād and Thamūd. There are references to communities of Jinn and men that have passed away (46.18/17; 7.38/36); and communities like individuals are said to have a 'term' (*ajal*) or appointed end of their existence. Life in the desert must have had many vicissitudes; two or three misfortunes in a row might make a tribe too weak to survive and force it to attach itself to a stronger body, thereby perhaps losing its identity. In the books of genealogies which give the descendants of the early Muslims for the first century or so of the Islamic era, it is remarkable how many lines die out completely, while others flourish and after a century have numerous representatives. Perhaps the Arabs saw in succession of occupancy something analogous to the passage of generations, and so to genealogy; the first of the verses referred to above about communities (*umam*) passing away is preceded by one about generations (*qurūn*) passing away.

Since history for the Arabs was thus a collection of interesting anecdotes about persons who had lived at some period in the past —a collection not in any way chronologically ordered—it is not surprising that we should find something similar in the Qur'ān. The element of the Qur'ān dealing with past history is chiefly the stories about earlier messengers, which have already been described for the light they throw on the Qur'ānic conception of the messenger. There is also some further material, mostly about Abraham, Moses and Jesus. For the most part the Qur'ān presents this material as a collection of isolated anecdotes, except that the stories about the messengers tend to have a common pattern. Indeed it would be more exact in many cases to say that the anecdotes are not recounted in full, but mentioned allusively in much the same way as pre-Islamic poetry makes allusions to the 'days' of the Arabs. Just as the allusions in poetry reminded the hearers (usually of the same tribe as the poet) of the glories of their tribe and so encouraged them to perform noble actions, so the references to previous messengers encouraged Muḥammad and the Muslims to endure bravely when things were difficult. Perhaps they were also felt as giving him a kind of spiritual genealogy, and showing the Meccans that his activities were not sheer innovation, (always hateful to Arabs) but followed closely on earlier precedents.

In the Qur'ānic references to previous messengers there can be seen faint beginnings of a chronological interest. In some of the groups of stories there seems to be no thought of chronological order; in *sūra* 21, for example, the order is: Moses and Aaron, Abraham, Lot, Noah, David and Solomon, Job, Jonah, Zacharias. In other cases the order may be intended to be chronological, though the point is not asserted; in several *sūras* there is found something like the order of *sūra* 54: Noah, 'Ād, Thamūd, Lot, Pharaoh. The most emphatic statement of chronological interest is in *sūra* 7 (69/67, 74/72) where 'Ād are said to be successors of the people of Noah, and Thamūd of 'Ād. With this it is interesting to compare 51.46 and 53.53/54, where Noah comes after 'Ād and Thamūd, but the words *min qablu*, 'previously', also occur. The most likely explanation of this nascent chronological interest is, not that the Muslims became aware of chronological data of which they had previously been ignorant, but that they became aware of the Jews' interest in chronology and their criticism of the Qur'ān for the absence of chronology in it.

The lack of interest in chronology, and more generally in the causal connection between events, which seems to be a feature of the Arab mentality and to be given an expression in the philosophical 'occasionalism' of many later theologians, is further illustrated by the treatment of Adam in the Qur'ān. Here again much effort is required if the occidental, or indeed the modern Muslim, is to place himself in the position of Muḥammad's first hearers. They were familiar with their Arab genealogies, which went back —we may assume—to 'Adnān and Qaḥṭān, but almost certainly no farther. It was probably only in the course of Muḥammad's career that he and his followers realized that there were also Jewish genealogies, which represented all men as sons of Adam and the Arabs as descended from Abraham's son Ishmael. The detailed biblical genealogies do not seem to have been known to Muḥammad and his contemporaries, and it was left to later Muslim scholars to link up the lines of 'Adnān and Qaḥṭān with the biblical genealogies. Thus the early Muslims, even when they came to understand in a general way that they were the sons of Adam, did not *feel* they were descended from him in the same way as they were descended from ʿAdnān or Qaḥṭān. Some of the passages in the Qur'ān about Adam and his posterity read as if they were about a race of beings completely distinct from the Arabs. From this it would not be correct to infer ignorance on the part of the early Muslims, but it would be correct to infer an absence of any strong interest in being descended from Adam; the point just did not touch any deep spring of emotion in them.

As has already been seen, there are numerous passages in the Qur'ān where human procreation and the development of the embryo are described as one of the 'signs' of God. There appears to be far less interest in the origin of mankind as a whole. We find such an account as the following:

> It is He who created you out of one living soul,
> and made of him his spouse
> that he might rest in her. (7.189)

In this passage, however, there is no hint that the common parent is Adam. The most explicit recognition of the fact seems to be earlier in the same *sūra* (7.27/26), where the 'children of Adam' are addressed and exhorted not to let Satan tempt them as 'he brought your parents out of the Garden'. There is also the description (7.172/171) of a strange primeval scene when God took the whole progeny of Adam from his loins and made them bear witness that he is their Lord (such at least is the usual interpretation, though the wording is a little vaguer); but both here and in a reference (19.58/59) to prophets 'of the posterity of Adam' it should be noted that it is not explicitly stated or implied that the posterity of Adam is the whole human race. While there is no record of any special attention to this event in the first century of Islam, from about that time onwards this covenant or *mīthāq* was prominent in the thought of ascetics and mystics.

The creation of Adam from clay is mentioned several times in connection with the story of the fall of Iblīs. In some verses Adam is not mentioned by name, but God merely says to the angels that he is creating a 'human being' (*bashar*) (15.28; 38.71), before whom they are to prostrate themselves. Iblīs refuses on the ground that he is nobler than the man since he is created from fire and not from clay; and he is therefore expelled and cursed. The interest of this story for the Arabs was doubtless that it gave an explanation of the existence of the evil spirits in which they already believed.

Some of the remaining references to Adam allow him a very special place in God's purposes, yet never explicitly because he is the first man. Thus in one place (2.30/28–34/32) God is said to have set him in the earth as a viceroy or deputy (*khalīfa*), presumably for himself. To justify the angels doing obeisance to Adam God teaches him the names of all things, these being unknown to the angels. In a sense this is a description of the special position of mankind in the world, yet there is no hint of this in the wording of the Qur'ān, and one must wonder if this implication of the passage was appreciated by the early Muslims. The seduction of Adam and his spouse by Satan—apparently it is always Satan and not Iblīs—is described several times (2.35/33 ff.; 7.19/19 ff.; 20.115/114 ff.). It is essentially a punishment for disobedience, however, not an event of cosmic significance and the source of a perversion of all mankind. In one version (20.115/114) God has originally made a covenant with Adam (*'ahidnā ilā Ādam*), which the latter breaks by his disobedience; but God relents and chooses him (*ijtabā-hu*). As a final problem may be quoted a verse which is generally agreed to be one of the latest references to Adam in the Qur'ān:

> God chose (*iṣṭafā*) Adam and Noah
> and the house of Abraham
> and the house of Imran
> above all beings, the
> seed of one another . . . (3.33/30)

A brief word may be added about the story of Noah. In general Noah is represented as a messenger sent to 'his people', and they are destroyed in much the same way as other peoples who do not listen to their messenger. The interest is in the unusual and fearsome form taken by the destruction. Once again there is no hint that it is the destruction of all mankind that is threatened. The flood is simply the destruction of one people among many, and the ship or ark the method by which God saved his messenger.

When one thus pays attention to what is *not* said in the Qur'ān, and refrains from filling in the absent details as was done by later Muslim scholars and others familiar with the Bible, a clearer picture is attained of the historical perspective of the Arabs in

Muḥammad's lifetime. Only those details of stories could be effectively used in the Qur'ān which addressed themselves to the Arab outlook. The Arabs were interested in the story of Iblīs because they were familiar with evil spirits; but they were not interested in descent from Adam or Noah, because these names were unknown to their genealogists. They were more interested in the birth of a human baby by the normal process than in the creation of Adam from clay. They understood something about covenants and even choice. They knew how killing could disrupt society, and the story of how one son of Adam killed the other was introduced (5.27/30–32/36) in connection with regulations dealing with murder. Altogether the treatment of Adam and Noah is a good illustration of how the Qur'ān, in adapting itself to the Arab mentality, imposes an Arab historical perspective (or lack of it) on the biblical material.

2. Relations to other communities

Part of the historical perspective in which Islam sees itself is the relationship which it conceives itself to have to other religious communities. Something has already been said about this incidentally, but the topic is sufficiently important to be looked at in its own right.

The general view of the Qur'ān is that Muḥammad is one messenger among many. For the most part each messenger was sent to a different community, and each community eventually had its own messenger. There was perhaps an exception in the Jewish and Christian communities, since they might seem to have had many messengers. It may be, however, that the Arabs thought of the communities as limited in time.[1] Thus the communities to which Noah, Abraham, Lot and Ishmael were sent were not regarded as in any way predecessors of the Jews; and for that there is justification, since several of these communities had disappeared. Moses was the messenger *par excellence* to the Jews, but it was not clear whether David, Solomon and Jesus were messengers to the same community or to others. The possibility of a community splitting up was certainly present to the minds of the Arabs of this period; they doubtless knew of this happening many times in the desert whenever a tribe prospered and became so numerous that it was unwieldy. At one point the people of Moses are said to have been cut up into twelve groups (*asbāṭ*) or communities (*umam*) (7.160); and it seems to be implied that the sending of Jesus to the Children of Israel led to further divisions.[2]

The problem and mystery of the divisions of mankind is given prominence. Several times in the Qur'ān there occurs some such phrase as 'Had God so willed, he would have made you one community' (5.48/53; 11.118/120; 16.93/95; 42.8/6). Originally the people (*qawm*)—presumably meaning all mankind—had been only one community, but then they separated from one another (10.19/20). Some communities erred and were destroyed, and others took their places, since each community (like each individual) has its appointed term to its existence. In particular the communities inhabiting Mecca (including that to which, according to the Qur'ān, Abraham and Ishmael had been sent as messengers) had passed away (13.30/29); and thus it was true that Muḥammad had been sent to a community which had not previously had any messenger (32.3/2; 34.44/33; 36.6/5).[3] From this it may be implied that, according to the thinking of the Meccan Arabs, there was no continuity between themselves and the inhabitants of Mecca in the distant past. Indeed it is not clear that there was any conception of 'the Arabs' as constituting in any sense a community; and it may well be, as has been suggested,[4] that it was only after the career of Muḥammad that the Arabs began to realize how much they had in common.

It must have been clear to the early Muslims, however, that the Christians and the Jews were in an outstanding position as religious communities. They knew that the Byzantines and the Abyssinians were Christians. They may also have known that there were numerous Christian groups in Arabia, and perhaps even that a large proportion of the inhabitants of Iraq were Christians. Even before the Hijra they may have known something about the Jews in Arabia, and they certainly learnt a great deal when they went to Medina. The far-spreading commercial interests of Mecca made it inevitable that the leading merchants should know something of the politics of their neighbours and the religious implications of their policies. In particular they must have known of the great struggle that had been going on between the mighty Persian and Byzantine empires through most of the second half of the sixth century. The wave of Persian successes culminating in the capture of Jerusalem in 614 is probably referred to in the Qur'ān (30 *ad init.*). On the usual interpretation of this passage the sympathies of the Meccans were with the

Byzantines, but the official policy of Mecca seems to have been one of neutrality. Neutrality was virtually essential if their trade was to continue, since they were concerned with the transit of goods from the Yemen (which was partly controlled by a Persian garrison) to the Byzantine markets at Gaza and Damascus; some Meccans also traded with Iraq.

The Meccan policy of political neutrality is probably closely linked with the adoption of Islam by many Meccans. Though there was a spiritual need for monotheism, Christianity and Judaism could not fully satisfy this need because of their political implications. For a Meccan to become a Christian meant subordination to the Byzantine empire; and in the case of Judaism there seems to have been a likelihood of similar dependence on Persia. There had in fact been an incident of this kind. Some fifteen years before Muḥammad began to receive revelations a Meccan, who had become a Christian, promised his fellow-Meccans that, if they accepted him as their prince, he would establish very favourable relations with the Byzantines; but this was not at all to the liking of the Meccan merchants, who preferred the higher, if riskier, profits of independence and neutrality, and they got other members of his clan to expel him. An independent revelation, which gave the Meccans and other Arabs a monotheism parallel to Judaism and Christianity, but without any political 'strings', was precisely what many were looking for.

The Muslims probably had little direct contact with Jews and Christians until they went to Medina, and there they found three Jewish clans and other smaller groups intricately mixed up in the politics of that oasis. The Qur'ānic view was that the message brought by all the messengers was the same in essentials, though from the first it must have been realized that there were particular instructions which might apply only to a single community (such as those about the she-camel of Thamūd). Nevertheless Muḥammad and his followers hoped that when they went to Medina the Jews there as well as the Arabs would accept him as prophet. Some at least of the Muslims seem to have turned to face Jerusalem when they prayed (like the Jews), and to have observed the Jewish Fast of Atonement. A few, however, even before the Hijra are said to have insisted that Mecca was the proper direction (*qibla*) to face in prayer. This divergence of opinion may have had political ramifications; it was said that a prominent Medinan leader, 'Abd-Allāh ibn-Ubayy, who had kept neutral in the feud which had rent the oasis, would have become prince of Medina but for the arrival of Muḥammad, and he was reckoning on the support of some of the Jewish clans. This fact may have largely determined the Jewish attitude to Muḥammad; at least it is known that, instead of accepting him as prophet, they began to mock and criticize him in a way that threatened to destroy the roots of the whole Islamic religious movement. They were able to argue that the Qur'ān could not be a revelation from God, since it claimed to be in agreement with their scriptures, and yet contradicted them.

In countering this argument and defining the relation of the Islamic community and religion to the Jewish, the Qur'ān develops the figure of Abraham. Abraham had appeared, like many other messengers, in stories about the punishment of wicked and disobedient peoples (e.g. 51.24 ff.). Then there are several accounts of how he turned from the idols worshipped by his father and his father's people (e.g. 37.83/81 ff.). The next stage (in a logical analysis) is when he is referred to as a *ḥanīf*. This word is something of a problem. It is apparently derived from a Syriac word meaning 'pagan', and is frequently used in this sense by Christian writers of Arabic. In the Qur'ān, however, *ḥanīf* is applied to one who is a monotheist but neither a Jew nor a Christian. It is possible that the connecting link between these two usages is that there was a form of the word in the language of the Nabataeans which 'meant a follower of some branch of their partially Hellenized Syro-Arabian religion';[5] such persons might be regarded as 'pagans' by the Christians and yet from another point of view might justifiably be considered monotheists. Whatever the derivation, there is no doubt about the Qur'ānic meaning—a follower of the purest form of monotheism. This is specially connected with Abraham, and he is often referred to as 'a *ḥanīf*, a Muslim'. It is also added that he is neither a Jew nor a Christian (3.67/60),[6] which, of course, is a simple matter of genealogical fact, since, according to the Bible, he is the grandfather of Jacob or Israel, the ancestor of the Jews, while other descendants of Abraham through Ishmael or Esau are not Jews.

This conception of the pure monotheism of Abraham led to a new conception of the historical relationship between the Muslims and the Jewish and Christian communities. The Jews and Christians were accused of having corrupted this religion, while the Muslims were restoring it in its purity. The claim that the religion of Muḥammad and his followers was the religion of Abraham in its pure form was strengthened by the Qur'ānic assertion that the sanctuary at Mecca had been established by Abraham with the help of Ishmael; and Abraham is said to have prayed that there would be a community submissive (*muslima*) to God among his posterity, taught by a messenger who was one of themselves (2.125/119–129/123). This provides a justification for the practice which was finally adopted by the Muslims about a year and a half after the Hijra and which became one of their distinctive marks, namely, the practice of facing Mecca in worship, or taking Mecca as *qibla*.

The assertion that Jews and Christians had corrupted the religion revealed to them was supported in many ways. The Old Testament gave much material; thus it was alleged that the Jews had broken the covenant made with God at Sinai by worshipping a calf (20.83/85–98), and that they had disobeyed some of the commands of God, such as the prohibition of usury (4.161/159). As a people whose culture was essentially oral, the Arabs would not be much impressed by the existence of a copy of the Jewish Bible, if there was one in Medina; but in any case the Qur'ān makes a number of points which weaken the Jewish argument that the Qur'ān must be in error where it differs from their scriptures. The Jews are alleged to have tampered with the scriptures in various ways: to have made additions to the revelation (apparently referring to their oral law), to have concealed parts of it from the Muslims (notably passages in which the Muslims believed that the appearance of Muḥammad as a prophet had been clearly foretold), and to have altered the meanings of words and made them oblique, whatever exactly these phrases may mean.[7]

While the alleged corruption of the pure religion by Jews and Christians accounted for many of the differences between these religions and Islam, there were some differences which could be explained in other ways. Among these were the different forms of worship, since the Qur'ān (22.67/66) mentions that God has 'appointed for every community a holy rite that they shall perform'. Some food restrictions, too, are recognized as having been imposed by God only on the Jews, but this has been done as a punishment for their greed and other sins (4.160/159; 6.146/147). With alternative explanations of the divergences between Islam and the religions with which it claimed to be identical in essentials, it was easy for the Muslim to feel that his community had the answer to the criticisms made of it by opponents.

Thus Islam grew into a consciousness of itself as a distinct community, different from the Jewish and Christian communities, yet able to hold up its head in their company. The definitive appearance of its will to differ from the Jews and to be itself may be said to be marked by the change of *qibla* just before the battle of Badr in 624. This led on to a proud and confident self-awareness and assertion of their individuality. 'You are the best community ever brought forth to mankind' (3.110/106). Likewise God says, apparently to the Muslims, 'We appointed you a midmost community that you might be witnesses to (or against) mankind, and that the Messenger might be a witness to (against) you' (2.143/137); the precise meaning of this is debatable, but it gives the Islamic community a position that is in some respect a special position. It is further implied that the Muslims are also superior to Jews and Christians because they recognize all God's messengers, whereas the Jews and Christians clearly reject some, notably Muḥammad.

> And they say, 'Be Jews or Christians, and
> you shall be guided.' Say thou: 'Nay, rather
> the creed of Abraham, a man of pure faith;
> he was no idolater.'
> Say you: 'We believe in God, and
> in that which has been sent down on us
> and sent down on Abraham, Ishmael,
> Isaac and Jacob, and the (twelve) Tribes,
> and that which was given to Moses and Jesus
> and the Prophets, of their Lord; we
> make no division between any of them, and
> to Him we surrender.' (2.135/129 f.)

There are also even wider perspectives opening up. In so far as the religion of the Jews and Christians has been corrupted, it would seem (according to one passage—42.15/14) that Muḥammad is to call upon them to abjure their errors. From this it is a short step to regarding Muḥammad's mission as one to all mankind.

> We have sent thee not, except to mankind
> entire, good tidings to bear, and warning . . . (34.28/27)
>
> Say: 'O mankind, I am the Messenger of God
> to you all,

of Him to whom belongs the kingdom of the heavens
and of the earth.
There is no god but He.
He gives life and He makes to die.
Believe then in God, and in His Messenger,
the Prophet of the common folk, who believes
in God and His words, and follow him; haply
so you will be guided.' (7.158/157)

There are other phrases which point towards the same conclusion, though a little more vaguely, since they could conceivably be interpreted otherwise. He is sent as a 'mercy to the worlds' (*raḥma li-l-'ālamīn*) (21.107), and he is 'the seal of the Prophets' (*khātam an-nabiyyīn*) (33.40). These are phrases which hint at a view which would see in Muḥammad and Islam the climax of world history and the consummation of all mundane activities. So at least it has seemed to many Muslims, and such seems to the modern occidental to be the implication of the phrases. Yet when we remember how different the seventh-century Arab's historical perspective is from ours, one wonders whether the phrases could have meant as much to him. Perhaps it would be safer simply to conclude that the Arab was assured that the Islamic community had a secure place in the world.

Part 2

The embodiment of the vision

Chapter 6

The achievement of Muḥammad's lifetime

1. From vision to embodiment

The previous four chapters have attempted to describe the vision of the universe (including the dimension of transcendence) which is expressed in the Qur'ān. The acceptance of Islam as a religion by men of many different races shows that this vision has a high degree of universality. Yet even in the Qur'ānic expression of the vision there has been some fusion of the universal elements with particular Arab elements. One of the universal elements is the awareness of human life as determined and limited by factors beyond human control and greater than man; but the precise form in which the omnipotence and creative power of God is described owes not a little to the nomadic Arab's experience of the determination of his life by 'time'. The particular Arab element is perhaps most noticeable in the distinctive historical perspective of the Qur'ān. To this extent, then, the vision at its very simplest is already embodied in Arab particularities.

The embodiment of the vision, at which we are now to look, is thus not something wholly novel, but only an increase of particularization. It might be called the bringing of the whole of life under the vision, and that for a vast community of millions of human beings. It should be clear, however, that this process cannot be compared to the actualizing of a blue-print of a machine. The vision is not a detailed plan which can be realized item by item. While a vision is being realized, the normal activities of the community continue, but gradually they come to receive a certain direction, as it were, from the vision. Men begin from where they are, and go on doing things as they have always done them until something becomes unsatisfactory and has to be changed. The unsatisfactoriness may be due to external events, or to an increasing awareness of inner contradiction. Whether the presence of the vision has contributed to the dissatisfaction with existing conditions or not, the vision tends to guide men as they set about making changes and modifications. In this all men's activities come to be, not prescribed by the vision, but in harmony with it and contributing to its fuller realization.

The remainder of the present chapter will give a roughly chronological account of Muḥammad's life and career.[1] This should provide a framework into which points already touched on incidentally can be fitted. Special attention, however, will be given to the ways in which the vision is gradually embodied, so that the continuing life of communities is subtly modified. The vision will be spoken of as a unity, though for Muḥammad himself it was only gradually being filled out in detail.

2. Mecca about 610, and Muḥammad's original message

When Muḥammad began to receive revelations, he and his first followers began to modify their lives in certain ways because of the revelations. This happened about the year A.D. 610. Our first task, then, is to try to understand the kind of life they were leading in Mecca about the year 610.

Mecca at this period was a prosperous commercial city. It stood on barren lava where no agriculture was possible, but it possessed a sanctuary; and the sacredness thus conferred on the whole region, especially during a particular month of the year, had led to the holding there of a successful annual fair at which considerable quantities of goods passed between the nomads and the sedentary populations. From such beginnings the Meccans advanced, not without unscrupulous dealings and the use of military force, until they controlled all the trade from the Yemen and other parts of South Arabia up to the Byzantine markets at Gaza and Damascus. They were also involved in other lucrative enterprises such as mining. The Meccans had benefited from the operation of the chief political factor in that part of the world, the old hostility between the Persian and Byzantine empires. Both had tried to gain influence wherever they could in the Arabian peninsula, but the Meccan policy of neutrality had been extremely successful.

The growing prosperity of Mecca had had repercussions within Meccan society. So far as the main clans of Mecca were concerned, there does not seem to have been any difference such as that between patricians and plebeians at Rome; but there had been developing an important distinction between those who had become successful merchants on a really big scale and those who, for one reason or another, had failed to do so. Perhaps what marked off the group of successful merchants was that they were able to act as entrepreneurs in organizing large caravans (and take the lion's share of the profits), whereas lesser men had to send their goods by someone else's caravan and could hope for only meagre profits. The great merchants were usually chiefs of clans, and were prepared to use their privileges as such in order to further business deals, but when it came to the responsibilities, their attitude was different; they tended to think more of business associates than of fellow-clansmen, and they shirked the chiefly duty of looking after the impoverished or unfortunate members of the clan.

As has already been noticed, the original message of the Qur'ān was relevant to this situation. It saw the root of the social tensions in Mecca as lying in the belief of the great merchants in the omnicompetence, indeed the omnipotence, of human planning and human wealth; and it therefore called on such persons to acknowledge the existence of higher powers and, in consequence, to act in the ways that would gain the approval of the higher powers. In particular they were to be generous, not niggardly, with their wealth, and to use some of it to relieve the needs of unfortunate members of the community. The old Arab conception of honour had broken down in the commercial environment of Mecca, but it was replaced, as a sanction for socially responsible conduct, by the Qur'ānic teaching that at the Last Judgment each man must appear before God as an individual to be recompensed for his good and bad deeds.

It would appear from a careful study of the social position of the first Muslims that they nearly all came from that section of the community which was most keenly aware of the social tensions or most exposed to the rapacity of the merchant princes. By the latter group are meant those 'weak' persons—persons without the full protection of a clan—who had no redress against unscrupulous dealing by the leading merchants. These were comparatively few in number, however. The majority of the early Muslims were men from what might be described as the stratum next to that of the top men—those who just failed to enter that inner circle of entrepreneurs where the large profits were to be made. There were younger brothers and kinsmen of the leading men, and there were senior men from families and clans which had somehow failed to 'make the grade'. Muḥammad himself had intellectual gifts and organizing ability which would have enabled him to become one of the leading merchants, but he was prevented from using his gifts by a general decline in the fortunes of the clan of Hāshim, and not least by the death of his own father.

The first Muslims, then, were men caught up in the wave of social discontent at Mecca resulting from its commercial prosperity and the increasing gap between the very wealthy and the others. These were the men who entered into the Qur'ānic vision, and who accepted it in the sense that they considered it a true picture of the world in which they had to live and act. This does not mean that they at once became ardent social reformers. The vision is not a plan for the attainment of social justice, even if it has implications that point in this direction. First and foremost the vision is a picture of the world as it *is*. It sees the world as a place where events are controlled by God and not by money and big business. This vision thus enabled men to feel they were living significantly, although by the standards of money and big business they were relative failures. The point of which at that period they were most conscious was perhaps that, however successful money and big business seemed to be for the moment, they would not continue indefinitely to be successful (unless they acknowledged God and abandoned fraudulent practices), since God would intervene to punish and destroy them. The chief thing the vision gave them, then, was encouragement to go on.

When men accepted the vision as a basis for living, it led to certain modifications in their activities. They spent time in worshipping God together; indeed the more enthusiastic seem to have spent much of every night in devotional exercises. They engaged in what they called *tazakkī*, but unfortunately we do not know precisely what they meant by this word. It is variously translated 'purifying of oneself' and 'almsgiving', but it is also said to mean much the same as 'being a Muslim'. It probably included avoidance of all the acts criticized by the Qur'ān in the great merchants, and possibly also some use of the money they had to help the unfortunate. In short it was the leading of a good life, with special emphasis on the points which required emphasis in seventh-century Mecca. In addition Muḥammad expounded the Qur'ānic vision to those whom he thought might respond, and other Muslims doubtless did something similar. They did not avoid the great merchants, but tried to get them to accept the vision and to show more generosity in the use of their money.

It may be concluded, then, that the first embodiment of the vision in the life of Mecca consisted in the specified changes in the lives of those who accepted it, together with appeals to other members of the population.

3. Failure at Mecca

According to the early authorities Muḥammad expounded his message privately to friends for three years before he began to preach publicly. At first the public preaching had some success, but gradually opposition developed until it became one of the contributory reasons for the emigration of some Muslims to Abyssinia. This last event is said to have taken place in the fifth year after the first revelation. The affair of the 'satanic verses' is to be dated about the same time. If we place the first revelation in the year 610, then the beginning of public preaching would be in 613 and the emigration to Abyssinia and the 'satanic verses' would be in 615. The chronological material for this period is scanty and inadequate, and so these dates are only approximate. Yet they are worth taking as a rough guide.

Two stages or phases can be logically distinguished in the hostile relations between the leading Meccan merchants on the one hand and Muḥammad and his followers on the other. The transition is probably marked by the affair of the 'satanic verses'. It is probable that opposition to Muḥammad's movement developed gradually as a consequence of some aspects of the message which he preached publicly. Although the main part of the message was presumably the call to acknowledge and worship God, there was also some castigation of the niggardliness and lack of concern for the unfortunate shown by the wealthy Meccans. It was doubtless this moral criticism which annoyed those against whom it was directed. They perhaps also felt that Muḥammad's claim to be in touch with a supernatural source of wisdom, combined with his other gifts, meant that he was bound sooner or later to be a serious candidate for supreme rule in Mecca, and therefore a threat to the controlling oligarchy. At this stage they cannot have felt—if they ever did—that his monotheism was likely to destroy the sanctity of the Ka'ba at Mecca, make it unsuitable for fairs, and so greatly reduce their trade; up to the time when he publicly rejected the 'satanic verses' Muḥammad had not attacked the worship of the Ka'ba. The chief threat to their profits from his preaching was from the abandonment of fraudulent practices and the making of provision for the needy. This stage of Meccan opposition to Muḥammad may be identified with the descriptions in the Qur'ān of how Muḥammad's opponents rejected the messenger and his message.

The second phase of Meccan hostility to the Muslims may be said to begin when Muḥammad denounced the 'satanic verses'. The affair has been described above (ch. 2, §5). When he accepted the verses as a genuine revelation, Muḥammad was attempting to come to some compromise with the leading Meccans. His realization of the falsehood of the intruded verses was *ipso facto* a realization that compromise was impossible. There could be no religious movement under Muḥammad which included most of the inhabitants of Mecca. He and his followers had to be a distinct body marked off from the pagans. The attitude is forcefully expressed in a short *sūra* (109):

> Say: 'O unbelievers,
> I serve not what you serve
> and you are not serving what I serve,
> nor am I serving what you have served,
> neither are you serving what I serve.
> To you your religion, and to me my religion!'

From this point onwards for the rest of Muḥammad's Meccan period the Qur'ān vigorously attacks the worship of idols and asserts that there is no deity except God.

This chain of events seems to imply some resurgence of paganism. So far as we can tell there was little effective belief in the pagan gods when Muḥammad began to receive revelations. Those of his fellows who were not crass materialists were, it has been suggested, 'tribal humanists' who might from time to time pay lip service to some local deity. The new emphasis in the Qur'ān, however, makes it almost certain that there had been some reassertion of paganism. This is only what might have been expected. A conflict of will between two groups of men is seldom fought out explicitly on the fundamental issues, but rather on those issues on which both sides are prepared to stand and do battle. The real issue in this case was the attack on the individual and social morality of the rich Meccans, but of course this was not suitable ground on which they could make a stand. The moral critique, however, was intimately linked with a certain picture of the universe, and it was obviously good defence tactics to attack some features of this picture and at the same time to offer an alternative picture. Even men who do not practise their traditional religion, rally to its defence if they think it is being attacked. Partly as a natural reaction to the spread of Muḥammad's religion, and partly as a piece of deliberate calculation, the leaders of the opposition to Muḥammad linked their policies with the traditional pagan religion. It is in this context that we must interpret the statement that Abū-Sufyān took the goddesses al-Lāt and al-'Uzzā along with the Meccan army in the expedition of Uḥud (A.D. 624).

One or two events have been recorded from this second phase of the opposition between Muḥammad and the pagan Meccans. Towards the end of the period, which lasted from about 615 to 622, there was increasing persecution of the Muslims. Owing to the fact that injuries to the person were liable to lead to blood-feuds, force could not be used against any Muslim except by senior members of his own clan. Thus many Muslims were largely exempt from persecution except of a petty kind, such as having garbage dumped outside one's door (as is said to have happened to Muḥammad). Those who were 'weak', that is, with little or no 'clan protection', did suffer to some extent. Slaves also had a difficult time, if their masters were active members of the opposition; and Muḥammad's chief supporter, Abū-Bakr, is said to have spent much of his money in buying enslaved Muslims who were being ill-treated. The leading merchants, of course, took coercive measures against junior members of their clans, and used threats of commercial discrimination against lesser merchants who did not fully support their policies.

The beginning of this second phase roughly corresponds with the event or series of events known as the emigration to Abyssinia. There is no reason for supposing that the emigration did not take place or that the lists of participants are not roughly accurate; yet much about the emigration remains obscure. It may have begun before the affair of the 'satanic verses', and the main reason for it may have been that some of the Muslims were already being persecuted; but there were probably other reasons also, since some of the emigrants remained in Abyssinia until 629—long after Muḥammad's establishment at Medina. Altogether eighty-three adult males are said to have gone, along with their dependants. The common version that they went in a body, some of them twice, is not supported by the oldest sources, and must be judged improbable. It is more likely that they went in small groups. Most of them returned to Mecca before the Hijra, and most, but not all, of these took part in the Hijra to Medina. A few, as just noted, remained until 629. Most of them presumably engaged in commerce while in Abyssinia.

Another event of the period is the boycott of the clan of Hāshim, which probably began about 616, and is said to have lasted for nearly three years. It is presented in the sources as a way of bringing pressure to bear on the clan of Hāshim to disown Muḥammad or at least to get him to stop propagating his religion. Most of the other main clans joined in the boycott, which meant that they were to have no business dealings with Hāshim and no intermarriage. This boycott is said to have been maintained for over two years. Since there is no record of any members of the clan (apart from Abū-Lahab) complaining about the boycott, there is some justification for surmising that, although the leading members of the clan did not approve Muḥammad's religious teaching, they were in full sympathy with his moral critique of the leading merchants. The boycott eventually 'fizzled out'. It had not been very effective, and, in so far as it was, it may simply have been making the strong men stronger.

About the year 619, soon after the end of the boycott, the chief of Hāshim, Muḥammad's uncle Abū-Ṭālib, died, and was succeeded by another uncle Abū-Lahab. This led to a serious deterioration in Muḥammad's position in Mecca. Abū-Lahab, as the honour of an Arab chief demanded, undertook to continue the protection of Muḥammad, although he was now in close business relations with some of the great merchants, and had sided with them against his own clan in the boycott. Soon after he became chief, however, some of his business associates made him realize that he could disown Muḥammad without any stain on his honour, since Muḥammad had spoken shamefully about Abū-Lahab's father (his own grandfather), asserting that he was in Hell. What exactly happened is not explicitly stated, but may be inferred from various data. Abū-Lahab must either have withdrawn clan protection from Muḥammad absolutely, or else made conditions which Muḥammad could not accept (such as ceasing to propagate his religion). What is recorded is that Muḥammad visited the neighbouring town of aṭ-Ṭā'if, where, instead of being honourably received as he hoped, he had the mob set on him, and was lucky to escape alive. Moreover, before entering Mecca again, he had to find the chief of another clan who was prepared to protect him, and it was only the third person he approached who acceded to his request.

With prospects for Muḥammad and the Muslims at their gloomiest, a ray of hope appeared when, at the pilgrimage of 620, some men from Medina showed themselves ready to accept Muḥammad's message. They interested others at Medina, and negotiations were carried forward at the pilgrimage of 621. Finally at the pilgrimage of 622 (in June–July) some seventy-five persons from Medina, representing most of the Arab clans, took an oath to defend Muḥammad as they would their nearest kin. Most of the Muslims in Mecca then began to migrate to Medina in small groups, Muḥammad himself coming last with Abū-Bakr and reaching the south of the oasis of Medina on 24 September. Thus was completed the Hijra, the breaking of ties between the Muslims and their kinsmen at Mecca.

Outwardly this was a failure to advance the embodiment of the Qur'ānic vision in the life of the inhabitants of Mecca. Yet the vision had not been without its effect even on those who opposed the Muslims. It had made the pagans aware of the contrast and contradiction between monotheism coupled with social justice and polytheism coupled with various malpractices. It had also forced them to choose, and for the moment they had chosen polytheism. Yet, even in making this choice, they might be said to be embodying something of the Qur'ānic vision, namely, its insistence on the contradiction between monotheism and polytheism. The previous 'vague monotheism', with its toleration of intercession of the deities at local shrines, was henceforward impossible. History shows that this slight and almost negative embodiment of the vision was a stage towards a fuller positive embodiment when most of the people of Mecca accepted Islam.

4. New possibilities at Medina

With Muḥammad's arrival at Medina there opened up before him the thrilling prospect of a much fuller realization of the ideas of his religion. His power was still strictly limited, however, in the year 622. As has been mentioned above, he was to be regarded as one clan chief among nine. Most of the inhabitants of the oasis, however, had recognized him as prophet, and this gave him prestige, though no specific administrative powers apart from that of adjudicating in such disputes as were submitted to him. The bitter feuds at Medina, in which peace had not yet been made, might have been expected to give Muḥammad opportunities to increase his authority; yet there is no record of this. It is possible, however, that he did much to smooth over difficulties before a critical point had been reached. Nevertheless, the chance of bringing in an impartial person of such prestige doubtless weighed much with many of the Medinan Arabs when they decided to accept Islam. Their contacts with the Jews of the oasis had at the same time made them familiar with monotheism, and perhaps also with the expectation of a religious leader who would come to set all things right. Thus Muḥammad came to Medina with his religious claims accepted, at least nominally, by the majority of the Arabs there, even though his political powers were no greater than those of a clan chief. This meant new opportunities for embodying his vision in ordinary life; in particular, his followers could engage in worship publicly, and were presumably joined in this by many of the men of Medina.

Medina also brought serious difficulties. One of the greatest of these was the presence of partly hostile Jewish clans. It was not that the Jews refused to recognize Muḥammad as a prophet, nor even that they engaged in political intrigue against him, serious as such attitudes and actions were. Much more serious was the Jewish attack on the ideational basis of Muḥammad's preaching. It had been claimed that the Qur'ān was a message from God and thus inerrant; and it had also been claimed that there was a large measure of identity between the Qur'ānic message and what was to be found in the previous scriptures. If the Jews, then, maintained that there were errors and false statements in the Qur'ān (because it disagreed with their Bible) and that therefore it could not be a message from God, they were threatening to destroy the foundations of Muḥammad's whole religious movement. If the vision were discredited, there could be no question of any embodiment of it.

At the level of ideas this threat was countered (as described in the last chapter) by the assertion that the Jewish (and Christian) scriptures had been corrupted. There were also military attacks against the Jews which may be briefly summarized here. In April 624, shortly after the victory of Badr, while the Muslims were flushed by that success and Muḥammad's political rivals at Medina temporarily eclipsed, he attacked and expelled the tribe of Qaynuqā', who had a central group of houses where they practised metal-work (including the manufacture of arms) and conducted a market; most of the houses were granted to emigrants from Mecca, who until now had been guests of some of the keener Medinan Muslims. In August 625, after the Muslims had recovered from the reverse at Uḥud, a second Jewish tribe was expelled, an-Naḍīr. At the siege of Medina in April 627 the remaining large Jewish clan, Qurayẓa, intrigued with the enemy, and after the failure of the siege it was forced to surrender and then punished, all the men being executed and the women and children sold into slavery. Finally in May/June 628 the oasis of Khaybar, which was almost entirely Jewish and had received the clan of an-Naḍīr as refugees, was attacked and captured by the Muslims, and the inhabitants made tributaries of the Islamic state. There were still a few small groups of Jews in Medina, but they were too cowed to voice any further criticisms of the Qur'ān. The dangers from the Jews had been averted.

Another of Muḥammad's difficulties was that of providing for the livelihood of the Emigrants, though this is one which he presumably foresaw before he left Mecca. The religious vision could not be said to be embodied in life simply by the practice of public worship, unless at the same time the worshippers were earning their livelihood by normal economic processes. But how exactly did the Meccan Emigrants do this at Medina, and to what extent were they dependent on the hospitality of the Muslims of Medina? Although there was still some poor but cultivable land available in Medina, it is difficult to suppose that the businessmen of Mecca contemplated taking to farming. There are indications that some at least of them engaged in commercial speculations in the market of the Qaynuqā', and there was doubtless more scope for this after that clan had been expelled. Up to spring 624, however, it would appear that the Emigrants must have owed much to their fellow Muslims in Medina. Yet one cannot suppose that Muḥammad contemplated them continuing as guests indefinitely. The chief alternatives open to them would seem to have been; either to organize long-distance caravans between Medina and Syria or Iraq; or to raid Meccan caravans. Since the first course would almost certainly lead to armed disputes with the Meccans, and the second involved something similar, hostilities with Mecca in some form or another would seem to have been inevitable.

It would be interesting to know whether Muḥammad realized

this inevitability before he left Mecca, or whether the point became clear to him only gradually; but it is not important to be able to answer such questions. What seems certain is that at least from the beginning of 624 he was aware that hostilities with the Meccans could not be indefinitely postponed, and decided rather to hasten the decision by provoking the Meccans. He had also to consider how to gain the whole-hearted military support of the Medinans. These thoughts must have been in his head as he sent out small expeditions to raid Meccan caravans, especially the expedition of Nakhla which was the first to gain a success and to shed Meccan blood (January 624). The story of Muḥammad's struggle with the Meccans over the next six years is well known, and a brief sketch will suffice in the present context.

The first important event after the expedition of Nakhla, and indeed one of the turning-points in Muḥammad's career, was the battle of Badr in March 624. On this occasion Muḥammad himself led a force of over 300 men to Badr, the nearest convenient point to Medina on the caravan route from Mecca to Syria. This was the first time Muḥammad had commanded anything like so large a force, and it was also the first time he had received so much support from the Anṣār (or Muslims of Medina). The aim of the expedition was to intercept a rich caravan returning from Syria to Mecca. The caravan itself eluded Muḥammad, but a force of some 900 men from Mecca had come out to defend it. This force and the Muslim raiding party found themselves in a position (perhaps in part contrived by Muḥammad) from which neither could withdraw without losing face. The ensuing battle was a great victory for the Muslims. Over a dozen leading Meccans and perhaps about fifty others were killed, and the same number taken prisoners, against Muslim losses of fourteen. Muḥammad regarded this outcome as divine punishment on those who had rejected God's message delivered by himself.

The Meccans had now received a challenge they could not ignore. The loss of many of their best men was not in itself irreparable, but the accompanying decline in the prestige of Mecca was very serious, and, if not arrested and reversed, must eventually lead to the loss of the Meccan commercial empire. About a year later, therefore, in March 625, a Meccan expedition of 3000 men invaded the oasis of Medina. Their horses were allowed to graze in unharvested grain crops, and, partly because of this, Muḥammad, against his better judgment, was persuaded to march out and engage in a set battle with them. The Muslims had a good position on the lower slopes of mount Uḥud (at the north of the oasis), but, as they moved forward after the defeated and retreating Meccan infantry, a flank attack by the 200 Meccan cavalry threw them into confusion, and many were killed before they could reform near their original position (where the cavalry could not assail them). The Meccans made no attempt to follow up this temporary advantage, despite the fact that the Muslim dead at Badr and Uḥud were still less than the Meccan dead—so that they had barely gained the standard blood-revenge of one for one, far less the magnified revenge of several lives for one which they had threatened. It must therefore be inferred that the Meccans themselves were so shaken that they could not take advantage of Muḥammad's discomfiture. Their infantry had been shown to be inferior, and their cavalry, with some of their horses wounded, could not attack the Muslims drawn up on a hill. An attempt to capture the numerous forts which dotted the oasis had no prospect of quick success. There was nothing to be done except to return to Mecca.

This battle of Uḥud has sometimes been presented, even in Muslim sources, as a serious defeat for Muḥammad, but this—at least from the military point of view—it certainly was not. The serious aspect was the religious or spiritual one. The victory of Badr had been taken as a sign that God was supporting them, and indeed fighting for them. The loss of life at Uḥud, therefore, seemed to be an indication that God had deserted them, or that they had been mistaken in the inferences they had drawn from Badr. It was some time before this line of thinking was checked by the insistence in the Qur'ān (3.152/147 ff.) that the reverse was permitted by God because the Muslims had disobeyed orders. Once this point had been made and accepted, confidence was restored.

For the next two years both sides prepared hard for a 'show-down' but avoided any major engagement. Muslim expeditions were going out in all directions, showing to the nomadic tribes the growing power of Medina, and occasionally gaining booty from hostile tribes. At last in April 627 the Meccans marched once again against Medina, this time with the 'grand alliance' they had been collecting, about 10,000 men in all, some being their allies, others induced to join by promises of money. Muḥammad had prepared for defence by having all the cereal harvest brought in early, and by digging a trench (in Arabic *khandaq*) wherever the main part of the oasis could be attacked by cavalry. Simple as this latter device was, it completely foiled the Meccans, for the Arabs were unaccustomed to sieges; and after a fortnight the uneasy alliance broke up and the besieging army melted away. The supreme effort to dislodge Muḥammad had failed.

After this Muḥammad's strength went on increasing, while the Meccans found trade more and more difficult because of Muslim raiding parties. In March 628 Muḥammad marched to Mecca with 1600 men, ostensibly to make the pilgrimage, but perhaps with hopes of much more. The Meccans, however, refused to let him enter the sacred area, but eventually concluded a treaty with him which permitted him to make the pilgrimage in 629 and stopped his attacks on their caravans. A breach of this treaty occurred in the latter half of 629 when a tribe allied with Muḥammad was attacked by allies of the Meccans. This led to Muḥammad marching on Mecca in January 630 with 10,000 men—a clear sign of his greatly increased power. The ground had been carefully prepared beforehand, by letting it be known that Muḥammad's terms would be lenient and honourable, and Mecca surrendered with hardly any fighting. Muḥammad entered in triumph, and tactfully but firmly assumed control of the city.

After about a fortnight spent in making new dispositions for the administration of Mecca and the surrounding region, and in destroying various pagan shrines, Muḥammad got news of a vast army of nomads concentrating not far to the east. The nomads belonged to the group of tribes called Hawāzin, old enemies of the Meccans, and the concentration may have been aimed against Mecca rather than Muḥammad. It was thus not difficult for Muḥammad to get a force of 2000 Meccans (probably the bulk of the adult male population of the town) to march with his original army against the common enemy. The two sides met at Ḥunayn, and for a time the issue of the battle was in the balance. Eventually, however, Muḥammad completely routed Hawāzin, capturing their camp with all their possessions and all their women and children; the one exception was that the inhabitants of aṭ-Ṭā'if, who formed part of the group, managed to regain their town and to hold it against Muslim attacks which, after a day or two, were called off.

Muḥammad was now the strongest leader in western Arabia. There was no chief anywhere near who could collect a force sufficient to meet him in battle. The Qur'ānic vision was thus embodied in Arabian life to the extent that there was a large tribal alliance in which the leaders accepted Islam and practised its way of life. This statement, of course, would bear elaboration in various ways. Instead of attempting this at the present stage, however, it is best to look at the remaining two and a half years of Muḥammad's life and then, in the light of his total achievement, to consider to what extent there had been an embodiment of the vision.

5. The final achievement

The great increase in Muḥammad's power resulting from the conquest of Mecca and the victory of Ḥunayn soon became apparent. Deputations came to him from most parts of Arabia, sent by tribes who wanted to be in alliance with him. In some cases—as had also happened earlier—one party in a tribe wanted to improve its position against its rivals in the tribe by gaining Muḥammad's support. In the area from the Persian Gulf to the Yemen there were many places where one faction was kept in power by Persian support, and it would seem that in general, with the collapse of the Persian central government about 629, these factions now turned to Muḥammad instead. In the north-west the tribes towards the Byzantine border had renewed their alliance with the victorious Byzantines; in the north-east were strong tribes, already thinking of raids on Iraq, now almost defenceless. Neither of these groups of tribes seem to have become Muslims at once, though the north-eastern tribes may have become allies of Muḥammad without accepting Islam. Apart from the north-west and north-east nearly every tribe in Arabia seems to have become a member of Muḥammad's alliance, or at least to have been represented by some subdivision. In sections of some tribes, however, dissatisfaction with the alliance had begun to appear even before Muḥammad's death, and after that event it swelled into the wars of the Apostasy which occupied the caliphate of Abū-Bakr (632–4). Thus by the time of Muḥammad's death on 8 June 632, the whole Arabian peninsula apart from the north was feeling Muḥammad's authority, though the extent of the control he could exercise over any particular tribe depended in part on the internal politics of the tribe.

The question we must now try to answer is how far the lives of those under Muḥammad's authority might be said to embody the Qur'ānic vision. Were they merely living their lives in the old way, but under a new leader? Or was there some new element in their lives? If so, what was this new element? It will be convenient to tackle this question by looking separately at the economic, social, political and religious-cum-intellectual spheres.

The acceptance of a new religious vision does not necessarily affect economic life. Muslim nomads continued to herd camels in the traditional fashion, and Muslim merchants to trade as they had always done, except that they were expected to avoid certain obviously fraudulent practices. Similarly the cultivators in the oasis of Medina continued to have their date palms and their cereal crops. There were certain changes, however. The commerce of Mecca had been disrupted for a time by Muslim attacks and threatened attacks. There is little information about what happened after the conquest of Mecca by Muḥammad. Presumably there was no further difficulty about caravans to the Yemen, but the hostility between the Muslims and the pro-Byzantine tribes in the north-west may have affected the caravans to Syria. We also know that some of the more talented younger Meccans preferred to abandon commerce and to take up positions in the employment of the 'state', that is, of Muḥammad, in leading expeditions and performing other administrative duties. This seems to have become the later pattern. By 650 the Muslims had acquired an empire, and the administration of this was more interesting, exciting and probably lucrative than organizing caravans on the route from Damascus by Mecca to the Yemen. This latter form of commerce doubtless flourished, but it was now only one of the minor activities of the Arab empire.

Again, while camel-breeding was the economic basis of nomadic life, it was modified—still at the economic level—by the practice of the razzia or raid. The razzia was almost a form of sport for the Arabs of the desert, but it also served certain economic functions. It made possible a redistribution of resources which might offset inequalities due to the weather or other natural forces; and at the same time the loss of life in razzias, though normally small, helped to reduce the pressure on the limited food supplies. The development of the Islamic polity at Medina subtly transformed the nomadic razzia. At first, if a party of nomads on a razzia against Medina went off with Muḥammad's camels, the Muslims would retaliate with a razzia against the particular nomads. Gradually more and more of the tribes in the neighbourhood of Medina became Muslims and allies of Muḥammad. This meant that all these tribes were now forbidden to raid one another, and Muḥammad took steps to see that this prohibition was effective. It would have been impracticable, both because of the Arab character and because of the economic situation, to stop razzias altogether; the Muslims are therefore encouraged to engage in razzias, but always against non-Muslims.

Thus the Muslim razzia comes to be commended in the Qur'ān as *jihād* or 'holy war'. This is essentially a transformation of a deep-seated Arab habit, arising from love of adventure and the ever-present lack of food. Those who took part in a Muslim expedition might be moved chiefly by desire for booty, and to this extent the *jihād* might seem to be no more than a razzia under another name. Yet there was an important difference. Another possible outcome of the expedition was the acceptance of Islam by the people raided. They knew, or were informed, that they could escape for ever from further raids of this type by becoming Muslims (or, in some cases, by accepting the status of 'protected persons' in the Islamic state). Moreover this was a form of surrender which brought no humiliation. In the century after Muḥammad's death many thousands accepted Islam in this way, and Muḥammad's little state became a vast empire. This could not have come about but for the Qur'ānic conception of the holy war, which in turn is linked with the distinctive conception of the Islamic community and polity. Thus the later Islamic state, even at the economic level, is in certain respects an embodiment of the Qur'ānic vision.

In the social sphere also, when people became Muslims, life went on much as before. This statement must be qualified somewhat, however. At the period when Muḥammad was forming his state at Medina Arabian society was already experiencing certain changes, some of which will be mentioned presently. In addition to this Muḥammad's activities slightly altered the character of society in the oasis of Medina. To begin with he brought the Emigrants with him from Mecca, and this had certain social repercussions; for example, the Emigrants found the position of women slightly different in Medina from what they had been accustomed to in Mecca, and there had to be readjustments. In the closing years of Muḥammad's life many nomads also settled in Mecca, attracted by Muḥammad's success; and this meant further adjustments. Thus in Qur'ānic passages revealed at Medina there are many regulations affecting the social life of this new mixed population at Medina.

Two points may be selected for amplification, namely, the regulations about inheritance of property, and the regulations about marriage. There is a set of complex arithmetical rules for dividing up the property of someone who has died. These appear to be designed to ensure that all the close relatives of the deceased, male and female, receive an appropriate share of what he leaves. Now this is very appropriate to the situation of the embryonic Islamic community. As was noted in an earlier chapter, the growth of commerce at Mecca had led to greater individualism; men used what had been communal property to advance their own commercial schemes, and then regarded the profits as belonging to themselves personally. Those women and children who had no honourable adult male to look after their interests were often defrauded. The matter was further complicated by variations between matrilineal and patrilineal family structure. The Qur'ānic regulations may be said to have accepted the trend towards individualism by regarding all property as individually owned; yet at the same time they acknowledge that relatives have certain rights in a man's property, so that he is in a sense only a steward of it on behalf of his family. The arithmetical proportions make the right of each relative quite definite, and in a way that seems perfectly fair.

The question of marriage is complex, and only the most important points can be mentioned here. As a preliminary it should be noted that the common assertion that prior to Islam an Arab married a large number of wives, and that the Qur'ān restricted this number to four, is almost certainly false; there is virtually no evidence to support it. For one thing the Qur'ānic verse itself (4.3) has no word of *restricting* men who had previously had ten wives, but rather encourages men (who presumably had only one or two wives) to marry up to four only. On the other hand, there is evidence—as good as can be expected—that matrilineal kinship still counted for much in several clans in Mecca and Medina. It is also known that where the matrilineal system was dominant the paternity of a child was sometimes disregarded, and it was common for a woman to have sexual intercourse promiscuously with a number of men. It is against promiscuity above all that the Qur'ānic marital regulations are directed. Important and characteristic is the institution of the '*idda* or 'waiting period', that is, that after divorce or the death of a husband a woman must wait long enough to ensure she is not pregnant before remarrying. For a woman married according to Qur'ānic regulations sexual relations with any man other than her husband are of course excluded. In such ways the Qur'ān actively supports the emergent social trend towards the patrilineal and virilocal family, and indeed, in a comparatively short period, establishes this and obliterates the traces of earlier forms of sexual and family association.

The political sphere has already been discussed to some extent (ch. 4, §3), and it has been shown that the polity created by Muḥammad could be regarded as a federation of Arab tribes according to pre-Islamic conceptions. It differed from such a federation not by its general structure, but by certain decisions about policy, namely, by the fact that the original full members were all Muslims, and by the refusal, wherever Muḥammad was strong enough, to admit further tribes to the alliance unless they became Muslims. There were Jews, Christians and other 'people of the book' under the umbrella of the Pax Islamica, but they were in a subordinate position and not full members of the alliance; this subordination was itself a form of relationship not unknown in pre-Islamic times. After the conquest of Mecca and victory of Ḥunayn, when Muḥammad's power was nearly absolute, this state of affairs meant that throughout the alliance the Muslim prayer was publicly observed, idols were destroyed and the Qur'ānic social regulations more and more put into force. Belief in God presumably became the norm; there is no mention of any attack on Qur'ānic monotheism apart from the semipolitical rearguard actions of retreating paganism. Thus the Muslim was able to feel that he belonged to a community which had been founded by God in that he had sent a messenger, and which was divinely guided in that the distinctive features of its way of life had been given to it by God in the Qur'ān. The Muslim was thus able to feel a deep confidence in the community and in his membership of it. In this way, despite the fact that the polity had still a traditional Arabian structure, the Qur'ānic vision may be said to have been very fully embodied at the political level.

Finally there is the religious and intellectual level. Here also something spectacular was achieved. It has been suggested above that polytheism was in decline (despite the external resurgence connected with opposition to Muḥammad), that the effective religion of the nomads was 'tribal humanism', and that there was a widespread trend, especially in places like Mecca, towards a vague monotheism. With the expansion of Islam the trend towards a vague monotheism was accelerated, and vague monotheism, even outside the Islamic community, came more and more to resemble Qur'ānic monotheism. The evidence for this is the way in which it was necessary for the political revolts against the Islamic state from 632 to 634 to have theological support, and the precise form taken by this support; there was no return to paganism, but instead several persons claimed to be prophets receiving revelations from God comparable to Muḥammad's. This suggests that the intellectual content of the Islamic vision had often been accepted even where Islam was not accepted.

We may conclude this review of Muḥammad's career, then, with the assertion that in the part of Arabia which was latterly under Muḥammad's control there had been a genuine embodiment of the Qur'ānic vision to a great extent. In many outward ways the life of Arabia went on unchanged, but it had also been subtly modified and transformed. Not merely were there thousands of Arabs observing the outward forms of Islamic worship, but the picture of the world held by these men was the Qur'ānic one, and this inevitably affected their aims in life. The latter point was all the more relevant because, through the integrative power of the Islamic religion, the Arabs were poised for a great territorial expansion, which would bring further demands for the embodiment of the vision in other aspects of the life of the community. This continuing process will be reviewed in the following five chapters.

Chapter 7

The religious aspect of later political developments

1. The great expansion, 632–750

The aim of the present chapter is to review the political history of the Islamic world, but in so doing to pay special attention to the religious aspect. In pursuance of this aim it is convenient to take as the first unit the period from the death of Muḥammad to the fall of the Umayyad dynasty, that is, from 632 to 750. When Muḥammad died at Medina in 632, no formal arrangements had been made for the continuation of the body politic he had created, though the leading Muslims were determined that it should continue. Since it was similar in some ways to a tribe, the choice of a leader could be made in somewhat similar fashion. After some discussion, because of the rivalry between the Muslims of Medina and the Meccan Emigrants, all agreed to accept as 'caliph' (*khalīfa*) or 'successor' of the Prophet one of the Emigrants, Abū-Bakr, who had in fact been Muḥammad's chief lieutenant since before the Hijra. He is the first of the four 'rightly guided' (*rāshidūn*) caliphs, but died after only two years. The other three were: 'Umar ibn-al-Khaṭṭāb (634–44), 'Uthmān (644–56), 'Alī (656–61). The First Civil War, however, broke out on the murder of 'Uthmān in 656, and 'Alī was not recognized as caliph throughout the caliphate, notably not by Mu'āwiya, governor of Syria, and a relative of 'Uthmān. Before there was any decisive military encounter between 'Alī and Mu'āwiya, the former was struck down by an assassin. After a weak attempt by 'Alī's son, al-Ḥasan, to gain the caliphate Mu'āwiya was speedily recognized everywhere as caliph, and thus became founder of the Umayyad dynasty. The most important caliphs of this dynasty are: 'Abd-al-Malik (685–705); al-Walīd (705–15); 'Umar II (ibn-'Abd-al-'Azīz) (717–20); Hishām (724–43).

Most of the reign of Abū-Bakr was occupied with the suppression of the revolts of a number of tribes against the centralized government in Medina. Something has already been said about these wars of the Ridda or 'apostasy'. Besides observing how such attempts to throw off the yoke of Islam had to adopt a quasi-Islamic basis, namely, leadership based on an alleged religious charisma, we note that they also established the principle that membership of the Islamic community or alliance was something from which neither individuals nor tribes could normally be released; the Qur'ān (16.106/8; etc.) had already stated that apostasy incurred serious divine displeasure. Before the death of Abū-Bakr in 634 the revolts had been quelled, and the Muslim state was ready to embark on, or rather to continue, its policy of expansion.

It is virtually certain that Muḥammad himself had foreseen the need for expansion (though he may not have suspected its great extent), and had made preparations by reconnaissances in force along the route to Syria and by alliances with Arab tribes on the borders of the Persian empire in Iraq. As mentioned above, an attempt at expansion beyond Arabia was made inevitable by the nature of the Islamic federation and by the transformation of the nomads' eagerness for the razzia into zeal for the Islamic holy war. For the ordinary Arab the chief reason for engaging in the holy war may still have been desire for booty; but the general pattern was altered by the possibility that the enemy might accept Islam and become members of the Islamic federation, because by this act they ceased to be a potential goal of a Muslim raid and instead became potential Muslim raiders. Unless raiding was to cease altogether—and economic pressure would probably make this impossible—it had to be directed outside Arabia.

In fact territorial expansion took place steadily throughout the period from the caliphate of 'Umar I to the fall of the Umayyad dynasty, with the exception of those periods when the energies of the Muslims were diverted by internal troubles; such were especially the period of the First Civil War (656–61), that of the Second Civil War (680–92), and the closing decade of the dynasty. It so happened also that at the precise moment when the Muslims were ready to burst out of Arabia there was virtually a power vacuum in the surrounding lands. A series of wars, extending over more than half a century until 629, had disastrously weakened both the Byzantine and Persian empires, and the latter was also experiencing dynastic troubles. Between 634 and 650 the Muslims had decisively defeated both empires, and indeed had sent the Persian administration reeling into dissolution; at the same time they had wrested from them Libya, Egypt, Palestine, Syria and Iraq, and had occupied most of Persia. The advance continued after the unsettlement caused by the First Civil War had subsided, but the major advances under the Umayyads were made after the Second Civil War in the years between 692 and 720. The coast of North Africa was annexed as far as Morocco, Spain (which then included Narbonne in southern France) was occupied with only slight resistance, while in the east a province was established beyond the Oxus and some settlements made in the Punjab.

Most of this spectacular expansion was achieved by armies consisting almost exclusively of Muslim Arabs. In the later stages—after 700—Persians shared in the fighting in the east and Berbers in the west, in both cases after becoming Muslims. The stabilization of the frontiers of the caliphate roughly at the points reached about 720 is partly due to the lack of manpower to occupy effectively any further territory. The much-discussed victory of Charles Martel at Tours (or Poitiers) in 732 was no more than the repulse of a Muslim raiding party, but it stopped the Muslims raiding so far afield in the future, since it made clear to them that the relatively small quantities of booty to be had north of the Pyrenees were no longer worth the effort expended in getting them. Something similar is perhaps true in the east.

It must also be noted that at an early stage in the expansion (during the reign of 'Umar) certain administrative measures were taken, without which the expansion would not have been so great. Firstly, it was decided—following precedents from Muḥammad's lifetime—that the conquered land would not be divided among the participants in the conquest, but would be left to its cultivators and the rents and taxes paid into the public treasury. From this treasury annual stipends were paid to all Muslims. By this scheme all able-bodied males were set free from making a living and enabled to give most of their time to military expeditions or to the work of administering the captured provinces. Arab manpower was thus deployed to the fullest possible extent in the work of expansion. The system seems to have continued into the eighth century, though the details are obscure. Gradually it must have been modified. With increasing prosperity the Arabs became disinclined to go on distant campaigns, and in order to raise sufficient troops some inducement beyond the stipend had to be given. By the end of the seventh century, too, many non-Arabs were becoming Muslims, but a large proportion of these, such as the city-dwellers of Iraq, were probably incapable of becoming good soldiers. This process of conversion must have accelerated the decline in the purchasing power of the annual stipend, which was probably coming about for other reasons, even if non-Arabs did not receive the same stipends as Arabs; and this meant that most Muslims had to have some means of livelihood other than campaigning. Though information about the breakdown of the system is scarce, it is clear that while it lasted it was a further embodiment of Islamic ideas, especially of the Islamic conception of the state, even if there was also some influence from the pre-Islamic conception of the tribe.

Much of the civil strife and some of the revolts during the period up to 750 were the outcome of personal rivalries or personal ambitions and had no basis in ideas. Such were the First and Second Civil Wars, at least in essence, and the revolt against ʿAlī which was crushed at the so-called battle of the Camel. On the other hand, we find involved in the First Civil War some groups of men whose political attitudes had a definite ideational, and indeed religious, basis, and who became the forerunners at the religious level of the sects of the Khārijites and the Shīʿites. Because their activities were based on ideas explicitly formulated they had much influence on the later development of the Islamic state and on the Islamic community's conception of itself.

The first Khārijites (Ar. Khawārij) were a small body of men who 'went out' (*kharajū*) or seceded from ʿAlī because they disapproved of some of his acts. Their primary contention was that the affairs of the state should be managed in strict accordance with the Qur'ān. They expressed this in the Qur'ānic slogan 'no judgment but God's' (*lā ḥukm illā li-llāh*). Though they were a different group from that which had been responsible for the death of the caliph ʿUthmān in 656, they held that that group had been right since ʿUthmān had failed to apply a Qur'ānic rule to one of his governors. This point was linked with their conception of the community. They spoke of the community of true Muslims as 'the people of Paradise', considering that they would all go to Paradise because of their uprightness of life and membership of the Islamic community. In their eyes a person who had committed a grave sin (that is, broken a Qur'ānic precept) had thereby forfeited his membership of the Islamic community—presumably because he was now one of 'the people of Hell' and because his association with 'the people of Paradise' would, as it were, contaminate them and endanger their chances of Paradise.

In spite of these high-sounding theories, in practice the Khārijites consisted of small bodies of men, varying from thirty to five hundred, who for shorter or longer periods maintained themselves in camp near cities or trade routes by what was little better than brigandage and terrorism. In the most extreme form of the theory the only true Muslims were those actually present in the camp of this particular group. This doctrine had the consequence, according to Arab traditional ideas, that everyone else could legally be murdered or robbed; it was no sin. Hence the brigandage and terrorism. Fortunately there were also more moderate forms of the doctrine. From about 690 there were Khārijites in Basra who wanted to go on living there although the governor was a non-Khārijite, and who therefore had to modify their doctrines to justify their conduct. The details of the process need not be described here, but it may be noted that they came to emphasize the fact that the non-Khārijite Muslims were at least monotheists (*muwaḥiddūn*).

It is important to try to lay bare the deeper significance of these facts. Examination of the sources gives no grounds for thinking that the Khārijites were moved chiefly by economic grievances. It would therefore seem that the fundamental reason for their revolts was a feeling of insecurity arising from the abrupt changes in their way of life. They came from tribes which had previously been nomadic; but now, though the campaigns might bear a slight resemblance to the old razzias, they were much more highly organized, and the individual must often have been conscious of curbs on his freedom. Then, after the campaign, instead of returning to the desert, they went back to camp cities like Basra, where again life was more regulated than in the desert. The likeliest explanation of the Khārijite movements is thus that these former nomads were impelled by a sense of insecurity to try to re-create on an Islamic basis the small intimate group with which they had been familiar in the desert. It is further likely, in view of the tribal affiliations of the early Khārijites, that most of them came from tribes where there had been a profound awareness of the dependence of the individual on his tribe. In such cases the tribe had been regarded as a charismatic community, that is, one with certain more-than-human qualities, in virtue of which it gave to the lives of its members meaning and significance; and these qualities were carried by the tribal stock.

Thus in their period of stress and insecurity these Khārijites had fallen back on an essentially religious conception of human communities. The Islamic community was ideally, as they conceived it, 'the people of Paradise', that is, a community which more or less ensured for its members entry into Paradise (something which made life meaningful and significant). This conception was rooted in the Qur'ān, but it was useful to have it emphasized again after the first wave of conquest when so much had changed; and it is interesting to follow the later history of the insight thus achieved or recovered. The final positions of the moderate Khārijites were not unlike those of another sect, the Murji'ites; but the latter were distinguished by their clear denial of one Khārijite thesis, namely, that the grave sinner was excluded from the community. An ethical rigorism like that of the Khārijites, which makes exclusion from the community the punishment for every sin, is politically impracticable, and a view like that of the Murji'ites (which allows, of course, for the punishment of criminals) is the only possible basis for a normal civilized state.

At a later date some Murji'ites were considered heretics because of their views on what makes a man a 'believer', that is, a member of the Islamic community. The chief doctrine of the early Murji'ites, however, was in essentials accepted by the main body of Sunnites, namely, the doctrine that grave sin in general does not exclude a man from the community. At the same time this main body accepted and developed the positive aspects of the Khārijite thesis, namely, that the Muslims were 'the people of Paradise' and their community a charismatic one. To avoid minimizing the seriousness of sin they evolved an elaborate doctrine according to which, though all Muslims, as 'the people of Paradise', would ultimately go to Paradise, they would first be punished for their sins; the punishment might take place either in this life or after this life in Hell, but, if the latter type of punishment was inflicted, its duration would be limited, and the man would in the end be moved on to Paradise. It also came to be accepted, following the Murji'ite discussions of membership of the community, that there was one sin which did exclude, namely, *shirk* or polytheism; but this point had good Qur'ānic support and was not disputed. It might also be remarked in this connection that one of the marks which assured Muslims that their community was a charismatic one was the possession of a God-given law, the Sharī'a. One of the curious consequences of this view was that it came to be held that it was a less serious offence to break one of God's commands than to say that a command was not really God's; to drink wine is less serious than to say wine-drinking is not forbidden by God. The breach of the command is an individual matter to be expiated by the individual, but the denial of the command is an attack on the divinely given basis of the community.

At the opposite pole from the Khārijites were the Shī'ites. The earliest were a small group of Arabs among the followers of 'Alī; then there were bodies of insurgents at various points until about 687; from then until near the end of the Umayyad period the chief expressions of Shī'ism were in underground movements. The distinctive Shī'ite belief was in the existence of supernatural powers in the clan of Muḥammad, the Hāshimites—powers which had been manifested in him, and which were transmitted or bequeathed to succeeding generations. In modern sociological terms this might be described as a belief in the charismatic leader. The actual charismatic leaders—first 'Alī, then his sons al-Ḥasan and al-Ḥusayn—were far from successful in their political activities. After the tragic defeat and heroic death of al-Ḥusayn at Kerbela in 680, leading a forlorn hope against an Umayyad army, a new idea was tried out; the leader of a revolt claimed, not that he himself was a charismatic leader, but that he was the accredited agent of such a person. The first example of this was al-Mukhtār, who led a rising in Kufa (685–7) and claimed to be the agent of another son of 'Alī, Muḥammad ibn-al-Ḥanafiyya ('the son of the Ḥanafite woman'); but there were other examples later. A variation of this idea was where a man claimed to be the agent of a leader who, though commonly supposed to be dead, was allegedly still alive in some secret spot and ready to return at an appropriate time.

The charismata were not confined to 'Alī and his descendants, but were sometimes held to belong to other Hāshimites like Muḥammad's uncle al-'Abbās and his cousin ('Alī's brother) Ja'far and their descendants. Eventually there came into existence a form of Shī'ite belief which considered the contemporary possessors of the charismata to be the descendants of al-'Abbās, and this belief was the basis of the movement which was responsible for the replacement of the Umayyad dynasty by the 'Abbāsid in 750. In its progress the 'Abbāsid movement was led by a man who was merely an agent of the charismatic leader, and it somewhat chauvinistically made use of other forms of Shī'ite feeling by not naming explicitly the leader for whom they were working but referring vaguely to 'him of the Prophet's house who shall be chosen'. The hopes thus roused, and the ensuing disappointment when an 'Abbāsid and not an 'Alid was 'chosen' for the caliphate, perhaps explain the difficulty which for a century the 'Abbāsid caliphs experienced in dealing with men of Shī'ite sympathies.

It was suggested above that Khārijism made its appearance among sections of the nomads of Arabia who believed that a man's life derived its significance from his membership of his tribe. Correspondingly Shī'ism seems first to have made its appearance among Arab tribesmen from South Arabia. This leads to a hypothesis complementary to that about Khārijism, namely, that in the time of stress and insecurity following on rapid changes in their way of life, these men turned back to the charismatic leader because for centuries South Arabians had looked to a semi-divine king as source and author of the salvation of the state. Despite their similar origin, or perhaps just because of it, Shī'ites and Khārijites were bitterly opposed to one another; each felt that the other was ruining the whole community's prospects of salvation. The Khārijites thought that the body of Muslims was bound to make the right decisions, whereas a single man could easily be mistaken; but to the Shī'ites exactly the opposite appeared to be the case—a single man with charismata was bound to be right, whereas a crowd of ordinary men without charismata was almost certain to be wrong.

Khārijism and Shī'ism are thus two rival elaborations of the Islamic vision, one putting the emphasis on one facet, and the other on another. Both facets—the ideas of the charismatic community and the charismatic leader—are present in embryo in the Qur'ān, but receive no emphasis. It is probable that acceptance of the ideas of the Qur'ān without any special emphasis was the attitude of many Muslims throughout the Umayyad period, so that one might speak of the central body or the general religious movement. It is to the credit of the Khārijites that they made Muslims more aware of the charismatic nature of their community. Though the main body of Muslims rejected some of the Khārijite conclusions they gradually came to accept the conception of the community as charismatic; and this conception probably played a large part in the progressive embodiment of the Qur'ānic vision by inspiring men to work at the elaboration of the Sharī'a, and in other ways. Similarly Shī'ism, though many of its views were rejected by the main body, made that body aware of its need for a leader who was more than human, perhaps aware of the fact that it had such a leader; even the 'Abbāsid caliphs were regarded as having certain charismata, though unfortunately 'Abbāsid theories of the caliphate left much Shī'ite opinion dissatisfied. This must not obscure the fact, however, that the 'Abbāsids were believed by their supporters to have charismata, and that therefore to this extent they were embodying more fully this facet of the Qur'ānic vision.

2. The establishment of Islamic forms, 750–950

From 750 onwards, nominally until 1258, the caliphate was ruled by the 'Abbāsid dynasty. The one exception was Spain, where in 756 one of the few Umayyad princes who had escaped from the 'Abbāsids managed to establish an emirate for himself and his descendants. Apart from this there were no major changes on the frontiers of the caliphate during the first two centuries of 'Abbāsid rule. The replacement of one dynasty by another, however, was more than a change of personalities. It marked a complete re-alignment of forces within the body politic. The political power of the traditional Arab element was considerably reduced. Up to 750 the caliphate had still been in some senses a federation of Arab tribes; and consequently when a non-Arab became a Muslim he had to become at the same time a 'client' (*mawlā*, pl. *mawālī*) of one of these Arab tribes. Since clientship implied an inferior status, this arrangement was felt by the non-Arab Muslims as a grievance; and part of the programme of the 'Abbāsids in their campaign against the Umayyads was to secure full rights for the clients. In particular this meant an increase of political power for the Persian and persianized Aramaean elements in the population; and it was in accordance with this that the capital and seat of government was moved from Arab Damascus to persianized Iraq. Much of the detailed work of administration was in the hands of the descendants of the civil service of the Persian (Sasanian) empire. The actual forms of government and of court ceremonial also tended to follow the autocratic Persian tradition, since the more democratic Arab forms, which encouraged long discussions, had shown themselves incompatible with the efficient control of a large empire.

While there was little change up to 950 in the external frontiers of the caliphate, certain regions within the frontiers came to be more or less withdrawn from the direct control of the caliph. This occurred when a provincial governor became so strong that he could insist on the caliph appointing a son or other relative as successor. One of the first of these semi-independent dynasties were the Ṭāhirids who ruled in the eastern part of Persia from about 820 to 872. Rather earlier the Idrīsids and Aghlabids had been virtually independent in Morocco, Algeria and Tunisia. The Ṭāhirids were followed in Persia by the Ṣaffārids and then the Sāmānids, the latter ruling most of Persia and also Transoxiana and part of Afghanistan. There were also various other dynasties in other regions. A new factor entered the situation when in 909 the Fāṭimids conquered Tunisia, for they were not content with the actuality of rule but claimed at the level of theory that they were the rightful rulers of all the Muslim lands. Their threat to the 'Abbāsids became more serious after their conquest of Egypt in 969.

Despite the appearance of these semi-independent or fully independent dynasties, the 'Abbāsids retained for a time a considerable measure of power. One of the steps which led to their undoing was taken when shortly before 850 they adopted the practice of relying on a bodyguard of mercenaries of Turkish or comparable origin. Before long these guards came to have so much power that they deposed caliphs and selected their successors almost as they pleased. Only those princes who were prepared to work along with the leading officers of the guard were likely to reach the caliphate; there was no law of primogeniture, and in any vacancy there were usually several members of the 'Abbāsid family equally suitable for appointment from a formal standpoint. During the later ninth and early tenth century military power came to count for more and more, until in 945 the caliph, denuded of military support, had to 'appoint', that is, recognize, one of a family of Persian war lords, the Buwayhids or Būyids, as governor of the central region of caliphate, including Baghdad itself. The Buwayhids professed the Imāmite form of Shī'ism (to be described presently) and under their rule the position in the caliphate of the Imāmites or moderate Shī'ites improved; but the bulk of the Muslims continued to be Sunnites, for one of the achievements of the period of two centuries from 750 was what might be called the establishment of Sunnism.

In their rise to power the 'Abbāsids had been supported not only by the 'clients', but also by a large body of Arabs with a genuine religious interest, who have sometimes been called the 'pious opposition' to the Umayyads, but might more appropriately be named the 'general religious movement', since there was a large, if amorphous, body of opinion neither Khārijite nor Shī'ite. We may picture these men sitting in mosques in the main cities of the caliphate discussing religious questions, especially questions of religious law, and forming something of a common mind on the many important points not explicitly dealt with in the Qur'ān. To be more exact, it was in each city that they tended to form a common mind, whereas views might vary greatly from city to city. From a legal standpoint these are often called 'the ancient schools of law';[1] and law was possibly the chief focus of their interest, though they also discussed other matters. Because of the support they had had from this movement, and perhaps for other reasons also, the 'Abbāsids gave a measure of recognition to the views of the movement, while at the same time exerting pressure to harmonize the divergent views of the local groups.

The image of the 'Abbāsids as upholding Islamic principles and ruling in accordance with them, in contrast to the Umayyads, who ruled according to secular or pagan Arab ideas, was part of their propaganda during their rise to power, and of their justification for their position after they were in power. The attitude of the 'Abbāsids to Islamic law shows that there was some foundation for their claim, but the contrast between them and the Umayyads has been heightened in the interests of propaganda. It has to be remembered that the historians from whose books we get our information were writing under the 'Abbāsids and that it might have been dangerous for them to antagonize their rulers. There is nothing to suggest that during the Umayyad period there was less personal piety among the caliphs and the leading men of the caliphate than under the 'Abbāsids. The Umayyads, however, were certainly not *seen* to be following Islamic principles in the same way as the 'Abbāsids. It may be that the ideas of the ancient schools and the general religious movement were still in too embryonic a stage for rulers to be able to recognize them; and in this connection it is relevant that Damascus was probably less developed than Medina or Basra. In other ways, however, the Umayyads were continuing to follow old Arab ideas and the practices based on them, which were not specifically Islamic; or else they would use ideas which might be labelled Islamic, such as the divine predetermination of all events, in order to justify reactionary political policies (the continuation of their own rule and the existing distribution of political power) which were on the whole out of harmony with the Islamic vision. Even if the central administration of the 'Abbāsids copied Persian precedents in many respects, yet the external recognition they accorded to the Islamic religious movement made possible the phenomenon which may be designated 'the establishment of Sunnism'.

One aspect of this phenomenon was the elaboration and development of Islamic law or the Sharī'a. The desire of the 'Abbāsid caliphs to have greater uniformity in law undoubtedly accelerated the development. At one time it had been apparently usual for men to say, 'The opinion of our school, or our associates, on this question is such and such'. If required to justify this, they might add that such had been the view of the leading member of the school in the previous generation. In course of time, however, the further justification was sometimes added that the opinion was in accordance with what might be inferred from a saying of Muḥammad's. The latter form of justification had an element of objectivity and was so clearly superior that any school wanting to maintain its own opinion against the alternative opinion of another school would try to justify it in this way. A further refinement came to be added in that evidence was required that Muḥammad had in fact said what he was alleged to have said—it would have been easy to invent sayings of Muḥammad. Because the cultural background of the Arabs had been oral the evidence that came to be expected was the chain of names of those who had passed on the anecdote containing the saying. This chain of transmitters, known as the *isnād* or 'support' of the anecdote, took some such form as the following: 'A reported that he had once heard B saying, I heard C telling how he heard D saying that once in certain circumstances he heard Muḥammad say . . .'

It was after the work of the outstanding legal thinker ash-Shāfi'ī (d. 820) that it came to be generally accepted that an opinion on some point of law not covered by the Qur'ān had to be based on such a saying of Muḥammad's. The anecdote containing the saying was known as a *ḥadīth* or *khabar*, in English 'Tradition' (the technical sense may be distinguished by a capital). The study of Traditions rapidly became a distinct branch of the studies of the general religious movement. It was soon realized that false Traditions were in circulation with sayings that Muḥammad could not possibly have uttered. The chains of transmitters were therefore carefully scrutinized to make sure that the persons named could in fact have met one another, that they could be trusted to repeat the story accurately, and that they did not hold any heretical views. This implied extensive biographical studies; and many biographical dictionaries have been preserved giving the basic information about a man's teachers and pupils, the views of later scholars (on his reliability as a transmitter) and the date of his death. This biography-based critique of Traditions helped considerably to form a more or less common mind among many men throughout the caliphate about what was to be accepted and what rejected.

Another factor contributing to the formation of a common mind was the practice of students to travel all over the Islamic world to listen in person to the most distinguished Traditionists. This helped to break down the isolation of the local schools. As a result of such travel it became common to find the same Tradition supported by different chains of transmitters. It also became common to find essentially the same Tradition with small variants, or even with considerable variants. This phenomenon occurs even in the Traditions which are accepted as 'sound'; outside the corpus of 'sound' Traditions there are great variations. Despite the variants, however, it would be fair to say that by the middle of the ninth century there was a large measure of agreement in the body of educated Sunnite Muslims. This agreement came to be stabilized by the recognition of certain collections of Traditions as canonical. The oldest of these collections are those by al-Bukhārī (d. 870) and Muslim (d. 875). The attainment of this wide consensus was a most important achievement for the whole development of the Islamic world. Yet it is one which is easily misunderstood by the modern scholar, since he thinks in terms of academic historical categories, whereas the men who reached the agreement were not academic historians devoted to the search for an abstract objectivity, but men deeply concerned with the ordering of society in their own century. The agreement they reached was essentially one about the structure of Islamic society and its way of life; and the result of their agreement was the marked stability of Islamic society as it passed through the political vicissitudes of more than a millennium.

While many members of the general religious movement became chiefly interested in the study of Traditions, others turned their attention rather to the legal principles which were justified by the Traditions. Such men were first and foremost the continuators of the ancient schools of law; but the growth of interest in Traditions led to revolutionary changes in the attitudes to legal matters. The details of this are difficult to follow, since it was common to ascribe to earlier thinkers doctrines which only came to be accepted at a later date. The outcome of this process was the replacement of the ancient schools of law by the great schools or rites which still exist, as well as by some minor ones which have disappeared. In some contexts the term 'rite' is to be preferred to 'school', since not only legal theories were involved but also practical matters affecting daily life, including some details of the ritual worship or prayer, as well as more strictly legal matters such as the rules for inheritance. The four great rites are the Shāfi'ite, the Ḥanafite, the Mālikite and the Ḥanbalite. The founder of the first has already been mentioned. The Ḥanafite takes its name from Abū-Ḥanīfa (d. 767), but was mainly developed by his followers. The Mālikites were the followers of Mālik ibn-Anas (d. 795) of Medina, and the Ḥanbalites of Aḥmad ibn-Ḥanbal (d. 855) of Baghdad. It is because of the formation of these schools or rites and the achievement of consensus about the Traditions that one can speak of Sunnism being established about the middle of the ninth century; but there is also a political aspect to be noticed.

The appearance of various groups of intellectuals with at least a modicum of recognition from the government led to changes in the balance of political power. Something like a standard curriculum for higher Islamic education was being evolved, with opportunities for specialization; and the products of this education constituted a new class of 'ulema' or 'scholars' (*'ulamā'*). Various careers were open to them, notably that of judge; and of course the judges had to be in close touch with the government. In general the ulema took the view that the caliphate should be administered according to the Sharī'a (which included the Qur'ān); and this was a matter which, though doubtless for the general good, also affected their personal interests and their interests as a class, since they were the only persons who could say authoritatively what the Sharī'a asserted.

Such a political attitude adversely affected another group of persons, the 'secretaries' or civil servants. These were professional administrators, who had virtually become a caste, since it was common for father to be succeeded by son. Some indeed were descendants of the men who had been administering the Persian empire before the Muslim conquest; and these men, though they had become Muslims in order to retain their jobs, were not deeply attached to Islam. All the secretaries wanted to increase theoretically the power of the caliph, since this would give them greater freedom in their administrative activity. In particular they wanted to get rid of the subordination of the caliph to the Sharī'a, since this meant that their administrative actions were ultimately subject to the control of their rivals, the ulema.

This obvious cleavage of interests was linked up with others. This matter is perhaps easiest to understand, but it may not have been the core of the complex of political interests which we find associated with the ulema and the secretaries, and which, because of the multiplicity, will here be called a 'bloc' and not a 'party'. Thus with the secretaries there sided many Persians, though not all, and likewise many men of moderate Shī'ite sympathies. The Shī'ites wanted a charismatic leader, and the secretaries wanted more power for the caliph. Now if the caliph could be regarded as a charismatic leader as the Shī'ites asserted he was, he would be able to override the decisions of the ulema. Since the secretaries were also bearers of Persian culture, it was natural that some Persians should side with them. So the 'autocratic bloc' came into being. The position of the ulema, on the other hand, implied that the caliph and his administration were subject to the Sharī'a. This appealed to the democratic or egalitarian attitude of many Arabs. It also appealed to all those persons who felt that the charisma required for the salvation of the Muslims was not that of a leader but that of the community as a corporate body. This grouping of interests created the 'constitutionalist bloc'.

These two complexes seem to have contained the main tendencies shown by Muslims in the ninth century. It is difficult to estimate the relative strength of the two blocs, but during the first half of the ninth century even the weaker must have been far from negligible, since the caliphs tried their utmost to gain and keep the support of both blocs, and also to reduce the tension between them. The most notable compromise policy which they attempted was when, under the influence of the theological sect of the Mu'tazilites, they introduced the Miḥna or 'Inquisition'. The Mu'tazilites had much influence over policy for most of the reign of al-Ma'mūn (813–33), though it was only towards the end that the 'Inquisition' was instituted. This was the requirement that all governors, judges and other senior officials should publicly make profession of the doctrine that the Qur'ān was the created word of God, not his uncreated word. In the light of what has been said about the opposing blocs, the political relevance of this doctrine would be clear. If the Qur'ān is God's uncreated word, then it is in certain respects an expression of his essential being; but if it is merely a word he has created, it is not necessarily an expression of his character, any more than other created things are, such as beasts of prey. The practical conclusion is that, if the Qur'ān is created, it does not have the ultimate validity ascribed to it by the ulema, and therefore may sometimes be set aside by the caliph. Thus the doctrine of the createdness of the Qur'ān weakens the constitutionalist bloc somewhat, though without giving the autocratic bloc all the support it wanted.

The policy of the 'Inquisition' was continued until the beginning of the reign of al-Mutawakkil (847–61), but it was apparently only at intervals that it was vigorously pursued. Most men yielded to governmental pressure and made the public profession, even when it was opposed to their convictions. Only a few resisted, and some of these were put to death. One outstanding upholder of the uncreated Qur'ān, Aḥmad ibn-Ḥanbal, was not put to death, presumably because he had strong public support in Baghdad, but he was forced to give up teaching and all public activities. Despite the outward success of the 'Inquisition' the policy underlying it was abandoned; and the reason is doubtless that it did not effect a reconciliation of the opposing blocs, and did not gain enthusiastic support for the régime in any quarter in order to offset the disapproval of many of the ulema. By 849 the 'Inquisition' had been abandoned, and the government had decided to rely for support on the constitutionalist bloc. This political decision and the policies that followed from it may be said to mark the establishment of Sunnism. From this time onwards the primacy of Sunnite forms in the 'Abbāsid caliphate was not questioned. The Sunnite legal rites had crystallized. The corpus of 'sound' Traditions was assuming its definitive form. There was beginning to be a measure of agreement about theological dogma, even though the 'rational' theology of al-Ash'arī and al-Māturīdī did not appear until after 900. Thus from about 850 the 'Abbāsid caliphate, and indeed the whole Islamic world, was essentially Sunnite, and the Shī'ites were no more than a tolerated minority.

There is something a little mysterious about Shī'ism prior to the year 900. This is indeed not surprising, since Shī'ism was in part an 'underground' movement. There are few contemporary documents, and in all later sources much is read back into the past. Thus the accounts make it seem that there was a body of men actively supporting the 'family'—the descendants of 'Alī through his son al-Ḥusayn—right through the ninth century from the coming to power of the 'Abbāsids in 750. Careful reading of the early sources, however, shows that this cannot have been the case. Just before 750 the 'Alids may have hoped to gain political power on the break-up of the Umayyad caliphate, but, once the 'Abbāsids had gained power, the 'Alids soon realized that it was virtually impossible to dislodge them and gave up their political ambitions. The 'Abbāsids were aware of their potential claim to the caliphate and kept them under careful surveillance; but the fact that at most they suffered light imprisonment shows that there cannot have been any serious revolutionary movement associated with the heads of 'the family' (the imams of the Imāmite Shī'ites) after the death of Ja'far aṣ-Ṣādiq in 765. The moderate Shī'ites were known as Rāfiḍites in the ninth century, and the sources show that some of them moved freely in court circles—a further indication of the tolerated character of moderate Shī'ism.

While moderate Shī'ism was little more than a political party aiming at a more autocratic form of government, there was a revolutionary type of Shī'ism which recognized the same six imams up to Ja'far as the moderates, but for seventh imam had his son Ismā'īl. The history of this Ismā'īlite Shī'ism during the ninth century is naturally obscure. It possibly took shape soon after the death of Ismā'īl, or perhaps not till later. By 909, however, there was a sufficient body of doctrine for it to be the basis of the Fāṭimid state in Tunisia, which conquered Egypt in 969, and founded Cairo to be its capital.

The decision of the caliph al-Mutawakkil and his government just before 850 to base their policies on the support of Sunnism must have made things difficult for the moderate Shī'ites, and they presumably set about looking for ways and means of maintaining their distinctive religious attitude. The decisive new step was taken by some leaders of the party at some time after 874. The eleventh imam, al-Ḥasan al-'Askarī, died in January 874, and his son Muḥammad the twelfth imam seems to have disappeared mysteriously shortly afterwards. It would presumably have been possible to find a successor, but it must have occurred to some of the leading men in the party that there were great advantages in not having an active leader who might prevent them doing what seemed best and who could always be made the object of 'Abbāsid reprisals. Someone must therefore have made the assertion that the twelfth imam was not dead but was 'absent' or 'hidden', and that in due course he would come back as the Mahdī, the messianic leader who would lead his followers to victory and set all things right. Most of those who have here been called 'moderate Shī'ites' seem to have accepted the doctrine; and the sect thus formed is known usually as the Imāmites or, from the fact of recognizing twelve imams, the Ithnā'ashariyya or Twelvers. They constituted an opposition to the 'Abbāsids which could be regarded as non-revolutionary, though the possibility of political revolution was not completely excluded for the future. In the early part of the ninth century a distinctive legal doctrine and rite were worked out, chiefly by al-Kulaynī (or -Kulīnī; d. 939). The Buwayhid war lords, who gained control of Baghdad in 945, professed the Imāmite doctrine, and did much to improve the status of the Imāmites and their legal rite; but it is significant of the relative weakness of the Imāmites that the Buwayhids did not challenge the dominance of Sunnism.

Thus by about 950 both Sunnism and Imāmite Shī'ism had attained the distinctive form which with few changes they were to keep for centuries.

3. The maintenance of Islamic society, 950–1800

After the fullness of the last two sections it may seem an abrupt change of scale to attempt to deal with 850 years in one section. The subject itself, however, seems to require this. Despite the magnificent proliferation of Islamic life during the period, religion and religious ideas in the narrow sense ceased to have much relevance to the activities of rulers and statesmen. This does not mean that the Islamic religion had no relevance, but that its relevance was limited, and can be brought under a few heads. First, however, let us glance at some of the chief among the kaleidoscopic political developments of the period.

From 945 to 1258 the 'Abbāsid caliphate was, with a small exception, ruled by war lords, that is, men whose rule was based primarily on the command of military force. At the centre of the caliphate the Buwayhids ruled for about a century, though latterly they were losing their grip and becoming divided among themselves. In 1055 the control of Baghdad fell to the Seljūq dynasty,

Turkish and Sunnite, which also retained control for about a century. The break-up of Seljūq rule was followed by a confused period in which there were many dynasties ruling smaller territories, while the 'Abbāsids for a time regained a small amount of power. Cataclysmic changes came with the Mongol invasion of the thirteenth century. Under Chingiz-Khan (d. 1227) the Mongols had entered Persia from the north-east, but for a time their energies were mostly directed elsewhere, and more than a quarter of a century had elapsed before the advance through Persia was continued. It was in 1258 that Baghdad fell to the Mongol Hulagu, and here as in many other places the Mongols with great savagery massacred large numbers of the inhabitants. The last 'Abbāsid caliph was among those put to death, and, owing to the numbness caused by loss of life and material destruction, he was not replaced. The Mongol terror was halted in Syria by the rulers of Egypt, the Mamlūks. Once they had attained power the Mongols were tolerant and indeed cultured rulers, and the eastern part of the former 'Abbāsid caliphate, divided in different ways from time to time, was ruled by various Mongol and Turkish dynasties until about 1500.

In the other part of the 'Abbāsid domains (Syria, Egypt and westwards) matters were complex. At times there were numerous small dynasties each ruling little more than a town and the surrounding region. Some of these dynasties might be partly dependent on stronger dynasties. The greatest state was that of the Almohads (al-Muwaḥḥidūn), which at its greatest extent stretched from Senegal to Tunisia and included what was left of Islamic Spain. The dynasty may be said to have ruled from 1130 to 1269, but the period of its outstanding power was from about 1150 to 1225. When the Almohads withdrew from Spain (as a result of dynastic disputes beginning in 1223), the Muslims were rapidly subdued by the Christian kingdoms, with the exception of the small kingdom of Granada in the south-east, which maintained itself until 1492. Egypt was under the Fāṭimids from 969 to 1169, under the Ayyūbids (the dynasty of Saladin) from 1169 to 1250, and under the Mamlūks from that date until the Ottoman conquest in 1517. From time to time the rulers of Egypt also controlled Syria.

Spain was the chief territory lost to the Islamic world during the whole period dealt with in this section, apart from the loss of some of the Ottoman conquests in Europe. At the same time the Islamic religion was spreading into West Africa, the Indo-Pakistani subcontinent and south-east Asia. The penetration of India had been begun under the Umayyads, but it is chiefly the accomplishment of the Ghaznavid dynasty, especially of Maḥmūd of Ghazna (reg. 998–1030). For a time the Ghaznavids also held parts of Persia and Transoxiana (nominally as subordinate to the 'Abbāsid caliph), but latterly they withdrew to their Indian domains, which they also extended, and maintained themselves there until 1186. They fell before an Afghan dynasty, the Ghorids, who further extended Islamic power in India. This led to the establishment of a Muslim kingdom at Delhi which lasted to the beginning of the sixteenth century, and for a time controlled most of north India (under the 'Sulṭāns of Delhi').

The centuries from 1500 to 1800 might be named the 'early modern' period of Islamic history. It is dominated by three empires, the Ottoman empire, the Persian empire and the Mogul empire. The earliest, most extensive and longest-lived of these was the Ottoman empire. The dynasty had established itself in the small town of Brusa in Asia Minor by the middle of the fourteenth century. Despite a decisive defeat by Timur-Lenk in 1402 the Ottomans continued to expand their dominions. The capture of Constantinople in 1453 was the conclusion of one phase of expansion rather than a fresh beginning. Another phase of expansion began in the early sixteenth century and made them masters of Syria and of the North African coast from Algeria to Egypt, while extending their European dominions. Iraq was taken from Persia about a century later. After this a decline set in. There was a gradual but steady retreat from the European conquests, until in 1914 at the end of the Balkan War only the present restricted territory was left, while the First World War detached the Asian and African provinces apart from Asia Minor. Even that was only saved by the resolute determination of Mustafa Kemal. The Ottoman empire came to an end and was replaced (to some extent) by the modern Republic of Turkey in the year 1922.

The Persian state of the last four and a half centuries is hardly important enough to be called an empire, but the term is convenient. The empire was the creation of Shāh Ismā'īl (1502–24), and has been ruled by his dynasty, the Safavids, and subsequent dynasties until the present time. There has been little change in the essential structure of the state, despite the far reaching reforms initiated by Riza Shah Pahlevi (1925–41). The distinctive feature of the Persian empire was that Shāh Ismā'īl made Imāmite Shī'ism the official religion of the state. Up to this time Imāmite Shī'ism had been spread through many parts of the heartlands of the Islamic world, and had not been a peculiarly Persian phenomenon. Now, however, Shī'ites in the Ottoman empire tended to be regarded as 'fifth-columnists', while life was made difficult for Sunnites in Persia. It cannot be contended that there was anything nationalistic in Shāh Ismā'īl's policy, but it had the effect of marking off Persia from the rest of the Islamic world, so that when nationalism appeared in the nineteenth century it found Persia a distinct entity already possessing some sense of unity.

The third of the 'early modern' empires was the Mogul; this word is, of course, a form of 'Mongol'. The first step towards its creation was taken in 1526 when Bābar, already ruler of Afghanistan, occupied the kingdom of Delhi; but it was in the early years of the reign of Akbar (1556–1605) that the empire expanded to cover most of the sub-continent. By about the middle of the eighteenth century the empire was in decline, and its territory rapidly dwindled until it received its *coup de grâce* at the Indian Mutiny in 1857. In the case of both the Moguls and the Ottomans there were internal weaknesses in the state which were responsible for the lessening grip on events, but both eventually fell before European powers.

We have now reviewed very briefly the vast panorama of Islamic history from the Atlantic to the Bay of Bengal and from the Sahara to the Jaxartes (Syr Darya). What part has the Islamic religion played in all this? In the higher reaches of policy it seems to have played very little. One of the great problems, for example, was how to maintain the unity of a ruling family or dynasty, how to effect smoothly the change from one ruler to another, and how to ensure that the person with power was always competent. On such matters little guidance was to be had from traditional Islamic views, which were essentially those of pre-Islamic Arabia, and not suited to the administration of large numbers of town-dwellers and agriculturists; so we find a variety of attempts to solve the problem, of which some were more successful than others, but of which none became universal. In the relationship, too, of Islamic states to one another Islamic religious ideas had little influence, and Islamic brotherhood did not prevent mutual conflict. Occasionally there was talk of the *jihād* (holy war) against non-Muslims, but this was usually when such war fitted in with policies already adopted on other grounds. There was often genuine enthusiasm for the 'holy war' among the rank and file, and perhaps at times among the rulers. It was also possible, however, to denounce as unspeakable heresy some view held by a Muslim enemy, thus making them infidels, and then as such to declare a *jihād* against them.

On the other hand, the rulers were always conscious of certain Islamic values. This was virtually inevitable for those who had been brought up in a setting of Muslim culture. In addition, however, they were aware of the strength of the Sunnite feelings among the populace and, if by nothing else, were forced by consideration of *raison d'état* to continue to allow the Sunnites to live by the Sharī'a. In other words rulers, if they wanted to go on ruling, had to make their domains part of *dār al-islām*, 'the sphere of Islam', that is, a place where a Muslim could live according to the forms of his religion. The Buwayhids and other Shī'ite dynasts were no exception to this. Even the Fāṭimids, though their rule was based on principles radically opposed to those of the 'Abbāsids, did not greatly alter the Sunnite structure of Egyptian society and its way of life. Thus one of the outstanding features of Islamic history is the maintenance of this social structure with little change despite the unending vicissitudes of the rulers.

The most likely reason for the enduring character of the social structure is that it is closely linked with increasing rigidity in the interpretation of the Sharī'a. In the formative period before the establishment of Sunnism jurists appear to have had considerable freedom in deciding particular novel cases according as they thought best. This was known as the exercise of *ijtihād*,which may be roughly translated 'independent judgment'. As time went on, of course, opinions had been pronounced on all the most important types of cases by distinguished jurists; and this in fact restricted the use of *ijtihād*, since it was always difficult for a man to contradict what accepted authorities had said in the past. Legal historians speak of the declining use of independent judgment as 'the closing of the gate of *ijtihād*', and one of the problems facing contemporary Muslims is said to be that of reopening this gate. It is not clear, however, at what precise period it came to be accepted by Muslim jurists that the gate of *ijtihād* had in fact been closed. The historians speak of the closure as effective in the tenth century, but al-Juwaynī and al-Ghazālī at the end of the eleventh century write as if it were still open in theory. Doubtless in these matters practice went before theory. It was clearly advantageous for the jurists and judges, when pressed by a ruler to give a judgment in his favour, to be able to say that they were bound by earlier authorities and were not competent to give the ruling he wanted. What may fairly be accepted was that a large measure of rigidity was implied in what has here been called 'the establishment of Sunnism'.

The maintenance of the Sunnite structure of society is undoubtedly the great achievement of the religious forces of Islam during the period of nearly a millennium now being considered. It was only won, however, at a certain cost. The ulema or religious scholars gained their point that there were certain matters which it was not in their power to alter. They also gained from the rulers a large measure of recognition for themselves as a class or rather corporate body within the community; but at the same time they became increasingly subservient to the rulers. The weakness of the position of the ulema was that all the good positions in the careers open to them were usually controlled by the rulers. In their rivalry for advancement the ulema were ruthless in their attitudes to one another. To be promoted one had to be on good terms with the rulers. A deviationist from the government line, no matter how well founded his deviation, was simply abandoned by his fellows and forfeited his chances of promotion. Such at least is the normal state of affairs, for which some evidence will be found in the first 'book' of al-Ghazālī's *Revival of the Religious Sciences* (*Iḥyā' 'Ulūm ad-Dīn*). From time to time in certain parts of the Islamic world circumstances may have favoured some collective action by the ulema, or a strong leader (like Ibn-Taymiyya) may have found sufficient support to enable him to stand against established authority; but this was the exception.

Apart from maintaining the Sunnite social structure during these centuries religious ideas influenced politics in only minor ways, or at least in ways that were relatively limited in space and time. It has already been observed that rulers made use for mainly secular purposes of the idea of the 'holy war'. The Safavid dynasty presumably made Imāmite Shī'ism their official religion in order to give their dominions greater unity and perhaps also to mark them off from the Ottoman empire. Indeed it seems to have been a common reason for the adoption and retention of sectarian views that they marked off a community from its neighbours. Distinctive doctrines and external religious forms could give greater cohesion to a community of merchants who, if they travelled to any extent, necessarily lived a somewhat scattered life. An example of this would be the followers of the Aga Khan at the present day, whose prosperity is not unconnected with their Ismāʿīlism. Distinctive doctrines and practices are frequent among the inhabitants of mountainous areas (like the Zaydite form of Shīʿism in the Yemen); and they seem to serve the purpose of isolating the mountain community and preventing them being dominated and swamped by the larger plain-dwelling community round them. The most ambitious attempt to use religious ideas for political ends was the Mogul emperor Akbar's construction of a universal 'divine religion' (*dīn ilāhī*) in order to unite his various Hindu, Muslim and other subjects.

For the sake of completeness it must be mentioned that in a few cases novel religious ideas appeared which had some influence in guiding and directing movements. Usually these were movements of revolt among small discontented groups, and they seldom had any wide importance. One such was the Nizārī form of Ismāʿīlism—which was distinguished from the Fāṭimid form by the recognition of Nizār instead of al-Mustaʿlī as successor to al-Mustanṣir in 1094. This doctrine then became the basis of the armed revolt of the so-called Assassins in various parts of the ʿAbbāsid caliphate, since it enabled the leaders of the Assassins to act independently of Fāṭimid Egypt when the latter was not prepared to engage in war. A novel conjunction of ideas proclaimed with fervour was at the basis of the movements in the western part of North Africa which led to the Almoravid and Almohad empires. Despite the political successes the ideas do not seem to have been of sufficient depth to have much lasting influence.[2] In their inception both the Almoravid and Almohad movements were genuinely religious movements though—a point the occidental finds it difficult to grasp—with political implications. The same is true of the Wahhābite movement which began in the latter half of the eighteenth century with genuine zeal for religious reform in a puritanical direction, but has also provided a basis for the modern state of Suʿūdī Arabia. If Wahhābism looks like having more influence in the long run than Almohadism, it is probably because it did not introduce any novel set of ideas but was rather an emphatic reassertion of some of the fundamental ideas of Sunnite Islam. On the whole, examples such as those mentioned in this chapter only serve to reinforce the assertion made earlier that the great political achievement of the

Islamic religion in the period from 950 to 1800 was the maintenance of the distinctive social structure.

4. The periphery of the Islamic world

So far the talk has been almost exclusively of what might be called the 'classical' lands of Islamic culture, or the 'heartlands'. Yet there are other countries where Islam is now the dominant religion, and where some scholars would see the real growing-point of Islam in the present century. These regions may conveniently be referred to as the 'periphery' of the Islamic world. The four regions to be considered here are: West Africa, East Africa, South-East Asia and China.

Two main stages may be distinguished in the islamization of West Africa.[3] The first stage began soon after the Muslim conquest of North Africa about 700 and lasted until about 1600. It consisted first of all of penetration by Muslim (probably Berber) traders across the Sahara into the grasslands and woodlands of the western and central Sudan. In many cases such traders from the north would intermarry with local families, often those engaged in local trade. The northern traders with their wives and children would form a little Muslim community, absolutely certain that its religion is superior to the local religion. Some of the local Sudanese traders would feel that to become Muslims would raise them in the social scale; and in any case the African animistic religions could mean little to traders who were moving about, since each could only be practised in the home village. With the growth and increasing prosperity of the Islamic trading community, rulers felt it politically necessary for them to be members of it, since the merchants were often the main support of their rule. From at least the eighth century there had been one or more large states in West Africa, often called 'empires', and it was in the later part of the pre-European period that the rulers of some of these were Muslims.

Despite the conversion to Islam of rulers, the influence of the religion in this first period was slight. West Africa was accustomed to various groupings within society, each with its distinctive religion. Thus Islam was the religion of the rulers and the trading community, while the rest of society followed its old religions, effectively insulated from Islamic ideas and practices. The position of the ruler, too, was conceived in traditional African terms. It is not surprising, then, that even among nominal Muslims the actual practice of Islam was minimal. The classical story is that of Mansa Musa, emperor of Mali from 1312 to 1337, who made the pilgrimage to Mecca and, while passing through Cairo, is said to have heard for the first time that a Muslim was not allowed to have more than four wives. Yet the absence of Islamic practices in the social structure does not necessarily mean that the link with Islam was weak. On the contrary, it would seem that many West African Muslims were conscious of belonging to a vast community, and were proud of their membership.

The second stage in the islamization of West Africa began about 1600, but the most significant changes did not appear till shortly before 1800. The factors which mark off the new stage are the decline of trade across the Sahara by the old trade routes, and the growth of new forms of trade through the ports on the coast created by the Europeans; by about 1800 slaves were the most important item of trade through the ports, and this had internal repercussions, since the slave-raiders were Africans. The interesting feature of this period in the present context is the emergence of the so-called (Islamic) 'theocratic states'. The first outstanding state of this kind was that founded in the first decade of the nineteenth century by Usuman ('Uthmān) dan-Fodio. Though this state later split up into the Hausa emirates of northern Nigeria, it left a trace of itself in the recognition by these emirates of the primacy of the Sultan of Sokoto. At least three other 'theocratic' states are to be found in West Africa in the nineteenth century.

All these states differ from the older empires in that the position and authority of the leader rest on Islamic ideas and not on traditional African ideas. The fact that the structure of these states is sufficiently similar for them to be given the name 'theocratic' suggests that they owe their emergence to common factors. Thus they would seem to presuppose a considerable diffusion of Islamic ideas in the areas where they emerged and many, at least nominal, Muslims. It is also likely that the change in the direction of trade and the consequent social dislocations, especially those caused by slave-raiding, were contributory factors. Islam has always been a religion of urban societies, and can provide a stable basis for life to men who have been uprooted from a tribal or village society; and doubtless the stricter observance of Islamic forms and rules under a forceful and confident leader gave uprooted men in West Africa a new security. The records show that the leaders interpreted the movement in theological and not in social terms; but this does not invalidate the sociological examination of the events. The theocratic states eventually disappeared, except where emirates continued under the British system of indirect rule, but they gave a fillip to the expansion of the Islamic religion. As more Africans were affected by the processes of uprooting and social dislocation, Islam has continued to expand.

In East Africa the contacts with Islam probably go farther back than in West Africa, and yet the expansion of Islam has been slower. This is partly due to the geographical character of the area. There are well-populated regions in the interior, especially round the lakes, but between these and the coast is an arid or semi-arid belt which is only sparsely inhabited. Arab merchants visited the coast before the time of Muḥammad, and their visits seem to have continued after they became Muslims, and to have led to the establishment of trading-posts. As elsewhere they intermarried with the local people, and there were groups of Muslims here and there which were mainly African in race. Zanzibar is said to have been occupied by about 750, and about 940 appears to have been ruled by a Muslim African dynasty. By the thirteenth century it is probable that the coast towns were predominantly Muslim; they were prosperous, and there are said to have been thirty-seven of them between Mogadishu and Kilwa before the coming of the Portuguese. The prosperity of the towns rested on the fact that they were entrepot ports; on the one hand goods were brought to them from the fertile parts of the interior, and on the other hand they were the termini of the seaborne trade from India, Malaya and the East Indies.

The Portuguese, shortly after the discovery of the route to India in 1498, began to interest themselves in East Africa. Some of the towns they occupied, some they sacked. The actual trade they tried to take into their own hands, but they seem to have been unable to form good relationships with the 'middlemen' who carried goods between the ports and the interior of Africa. The result was that trade languished and the coastal towns declined. The appearance of Ottoman Turks from Egypt in East Africa in 1585 and 1588 led to a temporary escape from the Portuguese grip and to a continuing desire for unity and independence under Islam. The Portuguese, however, soon reasserted themselves, and maintained control until the middle of the seventeenth century. By that time they were growing weaker everywhere in the East. The sultans of Oman, which had just gained its independence from the Portuguese, carried the war against them into East Africa, and by 1698 had brought all the coastal towns under their rule, though the local governors had a large measure of independence. The power of the sultanate, with its capital now at Zanzibar, was at its zenith about 1850; but later it declined as the European impact increased.

The Islamic religion does not seem to have begun to spread inland from the coastal area until the second half of the nineteenth century. One tribe, the Yao, about 1850 took to slave-raiding for the Arab market at Zanzibar, and became largely Muslim; but this did not commend Islam to other tribes. The renewed European contacts of the later nineteenth century and the schemes of European colonization have led to a process of uprooting and detribalization comparable to that noticed in West Africa. The Islamic culture of the coastal towns has attracted detribalized persons and given them some support, and has also spread into the interior as men there felt more of the stresses and strains of the modern world. This special form of Islamic culture is distinguished by its *lingua franca*, the Swahili language, which is essentially a Bantu language with a large number of Arabic loan-words. The creation of this Swahili Islamic culture seems to be the chief achievement of Islam in East Africa which is relevant to politics, and its relevance is perhaps still mainly in the future. (The name of the language is derived from the Arabic *sawāḥilī*, an adjective from *sawāḥil*, 'coasts'.)

The remaining regions may be dealt with more briefly. In South-East Asia the spread of Islam was largely the work of Muslim traders. Trade had been carried on between India and the Indies for centuries before the rise of Islam, and this brought with it Hindu culture and religion, and then Buddhist religion. In the latter half of the twelfth century a kingdom, partly Buddhist, partly Hindu, with its capital at Palembang in southern Sumatra, controlled the whole of that island as well as Malaya and western Java. This was replaced towards the end of the thirteenth century by an eastern Javanese kingdom with its capital first at Singhasari, then at Majapahit; this kingdom was powerful for a century, then declined, and finally disappeared early in the sixteenth century. Long before this Islam had been establishing itself. The Arabs may have begun to have a share in the seaborne trade soon after the time of Muḥammad. By the end of the thirteenth century there were sizeable communities of merchants in some of the ports of

Sumatra (like Perlak, visited by Marco Polo in 1292), and in some towns the prince had already become Muslim. The parallel with West Africa is noticeable.

From the fourteenth century onwards Islam kept spreading throughout the Indies and in Malaya, though there was a slowing down of the process during the Portuguese ascendancy in the sixteenth century—perhaps because the Portuguese had taken much of the seaborne trade from the Muslims. The expansion was by peaceful means, but when Muslim rulers extended their territories there would be material advantages for their subjects in the adoption of Islam. In contrast to what happened in the sixteenth century the period of Dutch rule from the seventeenth century onwards was one which favoured the spread of Islam. The chief point of difference with West Africa is that here Islam was confronted by highly integrated Buddhist and Hindu civilizations, and therefore was the bearer of religion only, not of culture also. There were more primitive peoples in the interior areas, and on the whole these did not become Muslim until they had become detribalized. As elsewhere, local customs and institutions were not much altered, not even the matriarchal social structure found in many areas. There was, however, a gradual trend towards a purer form of Islam.

The political relevance of Islam in the history of South-East Asia, apart from its general influence, is to be seen chiefly in two wars. The first of these was the rising of the Padris (1821–38). In 1803 three Sumatran Muslims, returning from the pilgrimage to Mecca greatly impressed by the Wahhābite movement in Arabia, set moving currents of religious puritanism, directed in part against the prevailing matriarchal institutions. Religious zeal, however, developed into a holy war against pagan Bataks, and the holy war was so successful from a military point of view that it led to armed conflict with the Dutch government, until the Padris had been suppressed. The other event was the war between the state of Atjeh and the Dutch which continued with quiescent periods from 1873 to 1910. In organizing popular support for this war a large part was played by the ulema, so that Islamic religious ideas became the focus of an anti-European revolt.

The fourth of the regions mentioned as peripheral is China, where there are estimated to be between ten and twenty million Muslims. These are found mostly in Sinkiang (or Chinese Turkestan) and in the western provinces of Kansu, Szechwan and Yunnan. One reason for not forgetting about Islam in China is that it presents a contrast with most other regions where Islam has taken root. The expansion of Islam, for example, does not seem in the first place to have been the work of travelling traders. In the province of Kansu the majority of the Muslims are considered to be descendants of Muslim mercenaries, called in about the year 755 to help the Chinese emperor against the Tibetans; they were probably mainly arabized inhabitants of Iraq, but there may also have been some of Turkish stock. Certainly most of the other Chinese Muslims belong racially to one or other of the Turkish peoples. In the late fourteenth century the Chinese government adopted a policy of isolation, and one of the results of this was that the Chinese Muslims became more Chinese. There were several risings of Chinese Muslims in the nineteenth century, followed by severe reprisals; but these seem to have been based chiefly on the feeling of common loyalty to the Islamic community, and not (as in other parts of the world) on some new contemporary expression of the Islamic religion. Before the advent of the Chinese People's Republic optimistic Muslims entertained hopes of the conversion of all China to Islam. A more sober estimate would be that, if Islam is to have political relevance in China, it must be in a fairly distant future.

The survey of peripheral regions may seem to have left out important Islamic territories which fall between the 'heartlands' proper and what we have treated as periphery. On the one hand there is Soviet Central Asia, and on the other Somalia, Ethiopia and the Sudanese Republic. The justification of omitting a separate treatment of these areas would be that, since they sometimes resemble the heartlands and sometimes the periphery, they would not add anything distinctive to a general survey. There are also three and a half million Muslims in Europe (other than Turkey), chiefly in Yugoslavia, Albania and Bulgaria; but this is a part of the periphery where Islam has been on the defensive, and indeed in retreat, for centuries. These European Muslims are unlikely to make any great contribution to the general life of Islam in the visible future, but influences from other parts of the Islamic world might some day lead to revival and renewal among them.

5. Islam's reaction to the impact of Europe and America

The outstanding event in the life of the Islamic peoples during the last two or three centuries has been the impact on them of the occidental world, first Europe, then America. This has not been a period when the political relevance of Islam has been specially noticeable, yet there are potentialities which should not be neglected. This occidental impact has no parallels in earlier Islamic history; it is much more profound than the impact of Greek thought between 800 and 1100, since it is not merely intellectual, but also economic, social and political.

In accordance with the view underlying this book—that economic and material factors have a certain primacy, as constituting the framework within which human life has to be lived—the economic, or more generally, material, aspects of the impact will be noticed first. The fundamental date for the beginning of the impact is 1498, the year when Vasco da Gama reached India after rounding the Cape of Good Hope. This event is a practical application of a new technique, that of long-distance navigation. The application of this technique, however, requires not merely certain knowledge and instruments, but also a certain attitude of mind both in the voyagers themselves and in those at the 'home base' who support them. It is noteworthy that no Muslim sailors from India or elsewhere, despite a long tradition of seafaring, ever completed the voyage to Europe or gained a share in the seaborne trade between Europe and the Indies.

The development of other techniques of communication greatly increased the force of the European impact, although it was still in the days of sailing ships that the invasion of Egypt by Napoleon took place—another landmark in the total story of the impact. Steamships took the place of sailing ships, and the journey from Europe to India was further shortened by the Suez Canal. Railways also came to play a part; the chief encroachment on the Islamic world in this way was by the Russians with the Trans-Siberian railway and its offshoots, which enabled them to occupy the emirates of Central Asia. Another form of communication in the nineteenth century was by telegraph and cable; while the twentieth century brought the petrol engine, which made possible the motor-car (including tracked vehicles for the desert) and the aeroplane. Another form of communication resulted from the European invention (or rediscovery) of the process of printing with separate types. These techniques and inventions led in the first place to wider possibilities for trade, and then to other forms of contact, such as the sending of Muslim students to Europe and the participation of Muslim statesmen in international councils.

At first, though long voyages by sailing ship were relatively cheap, trade was mostly confined to spices, silks and other luxury goods; but the steamship made it economically possible to transport large quantities of less valuable goods over great distances. By the beginning of the nineteenth century the Industrial Revolution was altering the European patterns of buying and selling. The Europeans wanted cheap raw materials, and could offer cheap factory products in return. On this basis intercontinental trade developed of ever-increasing volume. European financiers also entered in, and loans were given to encourage consumption of European goods in the old Islamic lands. The much later discovery of oil at first led to a similar pattern of exploitation by Europeans and Americans; but it had not proceeded far before the Islamic reaction was under way.

In course of time the economic interests of the Europeans led to political interference. The Portuguese were first in the field, followed by the Dutch, the French and the British. The struggle between the European powers led eventually to the establishment of the British Raj in India and of Dutch rule in what is now Indonesia. In the nineteenth century, beginning with the French occupation of Algiers in 1830, the Islamic states of North Africa came piecemeal under European rule. Apart from these instances of direct or semi-direct rule, there was much dictation of policy by European states in the nineteenth century, especially to the Ottoman and Persian empires. Because of military weakness and financial obligations they were forced to accede to the suggestions of 'residents' and 'ambassadors'. Despite such dictation some Islamic states were being gradually admitted to the family of modern states, which had at first been entirely occidental; ambassadors were exchanged; treaties were signed as between equals; since a definite frontier was one of the marks of a modern state frontiers were carefully delimited. At a later time came admission to the League of Nations and then to the United Nations Organization. This acceptance into the international state system led in its turn to a further impact of occidental political thinking. Islamic countries wanted to develop institutions which would be acceptable to the Europeans, so that they might feel that they were fully and genuinely sharing in the international life of the world. So they had parliaments, new codes of (European) law, first for commerce and then for other matters, and finally new law courts and new judges to administer these codes.

The direct social impact of the occident (as distinct from the repercussions of its economic impact) was not great. A measure of familiarity with the customs of occidental society was achieved by the students who came to the European universities, and a further measure came later from the cinema. The result of the social impact is perhaps to be chiefly seen in the widespread movement to give women a better place in society.

The intellectual impact, on the other hand, has been considerable. Muslims naturally came to have an understanding of the scientific thinking underlying European technology. In addition to studying the particular sciences they came to appreciate the philosophical positions implicit in the general scientific outlook. Because of Islam's historically deep-seated suspicion of Christianity they preferred anti-Christian to Christian exponents of modern thought. In Islamic lands Christian missionaries had little success in gaining converts and spreading specifically Christian ideas, but they made important contributions to the general spread of occidental ideas by education. The deliberate propagation of occidental political ideas was begun in the third decade of the twentieth century by Fascists and Communists, followed later by the democracies.

Such then was the total occidental impact on the Islamic world in the period since 1498 and more especially since 1798. There has, of course, been a comparable impact on the other ancient civilizations of Asia. From an early date there was a reaction to this impact among Muslims, beginning with the abortive attempts to send Muslim ships to Europe. The reaction may conveniently be dealt with under the same heads as the impact.

To the economic impact the reaction was the replacement (in suitable areas) of the old system of subsistence agriculture by the growing of crops to be sold for cash, such as cotton, rubber and tea. This meant involvement in the world economic system, and exposure of Muslim populations to the fluctuations of the world markets. There were also some attempts, chiefly in the twentieth century, to develop industries in Islamic countries so as to reduce economic dependence on the occident; and these efforts continue with growing success.

In the social sphere what is found is not so much a conscious response to the impact as unconscious repercussions. An important feature is the appearance of a new Western-educated middle class. Before the impact of Europe made itself felt there were, roughly speaking, two classes in the Islamic world; there was an upper class consisting of rulers, landowners, administrators and great merchants; and there was a lower class consisting of peasants, subordinate artisans, small traders, and the town proletariat generally. The new middle class, in contrast, consists of army officers, civil servants, professional men, skilled artisans and the like. The economic changes of the last century have on the whole led to increasing disparity of wealth. The upper class (or at least those sections of it that were forward-looking) benefited most from the introduction of European methods, and until recently have in most countries been increasing their economic and political control of affairs. In consequence the middle class is discontented, since it is aware that it is essential for the running of each country as a modern state. The Egyptian revolution of 1952 is one of the first signs of this middle class's assertion of itself.

In the internal political scene there was little change of control until the Egyptian revolution and other similar coups by army officers. The old ruling and upper class managed to retain its power by one strategem or another. There was a façade of parliamentary and democratic forms, but the unfamiliar institutions were easily manipulated by intriguing upper-class cliques to ensure that no real power went to the other classes. This absence of change in internal politics was in contrast to developments in external political relationships. The reaction to European domination was the obvious one of struggling to assert or reassert independence. In this struggle certain aspects of the European idea of nationalism have been used to unite the 'nation' and, in the international forum, to present a case which could not be gainsaid by the occidentals. At the time of writing (1966) the struggle has been successful nearly everywhere. The chief body of Muslims under non-Muslim rule is in India where there are reckoned to be forty million. There are twenty million in the parts of Central Asia belonging to the U.S.S.R., and ten million or more in China; in these cases there is a measure of self-determination, as indeed there is also in India, and in the countries of south-eastern Europe where there are Muslims. The Muslims of South Arabia are less than a million but, since the land is wholly Muslim, the appearance of foreign domination is clearer; there is a movement towards independence, however, and the chief questions now seem to be at what date and in what form independence is to come.

In going on to consider the intellectual and religious reaction it is important to note first of all the bipolar attitude of the Muslim is important to note first of all the bipolar attitude of the Muslim heartlands to occidental culture. On the one hand, there is great admiration for occidental political strength, technological achievement and material luxury, and this admiration extends into the cultural and intellectual field. On the other hand the determination not to be dominated politically by Europe and America is paralleled by a resolve to maintain some independence in the intellectual sphere also. Occidental ideas have been accepted and developed chiefly in the middle class as a result of their occidental education. One such idea already noticed is that of nationalism, which has been prominent in the struggle for independence, despite the difficulties of applying it in the Islamic heartlands, since the break-up of the Ottoman empire with its millet system has left most of the successor-states with intractable minority problems. Egypt has had to consider whether to speak of Egyptian (or Pharaonic) nationalism, to include the Copts, or of Arab or Islamic nationalism, to support her claims to leadership in a wider field. Iraq has, to mention no others, Sunnite Kurds and Shī'ite Arabs, who together considerably outnumber the Sunnite Arabs. With the attainment of independence the conception of nationalism ceased to give much guidance, and the middle class has turned instead to some form or other of socialism. The lower class, however, that is, the great masses of the people, have not accepted these occidental ideas except to the extent, for example, that nationalism was in line with their innate xenophobia. They are still firmly attached to traditional Islamic ideas, and are easily roused by the cry that Islam is being attacked.

The resurgence of Islam is a phrase frequently used nowadays, and there are indeed phenomena to which it applies, but it is important to look closely at the precise nature of these phenomena. The middle class in the course of its education has acquired the general scientific outlook of the occident, with emphasis on the secular and anti-religious aspects. It has thus become for the most part alienated from the traditional religion, yet without finding anything else to take its place, that is, any set of ideas by which to direct its life. This religious attitude is often accompanied by a kind of secular patriotic attachment to Islam as a cultural community. This seems to be one aspect of the resurgence, but it is hardly a revival of religion. Another aspect is to be seen among those, whether occidentally or traditionally educated, who appreciate the intellectual outlook of the occident, yet remain attached at the religious level to Islam. Such men are becoming aware that there is something at the heart of their religion which is not ultimately affected by occidental scientific thought, so that the Muslim can hold up his head proudly among the adherents of the great religions. This 'something' is ultimately what in this book has been called the Islamic vision. The problem for those who are attempting to recover from the occidental impact on the Islamic religion is how under modern conditions to continue to embody the vision in their lives.

The theme of this chapter was the religious aspect of political developments. In the modern period, the period of the occidental impact, religion is not prominent. The most important facts seem to be the alienation of the middle class and the tenacity of the masses. The latter is potentially a factor of great political importance in the present situation, but only provided a leader can arise who is able to reverse the identification of religion with social conservatism for one with social reform.

Chapter 8

The function of the religious intellectuals

1. Dogma and unity

The Islamic vision comes to men, at the intellectual level, in the form of ideas, and these are contained primarily in the Qur'ān. The men to whom these ideas originally came, however, were already for the most part members of the community, and the vision was in some sense embodied in the community. Yet it is difficult to state precisely the function of ideas in the life of such a community through long periods of history. Some might be inclined to dismiss the problem by saying that the only function of the ideas is to be believed by the Muslims. The sociologist sees much more in the problem than this. Now one idea is emphasized, now another. Some Muslims held that the Qur'ān was the created Word of God, while others maintained that it was uncreated. It has been suggested above that this theological point was linked with a great struggle between two blocs of Muslims, a struggle that had an important political aspect. The sociologist would therefore seem to be justified in asking how the theological point is related to the political aims. It is quickly apparent, too, that the relationship is not a simple one. The 'autocratic bloc' did not adopt their political views simply because they believed that the Qur'ān was created, nor could the belief be regarded as the product of their political views.

This problem of the function of religious ideas in a community is indeed a vast one with many ramifications and cannot be tackled in its entirety in the present volume.[1] For the moment all that is insisted on is that the problem exists and is a complex one. Religious ideas have clearly had an important place in the ongoing life of the Islamic community. They have been handed down from generation to generation, as the Qur'ān was memorized, so that in one sense the same Qur'ānic ideas underly the whole life of the

Islamic community. Yet a brief survey of the intellectual history of the Islamic world shows that more was being done with the ideas than simply transmitting them and memorizing them. Among the processes to be observed are the apologetic interpretation of Qur'ānic texts and the increasing definition of dogma.

Apologetic interpretation occurs in the course of disputes within the community. In the course of such a dispute as that about the created or uncreated character of the Qur'ān one side would produce certain texts, claiming that these supported its view. The opponents would then assert that these texts really meant something else, while there were others which clearly proved their own case. Both sides would then enter into furious arguments over these texts and others, each trying to strengthen its own case and weaken that of its opponents. More theoretical questions might sometimes be brought in, such as the question whether a particular verse was originally intended to be of general or particular application. There were extremists who produced the weirdest interpretations of certain texts—interpretations which were rejected by virtually all Muslims. In the end any important group or body of thought within the Muslim community achieved a measure of agreement within itself on the interpretation of the Qur'ān. This agreed interpretation was adapted to their general view of *the* meaning underlying the Qur'ān as a whole, or, in other words, the Islamic vision. Within the main body of Sunnite opinion, although there were sectional divergences, there was a wide measure of agreement about the interpretation of the Qur'ān.

The process by which dogma becomes increasingly definite is also to be observed in the history of Islamic thought. Unfortunately there is in the contemporary occident serious misunderstanding of the function of dogma in the life of a community. This is largely due to the way in which dogma has frequently been used in the last century or so by conservative elements in a community in order to resist apparently desirable forms of adaptation to changing circumstances. In the formative stages of the life of a community dogma has an important positive function, since it is the formula recording agreements reached after matters have been long disputed. Some of the points to be mentioned in the next section led to bitter disputes with many ramifications. After such a dispute most of the parties concerned come eventually to agree that a certain view of the matter is the true one. This agreed view is expressed in a concise formula, such as: 'the Qur'ān is the uncreated word of God'. Once a point of belief has been 'defined' in this way it is a dogma, something fixed, which is generally accepted and not further disputed. The dogma is not the Islamic vision itself, but the expression of a facet of that vision. The acceptance of the dogma by the bulk of the community is not a decision to hold a particular intellectual belief in dogged obstinacy through thick and thin. It is, on the contrary, the decision that the agreed formula best expresses a facet of the vision by which the community is already living. In other words, the dogma is not something new in itself, but merely makes definite what has already been present vaguely or indefinitely in the vision accepted or followed by the community. To reject the dogma is tantamount to leaving the community, but one can sometimes avoid this by attaching oneself to a splinter community based on an alternative dogma.

Something will be seen in the next section of the process by which more and more points of dogma are made definite. It will also be seen in this process, however, that many formulations are put forward for the acceptance of the community which fail to gain that acceptance. It follows that there is something tentative about the efforts of theologians to formulate dogma. Thus in the creed known as the *Kifāya* of al-Faḍālī (d. 1821) it is stated that every Muslim is obliged to know fifty articles of belief, together with a proof of each; and several of these articles involve a subtle distinction between *ṣifāt al-maʻānī* and *ṣifāt maʻnawiyya*. This dogmatic formulation has obviously never been accepted by the Islamic community as a whole. If what one theologian puts forward as a dogma can thus be rejected by the community as a whole, may a dogma accepted by most of the community ever be revised later? The answer to this is not altogether simple. In so far as the community is based on the vision and not on any expression of the vision in a dogma, it would seem that revision of the expression is theoretically possible. On the other hand, if a dogma on a fundamental point has been unquestioningly accepted by a community for centuries, it is difficult to alter it without appearing to abandon the vision. Nevertheless there are Muslims nowadays who are trying to reinterpret the verses of the Qur'ān supporting the practice of having four wives, which has been characteristic of Islam for centuries, and who hold that the words 'if you fear that you cannot act equitably, then one only' (4.3) virtually makes it impossible for a Muslim to have more than one wife. It must be admitted, however, that this is not one of the central matters, and on the whole it seems unlikely that these could be changed.

This consideration of Islamic dogma leads to a further question about the unity of the Islamic religion over many centuries and in many regions of the world. In what sense can Islam or any other religion be said to remain a unity? The process by which dogma is increasingly defined is itself a change of a sort in the religion. The Muslims who lived under the first four 'rightly guided' caliphs had no set of credal beliefs such as that later formulated by al-Ash'arī (d. 935). Yet it could be maintained that this was not a change in substance, but that the creed merely made explicit what had hitherto been implicitly believed. Alternatively one could say that the essential vision is the same, but that the verbal expression of it is fuller. Any such statement, however, leaves the door open to another type of alteration, namely, the alteration required to meet changing modes of thought in non-theological spheres. An example of this would be the way in which the existence of God has now to be explained to men who normally think in terms of the modern scientific outlook; such men may find it difficult to find a place for the creative act of God in the obscurity of the origins of the universe, or to know how to answer the assertion that the idea of God is merely a 'projection'. Thus the unity of a religion must at least be compatible with differences of emphasis from time to time.

The view that Islam is something absolutely unchanging has been popular with Muslims in the past and is still held firmly by some. Similar views are indeed held about other religions by their adherents. In the case of Islam such a view doubtless owes something to the outlook of the Arabs of the desert. These lived in a static society where there was a deep conviction that safety was to be achieved by following meticulously in its details the manner of life of their ancestors. Innovation (*bid'a*) was to be avoided like the plague since it normally led to disaster. It was therefore not surprising that the exact following of the manner of life of Muḥammad later became an ideal for Muslims; and that the word for heresy in religious doctrine or practice was simply 'innovation'. Apart from this aspect of the Arab outlook the view that a religion is unchanging has much to commend it. A religious community has some of the features of a single living organism. Yet the difficulty inherent in the view appears when one tries to say precisely what is unchanging through a long period of time. If one defines the permanent element too fully, many persons are excluded who are normally reckoned Muslims; but if, in order to include all such persons, one says, for example, that the only permanent elements in Islam are the Shahāda (confession of faith), the five daily prayers and the fast of Ramaḍān, this is far short of a statement of the essence of Islam as it is commonly understood. It therefore seems better to say that the essence or kernel of Islam, which is unchanging, cannot be adequately expressed in words, but is rather what has been called in this book 'the Islamic vision'.

The difficulty of regarding Islam as a unity is also made clear when one considers the various sects and the variations in practice from region to region. It is commonly agreed, of course, that both Sunnites and Shī'ites are Muslims, though each group would maintain that its own form of Islam is superior to the others. In some sense both Sunnism and Shī'ism are expressions of the Islamic vision, but it is difficult, if not impossible, even for the impartial observer, to put into words what they have in common. The difficulty is made only the more intractable when Zaydites, Ibāḍites and Ismā'īlites are mentioned; and the Aḥmadiyya from Qadian arouse a storm of controversy. The heart of the problem is to decide how far deviation in doctrine or practice must go before a group is excluded from Islam; and in this respect the position of the academic scholar differs from that of the administrator. The scholar may admit a strong continuing influence of the Islamic vision, where the administrator is justified in treating a group as being no longer Muslims. On the other hand, it is worth remembering that al-Ghazālī in *Fayṣal at-Tafriqa bayn al-Islām wa-z-Zandaqa* gave a warning against declaring men infidels on insufficient grounds; and there is always a temptation for the mass feeling of a dominant majority to use the cry of *kufr* or *shirk* (unbelief, polytheism) against a minority which is disliked.

Similar difficulties arise when one considers the variations in local practice in various countries. In peripheral countries in particular Muslims often retain much local custom. Some occidental observers have gone so far as to say that there is not one Islam but many—a different religion in each country or region. The very fact that such a view can be put forward suggests that the question whether Islam is one or many is not a question that can receive an objective answer, since whatever answer a scholar gives is partly based on his subjective interests. Perhaps we should boldly grasp the nettle and admit that the unity of Islam is a 'projection', but then go on to contend that its projective character does not make it an invalid idea. The word 'projection' is commonly taken to mean that some quality is read into the phenomena by the observer although it has no basis in them. There is another possible interpretation of 'projection', however. It may be that in certain cases we have to begin by reading, say 'unity', into the phenomena, but that, once we have done so, we are able to perceive that there are elements in the phenomena capable of becoming adequate bearers or supports of this idea of unity. In the case of the unity of the religion of Islam such an element would be the fact that, of those whose lives embody or have been largely influenced by the Islamic vision, almost all would publicly profess that they accept the vision which came with the Qur'ān, that is, that they accept the Shahāda.

In this manner the conception of a vision, or way of looking at the universe and man's place in it, makes it possible to affirm the unity of Islam through centuries, and yet also to accept a sociological view of religion, namely, as an aspect or facet of a communal life which in one sense is unchanging and in another is constantly adapting itself to changing circumstances.

2. The great doctrinal disputes

After these general considerations about the function of dogmatic development in the life of a community, we may turn to look at the most important disputes in the life of the Islamic community. Something has already been said from the political angle about the early disputes connected with the Khārijites and the Shī'ites, so the treatment of these from the dogmatic or doctrinal angle may be brief.

The Khārijites first came into prominence during the caliphate of 'Alī (656–61) with their insistence that the Qur'ān was to be the ultimate standard of authority in the Islamic community. Administrative decisions were to be based on it, and the conduct even of rulers was to be judged by it; those who failed to obey it, as they alleged 'Uthmān had failed, were worthy of death. In their thinking the conception of the community played a very important part. They spoke of the body of Muslims as 'the people of Paradise', and seemed to think that membership of this body was a guarantee that a man would ultimately attain Paradise. Presumably they felt that a sin (disobedience of a Qur'ānic precept) imperilled the future bliss of the whole community, and for this reason they put the sinner to death or expelled him from the community. In all this they seem to have been trying to bring into Islam a value associated in many cases with the pre-Islamic tribe, namely, the conception that the tribe through the tribal stock gave nobility and significance to the member of it.

Some of the critics of the Khārijites maintained that it was wrong to exclude a man from the community because of sin. However this might be in the desert, where a man expelled from one tribe could usually find another to give him protection, it was clearly impracticable for a stable urban civilization to expel its members for every sin. On the other hand, the view put forward by some Muslims that, where a man was a member of the community, sins did not matter, appeared to belittle the seriousness of sin. Crimes certainly had to be punished, but not all crimes could be punished by death or exclusion from the community. This view was apparently accepted by most Muslims. The problem was how to reconcile the presence of criminals in the community with the fact that it was a community of persons destined for Paradise. The first attempt to solve their problem was that of the Murji'ites ('postponers') with their conception of 'postponement' (*irjā'*), namely, that the practical administrator need not decide whether the criminal was ultimately destined for Paradise or Hell, but might 'postpone' that decision and leave it to God at the end of the world. Some pious people, however, objected to associating with sinners as if they belonged to the people of Paradise. As the centuries passed the view was more and more accepted that the community was a charismatic one, membership of which guaranteed ultimate admission to Paradise. The seriousness of sin or crime was upheld by insisting that it must be punished; this punishment might be either on earth or in Hell, but, if the latter, it would be for a limited period and the sinner would at length enter Paradise, provided he had remained a member of the Islamic community.

Out of these discussions, therefore, there grew a further debate about the conditions of membership of the community. This is linked with the conception of *īmān* or 'faith', but the connotations of the English word and its European equivalents are misleading when one is dealing with the Islamic discussion. Linguistically, of course, *īmān* means 'faith', but in the Islamic context it is regarded primarily as that which constitutes a man a *mu'min*, a believer or member of the believing community. For this reason the word *īmān* will be retained. In the discussions various elements were distinguished, usually those connected with the heart, the lips and the members. The heart, the seat of the intellect, was concerned with the acceptance of the articles of the creed; the lips gave the public profession or witness; while the members had the office of executing the various religious duties including the performance of public worship. There was much scope for dispute about the necessity for all three elements in *īmān*; in particular many theologians belittled the outward acts and thought they were not an essential part of *īmān*. Bound up with this was a further dispute whether *īmān* could increase and decrease or was one and indivisible. Eventually the consensus moved towards the view that the only sin that excluded a man from the Islamic community and from Paradise was *shirk*, polytheism, the acknowledgment of deities other than God. In this way a balance was attained. Only *shirk* led to forfeiture of membership of the community and so to Hell; other sins would be punished, but, since membership of the charismatic community was retained, the sinner would ultimately reach Paradise. (The sin of apostasy—*ridda*, *irtidād*—which might have been thought relevant to this topic seems to have been neglected by theologians and discussed exclusively by jurists.)

Contemporary in origin with the Khārijites and often their bitter opponents were the Shī'ites, who have also been described already (pp. 119–21) at a mainly political level. They emphasized the belief that salvation is to be looked for, first and foremost, from the charismatic leader. Procedure of a democratic type, they were convinced, could only lead to disaster since ordinary men without any charisma were bound to make bad decisions. Only the divinely endowed leader could guide the community to safety. Such beliefs are probably to be connected with the long tradition in South Arabia of semi-divine kings, for a large proportion of the early Shī'ites came from South Arabian tribes. Also involved in the Shī'ite conception was the common Arab belief in the nobility of certain stocks. In particular, because of the special gifts manifest in Muḥammad, the Shī'ites believed that the stock of the clan of Hāshim was of exceptional merit. The older Arab idea was that nobility and outstanding gifts were due simply to heredity, so that every member of the particular clan or family had the gifts, at least potentially. Another idea also came to be present, namely, that charismatic gifts of a unique kind were possessed by only one member of the family at a given time, and that this unique person, the imam or 'leader', had always to be designated by his predecessor. The later Imāmites considered that 'Alī had been designated by Muḥammad as imam after him, al-Ḥasan by 'Alī, and so on to the twelfth of their imams. The original 'Abbāsid claim to the caliphate was that they had become imams by designation; and they gave details of the line of transmission. About the year 780, however, they adopted an alternative claim or rather justification of their position, namely, that from the death of Muḥammad the imamate had rightfully been in the house of 'Abbās.

Another doctrinal development found among the Shī'ites, is that which is sometimes called by the generic term 'messianism', meaning the belief that deliverance is only to be expected from a supernatural leader or one sent by God. This may take the form either of the belief that the Deliverer is actually present or of the expectation that he will appear in the near or distant future. Among the Shī'ites, after the failure of the revolt of al-Mukhtār and more particularly after the death of Muḥammad ibn-al-Ḥanafiyya in 700, the idea began to spread that he, their imam, was not dead but in concealment (*ghayba*), and that at the proper time he would return as the Mahdī to set everything right. The practical effect of such an idea is to make men quiescent in acceptance of their present lot by offering them the hope that one day it will be changed for the better. The conception of the 'hidden imam' was probably also used by the Ismā'īlites early in the ninth century, but there are many obscurities in their history. It was certainly used by the Imāmites about the end of the ninth century and applied to the twelfth and last of their imams. The persistence of this idea among large numbers of Muslims shows that it meets some deep need of men, if not of all men at least of many men. One of the desiderata for the unification of Islam at the present time is the discovery by the Sunnites, without abandoning the essentials of their own position, of some way of meeting the needs of the Shī'ites.

Another important dispute was about what an occidental would call 'free will and predestination', though this was not exactly how the Muslims thought about it. The idea of 'freedom' meant nothing to the pre-Islamic Arab, though he distinguished between the slave and the free man. In Islamic theology this problem is discussed as the problem of the *qadar*, where *qadar* means something like 'power to determine events'. The debate was focused on whether this power belonged to God alone or was shared by men. Those who wanted to assert some power for men were known by the nickname of Qadarites. In an earlier chapter it has been seen that the Arab of the desert had a deep conviction that the main aspects of his life were all determined by the sum of forces which he called 'Time', and that man was powerless to alter these things. The Qur'ān, too, criticizes the confidence of the Meccan merchants in their own power. Thus the first Muslims would have little inclination to exaggerate human power. As Islam spread in Iraq and Syria, however, among Christians and others who had long been under the influence of Greek civilization with its emphasis on human achievement, something of this outlook was brought into Islam. The point had a political reference, too. The Umayyads seem to have argued that, since they in fact ruled (*sc.* since they had been given the rule by God), any attempt to revolt against them must be disobedience towards God. Political opponents of the régime had thus to find a theological justification for their opposition. Part of this justification was the insistence that man had power over against God, and that he was not obliged to obey a ruler who himself had disobeyed God's commands and ruled unjustly.

After the replacement of the Umayyads by the 'Abbāsids the dispute continued, but the political implications had largely disappeared, so that it might now be regarded as an attempt to reconcile differing cultural backgrounds. In particular the opponents of predestination were anxious to maintain not man's power as something ultimate, but God's justice. The fundamental argument was that, since God rewarded and punished men on the Last Day according to their acts, they must be genuinely responsible for these acts and be the doers of them. From this point onwards complications entered. It was seen that a simple act like shooting an arrow required the cooperation of natural forces, so that it was difficult to say what the essential act of the man was. It could be regarded as the movements of his body (such as the stretching of the bow), but the powers to make these movements were given by God. Soon it was realized that the question was not one of physical or bodily power, but of power in the sense of volitional ability (though no word for 'volitional' was normally used); and further—strange as it seems to an occidental—both parties agreed that power in this sense was created by God. The crux of the matter then became the question: was it power to do only what in fact the man did, or was it power to do either that or the opposite? If it was the former, as the upholders of God's *qadar* claimed, then it would be simultaneous with the act; but if it was power for alternative acts, then it must be before the act in the moment of choice when it is decided to do this act and not that act.

A compromise formula on this point was produced by the Ash'arite school of theologians, though the essential conception of 'appropriation' (*kasb*) was invented before al-Ash'arī. According to this formula, God creates a man's act, and the man 'appropriates' (or 'acquires'—*kasaba*) it. The latter term is a technical one, intended to convey that there is just a sufficient relation between the man and the act for it to be called 'his' act; he is thus responsible for it and may properly be rewarded or punished. Everything else is ascribed to the continuing physical and psychological forces which in their totality are seen by the Muslim as coming from God and being essentially his activity. The formula is thus an attempt to maintain divine omnipotence without making man a mere automaton. It should be added that critics of the Ash'arites considered that they failed to allow man any genuine responsibility. Doubtless what they were chiefly concerned to uphold was the conviction—derived from the experience of the Arab in the desert—that nothing could happen to a man that was not willed by God. This conviction is a source of inner strength, and could not lightly be set aside; but it is difficult for anyone to reconcile it with a genuine confidence (probably derived from the Greeks) in the efficacy of human endeavour.

Before the dispute about the *qadar* had begun to fade away another dispute had begun, namely, that about the createdness or uncreatedness of the Qur'ān. It is not clear how this dispute began. The Qur'ān clearly had a temporal character; it had appeared at particular points in time, and had references to many historical events. That it should be eternal was far from obvious. Presumably the assertion that it was uncreated was made to refute an emphatic statement of its created character. It has been suggested by occidental scholars that the formulation of the doctrine of uncreatedness owes something to the Christian doctrine of Jesus as the uncreated Word of God; and this cannot be ruled out as a secondary factor. The vehemence of the debate within Islam, however, must have been due to the political implications of the two views (as explained above). The one party, including most of the ulema, had to insist that the Qur'ān was the uncreated Speech of God, because they claimed that it was the foundation on which the Islamic polity and society should be based. The other party, which held that the Qur'ān was the Speech of God but created, were maintaining in this way that the Qur'ān, though perhaps manifesting the power of God, was not an expression of his essential nature. This dispute also had ramifications. There were Qur'ānic texts which could be made to support the one view or the other. There were also subordinate arguments about the status of verses written or spoken; according to Islamic ideas these were clearly created, but a distinction could be made between the written shapes or the sounds, which were created, and that of which they were expressions, the uncreated Qur'ān.

It was apparently out of the dispute about the Qur'ān that there developed the more fundamental one about the attributes (*ṣifāt*) of God. The Ash'arites and other rationalistic Sunnite theologians held, for example, that God has a knowledge which is not his essence, yet not other than his essence. This might be paraphrased by saying that God's knowledge has a hypostatic character; it is in some sense a distinct existence on its own, and yet in another sense not distinct. Seven attributes were treated in this way and given a special place as 'essential' (*dhātiyya*) attributes: knowledge (omniscience), power (omnipotence), life, will, hearing, seeing, speech. Other attributes like 'creating' were described as 'active' (*fi'liyya*). This doctrine of the attributes should quickly convince anyone that Islamic theology is far from having the simplicity sometimes ascribed to it.

The only other dispute to be mentioned here is that about the difference between miracle and magic. This arose out of the attempts to give a rational proof of Muḥammad's prophethood. The general line of thought, which possibly came originally from Jewish or Christian sources by way of denial of the prophethood of Muḥammad, was that a prophet comes before the people to whom he is sent and says to them, 'I am a prophet sent to you by God with a message for you, and the proof of this is that such and such an abnormal event will occur at a certain time'. The underlying theory is that the event mentioned, being abnormal, can only come about by special activity on the part of God, and that God will only act thus to confirm the fact that the prophet is speaking the truth. In the course of time, however, it was realized that an extraordinary event was not necessarily a miracle. The evidentiary prophetic miracle could easily be distinguished from the 'graces' (*karamāt*) of the saints, for the latter were preceded by no claim to bring a message; it is possible that the alleged miracles of the 'martyr' mystic al-Ḥallāj (d. 922) were a factor in opening up the discussion. By the end of the tenth century the subject was of sufficient interest for the Ash'arite theologian al-Bāqillānī (d. 1013) to write a book on the distinction between the evidentiary or apologetic miracle (*mu'jiza*) and the graces of holy men, legerdemain, magic and spells. The subject was still of importance a century later, and al-Ghazālī imagines a man saying: 'two is greater than ten, and to prove it I shall turn this rod into a serpent' (which of course is the miracle of Moses and Aaron); but even if we see him doing this, continues al-Ghazālī, we are not convinced that two is greater than ten, since this is an unshakable mathematical truth, and we merely wonder how he performed the trick. Such difficulties were eventually resolved to the satisfaction of the Muslim disputants, and the dispute faded away leaving the conviction that there were rational grounds for accepting the prophethood of Muḥammad.

Theologians will always find something to argue about, and it cannot be said that this was the last dispute in Islamic theology before the modern period. Later writers have not been very fully studied, with the exception of Ibn-Taymiyya (d. 1328), but it would seem that most of the later disputes were concerned with variations of emphasis and formal matters rather than important points of substance. The development of Islamic theology in the medieval period may therefore be left here.

3. Revelation and reason

While theological dogma was evolving in the way just sketched, the dogmatic disputes were being crossed by another dispute, namely, that between the opponents of reason and the believers in it. In certain parts of the life of Arab society there was a deep-seated suspicion of reason. In the desert men apparently felt that it was best to live by the *sunna* or standard custom of one's tribe rather than by any calculation of advantages; perhaps there had been more occasions when calculations went wrong than when they succeeded. Certainly there soon appeared among some sections of the Islamic community a strong resistance to the use of rational argument. This was so even in legal matters, where it often happened that Muḥammad had not explicitly pronounced on some particular point, though he had done so for something similar. The conservatives in respect of reason tended to hold that you could not make valid inferences from Muḥammad's statements to completely fresh cases. On the other hand, there were those who held that it was right and proper to make rational inferences in order to have a firm rule to guide practice. A prominent early upholder of the use of reason in the legal field was Abū-Ḥanīfa of Kufa (d. 767), from whom the Ḥanafite legal rite is named. Out of the Ḥanafites came al-Māturīdī (d. 944), the founder of a school of rational theology comparable to that of the Ash'arites.

The opposition to any employment of reason in religious (including legal) matters was strong, and at first was supported by most members of the 'general religious movement' and their successors the Traditionists. A favourite argument was that, since Muḥammad and his Companions had not used reason in this way, to do so was 'innovation', *bid'a*, that is, heresy. Because the main central body of Sunnism thus fought shy of reason, the use of reason tended to be more developed by extremists of one kind or another, whose views on dogmatic questions were not accepted by the central body. Among the early exponents of Greek philosophical methods and indeed of Greek philosophical ideas were the Mu'tazilites. By the end of the ninth century the Mu'tazilites were claiming that they were the followers of certain 'Traditionists' of the early eighth century, but it was only at the end of that century that they came into prominence in the persons of Abū-l-Hudhayl and an-Naẓẓām at Basra and Bishr ibn-al-Mu'tamir at Baghdad. These men may be regarded as the founders of rational or philosophical theology in Islam. They were by no means free-thinkers, as was supposed by some nineteenth-century occidental scholars, but were zealous apologists for Islam who used Greek ideas and logical weapons in defence of their religious views. Sometimes they were too adventurous in their speculations, but this is a good fault in pioneers. Unfortunately they also tended to hold dogmatic views to which the main body of the Sunnites objected—the createdness of the Qur'ān, the assertion of man's *qadar*. In the reign of al-Ma'mūn (813–33) some members of the sect were influential in government circles, and it was largely they who inspired the policy of the 'Inquisition' (Miḥna) which lasted from 833 to about 849 (see p. 127f.). They had probably always been a small sect without much popular following, and with the abandonment in

849 of the policy they inspired they became even smaller and more academic.

The attitudes of men like the Mu'tazilites were likely to increase conservative distrust of reason. The Mu'tazilites may be said to represent the Hellenistic element in the culture of ninth-century Iraq; not merely did the use of reason come from that source, but also dogmatic positions such as the insistence on man's ability to determine events. The latter, perhaps even more than the use of reason, was abhorrent to the representatives of the Arabic element in that culture. Something violent was clearly needed to break down the barrier of distrust between the two sides. This 'violence' was provided by the 'conversion' of al-Ash'arī about 912. He had been educated in the school of the Mu'tazilites at Basra, and was one of the most promising pupils of the head of that school, al-Jubbā'ī (d. 915). At about the age of forty (doubtless a conventional figure) he experienced a complete inner reversal. He turned away from the Mu'tazilite views of his teacher and adopted those of the anti-rationalist Traditionist and jurist, Ibn-Ḥanbal (d. 855), who had been a leading champion of the uncreatedness of the Qur'ān at the time of the Inquisition. In abandoning the Mu'tazilite dogmatic positions, however, al-Ash'arī did not abandon the types of argumentation he had learnt, but began to use these to defend Sunnite dogma. It is difficult to know all that lay behind his change of heart; but the most significant fact is that it occurred. If the Mu'tazilites may be regarded as the first wave of the onslaught of Greek thought against Islam, then its repulse is largely the work of al-Ash'arī, though his Ḥanafite contemporary al-Māturīdī was working towards a similar end farther east in Samarqand.

For nearly two centuries after al-Ash'arī the rational theologians were content to digest and assimilate this first dose of Greek ideas. While they were doing this, a second onslaught of Greek thought was being prepared, this time in a definitely philosophical form—namely, in the philosophies (of Neoplatonic inspiration) of al-Fārābī (d. 950) and Ibn-Sīnā (d. 1037). Technically a very high philosophical standard was attained in the schools in which these philosophers grew and which they helped to develop; but they were entirely separate as institutions from those concerned with Islamic higher education, which was essentially juristic and theological. Philosophy was associated with the other Greek or 'foreign' sciences, notably medicine. Though there were no great philosophers in the east after Ibn-Sīnā, it seems to have been felt at the end of the eleventh century that philosophy was in danger of weakening the central Sunnite position (perhaps through its connection with Ismā'īlism), but no one among the theologians knew sufficient philosophy to be able to refute the philosophers in language they could appreciate. Eventually this task was undertaken by al-Ghazālī. He obtained copies of the main works of the philosophers, and by personal reading without a teacher (as he tells us in his autobiography) gained such a grasp of their philosophical system that he could expound it more lucidly than any contemporary philosopher, and he in fact did so in a book entitled *The Aims of the Philosophers* (*Maqāṣid al-Falāsifa*). This he followed by a devastating critique of certain of their views in *The Inconsistency of the Philosophers* (*Tahāfut al-Falāsifa*). Yet he was far from rejecting the system of the philosophers in its entirety. On the contrary he was very interested in logic, especially in the Aristotelian syllogism, and may be credited with introducing logical studies into Islamic theological circles, where they became a prolegomena to theology proper. Whether this was altogether a good thing may be doubted, since Islamic theology is generally agreed to have become too intellectual in later centuries; but this over-intellectualization of theology may also be due to other causes. Philosophy of the Neoplatonic type certainly disappeared in the Islamic world, apart from its late flowering in Spain in Ibn-Ṭufayl (Abubacer) and Ibn-Rushd (Averroes); and the latter had much more influence on Christian Europe than in the Islamic world. This was the second wave of the onslaught of Greek thought; and its repulse in part and acceptance in part was largely the work of al-Ghazālī.

Despite the achievements of rational theology, there continued to be a body opposed to all use of reason in this way. This was the Ḥanbalite school or movement. Despite the professed allegiance of al-Ash'arī in dogmatic matters to their eponym, Ibn-Ḥanbal, the later Ash'arites were anathema to the Ḥanbalites. In the Islamic world as a whole the Ḥanbalites were apparently a small school, but the populace of Baghdad had a large percentage of fanatical Ḥanbalites who could easily be induced to demonstrate or riot. The Ḥanbalite doctors rejected all arguments except direct observations on the sayings of Muḥammad in Traditions or on verses of the Qur'ān. The school reached its greatest height in Ibn-Taymiyya (d. 1328), whose influence was felt for several centuries. He lived mainly in Damascus, then part of the Mamlūk state with its capital in Cairo, and was active in combating what he considered to be the intellectual and moral corruption of the time. One of his feats was so to master the logic taught by the rational theologians that in a 'refutation' of their position he was able to make some true and acute criticisms of logical procedure.

The very existence of such a work shows that the anti-rationalist attitude of the Ḥanbalites was no mere obscurantism, but was based on insight into the fact that religious truth cannot be reduced to rational propositions. The language of fundamental religious experience (for example, as this is presented in the Qur'ān) has an element which may be termed 'poetical', not in the sense that it is imaginary, but in the sense that it expresses truth in concrete images which move men more deeply than mere rational considerations. Such images may also be called 'symbolic'. They not merely represent something in the objective world, but they evoke a response in men and a release of psychical energy. During the last century or two the function of symbols has been almost forgotten by modern man, but once again we are coming to understand something of their working in us and of their potency. An important line of thought here is that connected with the Jungian conception of archetypes.

The rationalists and the anti-rationalists each in their own way have a place in the expression of the Islamic vision. The former express the common human need for logical consistency in one's world-view, especially in its application to religious matters. Certainly the theologians of Islam achieved a high degree of consistency in their intellectual synthesis of Islamic belief, and in general did not omit too much. Yet the anti-rationalists, insisting on the inability of reason to comprehend all that is contained in religious symbols or archetypes, whether they are expressed in Qur'ānic language or in some other way, have preserved something which is of great value at the present time. The revival of a religion only comes about as men learn to look afresh at the original images, allow themselves to be moved to respond to these images, and so bring about in themselves a new release of psychical energy.

4. The modern period

Between the formative period of Islamic intellectual life which has just been considered and the modern period marked by the impact of Europe there lie at least four centuries when the Islamic world in certain respects was somnolent and decadent. During these centuries the life of the Muslim intellectuals was lived more and more in narrow grooves. Instead of producing new works in the various branches of knowledge with which they were concerned, they were content to write commentaries on the older works, often even commentaries on the commentaries. So accustomed did scholars become to books with a main text in the centre of a page and a commentary round it, that this layout was extended to printed books, and even retained when the work on the margin was far from being a commentary on the central text. The result of such developments was that, when Islamic countries about 1800 began to respond to the European impact, the religious intellectuals were so affected by the endemic rigidity and ankylosis that they were unable to give a lead in the adaptation of Islamic life to the new situation. To appreciate this failure to respond and its consequences it is necessary to look more closely at the reasons; and in order to do so we have to go back many centuries.

Various groups among the religious scholars of the later Umayyad period, that is, in the 'general religious movement', supported the 'Abbāsids in their bid for power, and in return these religious scholars received a measure of recognition from the 'Abbāsid régime. Their ideas about the law were accepted to some extent, and appointments to the position of judge were increasingly made from their number. Gradually Islamic higher education became more organized, the distinction between the scholar-jurists or ulema and other men was clearer, and all judges came to be appointed from this class. Up to a point this was a great success. The reverse of the medal, however, was that the career of the jurist was entirely controlled by those who made the appointments to judgeships and other offices open to a jurist. This was normally the caliph and his ministers; and the result was the complete subservience of the religious intellectuals (with one or two outstanding exceptions) to the ruling institution. The Inquisition of 833–49 made it obvious that the ulema as a class or corps had not the strength to resist the rulers.

This subservience to the rulers had various unfortunate results. It meant above all that the ulema in general came to be chiefly concerned with their own prospects of promotion and to neglect the functions which it is the business of the intellectual to perform on behalf of his community, such as seeing that its intellectual or doctrinal basis is relevant to its contemporary needs. Apart from the innate Arab dislike of innovation they were moved to avoid novelty, we may suppose, by the consideration that novelty in their formulations was unlikely to be acceptable to the rulers and would therefore hinder rather than enhance their chances of promotion. Instead they turned and devoted great ingenuity to the elaboration of some of the more intellectual and abstract aspects of the subject, where there was little chance of practical application, but where they could show off their skill in argument. The final result of this process was that the ulema came to be out of touch with ordinary life, living entirely in the restricted intellectual world that they shared with the other members of their class. The one point at which there may be something to be said for rigidity is that in certain cases it might enable a judge to resist pressure from the government to go against strict justice in the interests of administrative convenience; for the judge could reply that it was not within his competence to vary the application of the law except within certain limits set by precedent.

Muḥammad 'Alī of Egypt at the beginning of the nineteenth century was one of the first Muslim rulers to become aware of the need for responding vigorously to the European impact. He saw the need for a modern army, and further saw that the officers of such an army required an education of the European type. So he set about providing such an education for them. Since it was utterly unlike the traditional Islamic education, the ulema paid no attention to it. Before long there were two competing systems of education in Egypt, and the intellectual life of the country as a whole was flowing in two completely separate channels. The old system began with the Qur'ān schools in the villages, and ended with the ancient university of al-Az'har in Cairo. The new system had primary schools, secondary schools and universities, all on the European model. At first in the European-type schools there was practically no teaching of the Islamic religion, largely because nobody had any idea of how to adapt traditional Islamic teachings to the outlook of the average pupil in this type of school. The products of the new educational system had mostly little interest in religion. If they still practised their religion, they had presumably an intellectual justification of their position which satisfied themselves, but they had no desire to communicate this to others, and might have found difficulty in doing so. No intellectual leaders had arisen to guide educated Muslims of the new type into a positive attitude to their religion, and to show them how to meet the attacks on religion in general made by the European writers whom they read (for they read the anti-religious writers of Europe but hesitated about the pro-religious, since these were Christian). Although what has been said in this paragraph applies in the first place to Egypt, something similar was true of most other parts of the Islamic heartlands.

Attempts to bridge the gulf between the two mentalities began in India. One of the causes of the Indian Mutiny in 1857 was that, while the Hindus gladly accepted European culture and education, the Muslims were suspicious of it and stood aloof. The result of this was that the Hindu community's wealth and influence in the country were increasing at the expense of the Muslim community's. After the Mutiny Sir Syed Ahmad Khan worked hard to get Muslims also to accept European culture, and was successful in founding in 1877 the Muhammadan Anglo-Oriental College (which in 1920 became the University of Aligarh). Syed Ameer Ali in 1891 published *The Life and Teachings of Mohammed, or the Spirit of Islām* (with a revised edition in 1922 called simply *The Spirit of Islām*), and in this work gave the educated Muslim reasons for being proud of his religion before Europeans. The first notable theologian, however, to attempt the adaptation of dogmatic theology to the modern outlook was Muḥammad 'Abduh of Egypt (1849–1905) with his *Risālat at-Taw'ḥīd*. This book was epoch-making in that it broke with traditional forms of theological arguing and writing, and thus began the vast labour of *aggiornamento*. There have been other movements since, but the trends are not yet clear. Such works of intellectual adaptation tend to fall under the heading of 'general literature' rather than theology; that is to say, the authors are general writers and not professional theologians.

Relating Islamic dogma to modern (predominantly occidental) scientific thought is only one small part of the task of the Muslim intellectual at the present time. He has also to consider the relevance of the Islamic vision to the other social and political needs of today. One could say that, in the period when Islamic countries were working for independence, an important contribution was made by Islamic patriotism and what is now called the Islamic resurgence. Now the accent is moving to the building up of Islamic society within each state. Has the Islamic vision and its previous embodiments in social life anything to contribute to this? Or is more to be learnt from occidental ideas of socialism and communism? There is certainly a ferment, and men are beginning to move in various directions. So far no great leader has emerged able to focus on the present situation all the insights of centuries of Islamic tradition. He may conceivably emerge yet—we wait to see.

Chapter 9

The expansion of the Islamic world view

1. The problem of cultural contrasts

It is the normal condition of a human being to have a world view which goes far beyond his present position in space and time. Yet in this respect there are wide variations between different cultures. The product of modern European or American education thinks of a universe which is measured in terms of galaxies and light-years, whereas a man from a primitive tribe may have only the haziest ideas of what lies beyond the territory of his own and the neighbouring tribes. The Arab of the desert in the early seventh century probably knew something of the Byzantine and Persian empires and had some ideas of the past history of the tribes of the Arabian peninsula, but, comparatively speaking, his world view was a restricted one. For literature the Arab had little beyond his poetry—dealing with aspects of desert life and traditions of the tribes—and a store of maxims or proverbs, together with memories of great feats of oratory.

This was in sharp contrast to the rich civilization of Iraq (and to a lesser extent that of Syria and Egypt). In Iraq there were patterns of culture stretching back to Sumer and Akkad. Superimposed on these was the intellectual heritage of Greece, which went back to the time of Alexander and was now transmitted chiefly by Christians. Greek astronomy and philosophy provided a cosmology far in advance of that of the nomadic Arab, while Greek medicine and other sciences added to the comfort and luxury of daily life. The historical tradition of the Bible set human life in a broad perspective. Altogether the best educated men of Iraq in A.D. 600 had reached a high level of civilization. When the Arabs settled in Iraq the more intelligent among them must have come to realize the vast differences in intellectual and material culture between themselves and the upper strata of society in Iraq.

The problem became acute when some of the Christian *dhimmīs* became Muslims, for they brought with them their intellectual world, suffused as it was with Christian ideas and values. While such people remained Christians, it was possible for the Arabs to avoid critical encounters with them, largely (as already noted) by the doctrine of 'corruption' or *taḥrīf*, which, just because it was vague, could be used to parry intellectual attacks from many directions. With the conversion of Iraqī intellectuals, however, the problem could no longer be avoided in this way. An educated man cannot indefinitely keep his religion in one compartment and his cosmological thinking in another; they have to be brought into relation to one another. By the eighth century, or even earlier, it was necessary to consider whether, for example, the cosmological and historical elements of the Christian world view could be dissociated from all that was specifically Christian, and instead brought into some relation with the central ideas of Islam. Until this was done, the Islamic vision could not be said to be truly embodied in the culture of the newly conquered provinces of the Middle East.

Two processes may be distinguished. First, there was the development of what the Arabs already had, and within this development one can distinguish the religious and the secular sphere. Second, there is the acceptance and incorporation of the most important things from non-Muslim culture, and this comes about in such a way that in the process Islam replaces Christianity as the vehicle of nearly all the culture of the Middle East.

2. The expansion of the Arab religious heritage

The Arab contribution to Islamic culture consisted first and foremost of the Qur'ān and the central core of religious ideas enshrined in it. All this was developed in various ways.

The most obvious way was by interpretations of the text. The Arabic language lends itself to many possibilities of interpretation even at the purely grammatical level. This may be most simply illustrated from the Traditions about Muḥammad's call. When the angel first said to him *iqra'*, 'recite' or 'read', he is said to have replied *mā aqra'u*, which may mean either 'I do not read' or 'what shall I recite?' Later, apparently, the exponents of the two views produced two further Traditions, one of which had the words *mā anā bi-qārin*, which can only be 'I do not read', while the other had *mādhā aqra'u* which can only be 'what shall I recite'. Difficulties of this kind are found in connection with the interpretation of the Qur'ān, though they are seldom so striking. Difficulties of interpretation may also affect the choice of textual reading. Thus 74.5 normally runs 'flee the *rujz*', though there is a variant *rijz*. Though many of the old scholars regard the two forms as equivalent, and al-Bayḍāwī reads *rijz* in this verse, while giving *rujz* as a variant, the word *rijz* tended to be taken as meaning 'punishment', and a command to Muḥammad to flee punishment would imply that he had done something worthy of punishment. *Rijz* can also mean 'conduct leading to punishment', and this is not theologically objectionable, but it seems to have been felt that the vaguer *rujz* was preferable here, especially since it is also said that it means 'idols'.[1]

Even after some agreement has been reached on the meaning there may be differences of reference. Thus 85.4–7 means roughly as follows:

> . . . slain were the Men of the Pit
> the fire abounding in fuel,
> when they were seated over it,
> and were themselves witnesses of what they did with the believers.

But to whom does this refer? Who are 'the Men of the Pit' (*Aṣ'ḥāb al-ukhdūd*)? In his commentary on the verse aṭ-Ṭabarī gives at least four apparently different incidents to which the description was referred by different scholars. In other cases the person referred to might admit of no doubt, but the Qur'ān might refer to him allusively without telling his story in detail. This was especially the case with figures from the Old and New Testaments. Such references left scholars, not to mention story-tellers, great scope for filling out the stories from biblical or extra-biblical sources.[2]

Closely connected with this matter of the persons or incidents referred to in verses of the Qur'ān was that of what are known as 'the occasions of revelation' (*asbāb an-nuzūl*). Many passages of the Qur'ān were revealed on some particular 'occasion' in the career of Muḥammad, for example, just before or after one of his battles, at the time of the change of *qibla* (direction faced in prayer), or when he was contemplating marriage with Zaynab, the divorced wife of his adoptive son. In course of time there were accounts—sometimes conflicting with one another—of the 'occasion' on which a great many passages were revealed, though not by any means all. Some of these 'occasions' are simply the inferences or conjectures of scholars, often justified but sometimes unjustified. In respect of other 'occasions' the accounts may preserve some genuine historical material. At first the 'occasions' were simply mentioned at the appropriate point in the commentaries on the Qur'ān; but after a great volume of such material had been accumulated books were devoted entirely to this, notably one by a great commentator of the Qur'ān, al-Wāḥidī (d. 1075).

This branch of study, again, was linked with the biography of Muḥammad, which itself was somewhat complex. It might be thought that the Traditions (the anecdotes about the sayings and doings of Muḥammad) were the primary material for the biography, but this is not the case. The Traditions were developed for legal—or sometimes political or theological—purposes. Muslim scholars early realized that many were being invented, and the discussion as to which are authentic has continued through the centuries. What must be noticed, however, is that many of the stories, *even if they are authentic*, give practically none of the kind of information the biographer wants. Thus there is a Tradition that Muḥammad once passed a man beating a slave and said to him, 'Do not beat him, for God created Adam in his [the slave's] image.' This particular Tradition is probably unauthentic, since it is clearly an attempt to find a meaning for the Old-Testament phrase 'God created man in his image' which would be theologically unobjectionable; the dominant trend in Islamic theology emphasized the dissimilarity of man and God, and found it difficult to accept any resemblance. Yet the story, even if it were authentic, would not give anything of value to the general biographer of Muḥammad.

The biography of Muḥammad or *Sīra*, however, did become a branch of study at an early perod. We possess a recension of the *Sīra* of Ibn-Is'ḥāq (d. 768), and we know something of his predecessors. For the main part of Muḥammad's career—the period after the Hijra when he was at Medina—we have a core of genuinely historical material dealing with his expeditions or *maghāzī* in chronological order; and into this have been inserted where appropriate other types of material such as Traditions or anecdotes, and material from Qur'ānic commentaries (dealing mainly with 'occasions of revelation'). Poems are also quoted; and these, if genuine, are usually contemporary. In the *Sīra*, then, there is a large volume of material which helps to fill up the intellectual world of the Muslim, whether we call this material religious or historical.[3]

Out of the Traditions there arose another scholarly discipline, which was indeed more closely connected with them, namely, jurisprudence. This began with little groups of men discussing practical legal questions in the mosques of the chief cities of the Islamic world, and ended in jurisprudence becoming the centre of all Islamic higher education. This included some discussion of questions which would now be reckoned to belong to epistemology, such as some of those concerning 'the roots of law' (*uṣūl al-fiqh*). The speculative interest is prominent in some of the writings of al-Ghazālī (d. 1111), notably his last work on legal theory, *Al-Mustaṣfā*. The great majority of Islamic jurists, however, did not pursue their epistemological studies beyond what was of practical importance. On the whole the Muslims of the Middle East did not have the speculative urge of the Greeks.

It is worth pausing for a moment to consider this point. It cannot—one feels—be entirely accidental that jurisprudence became central in Islamic education. It is likely that there is some connection with the desert background of Arab life. Nomadic tribes are only able to keep themselves alive in the desert where there is a high level of human excellence, that is, a high level of attainment in the skills required for living together. This includes developing a sensitivity to personal relationships. As a university teacher in Britain in the twentieth century one notices that Muslims from the Middle East are much more aware of one as a person than the average British student, who tends to treat one as a cog in the machine. The Middle Easterner—and the same is true of most other Asians and Africans—never forgets that he is dealing with a person, even if it is only as someone whose favour must on no account be lost, and whose good opinion may perhaps be gained by suitable presents. Now jurisprudence is concerned above all with human relationships in society. It may be regarded as the intellectual expression of a deep concern for persons. Since Islamic society placed jurisprudence at the centre of its intellectual life, this would seem to show that in its general attitude to life an important place was held by this interest in human relationships within society.

In this there is a contrast to the Greek attitude. The Greeks were curious about the material world around them, and this curiosity or interest developed intellectually into scientific and philosophical cosmology. The Greeks, of course, were also interested in the ethical and legal basis of urban life. Yet there is a contrast, and it becomes clear in the fate of Greek philosophy in the Islamic world. At first there was great enthusiasm for philosophy in certain circles, but eventually the intellectuals of Sunnite Islam accepted only those aspects of philosophy which could be made subservient to theology, and lost all interest in cosmological study and speculation, even at the level of the natural sciences. (Muslim reactions to Greek thought will be discussed more fully in section 4 of this chapter.)

The existence of this interest in human relationships in society makes one wonder how far it has influenced some of the great developments in Islamic history. It has already been explained how the theological dispute about the Qur'ān as the Word of God, namely, whether it was created or uncreated, is linked with the struggle between the ulema and the 'secretaries' for control of the Islamic empire. The connection between theological dogma and political movements is not, of course, peculiar to the Islamic world, but is almost universal. What may be singled out for mention, however, is that this struggle came to be focused on the question of the ideal structure of society—should one trust the divine inspiration of the Sharī'a or the divine inspiration of the imam?

Whatever answer may be given to this very general question, it is certain that there was a constant search among Muslims for Qur'ānic verses or 'sound' Traditions to support theological and political opinions. Much ingenuity could be shown in this. Thus the believers in the createdness of the Qur'ān quoted the verse 'We have made it (*ja'alnā-hu*) and Arabic Qur'ān' (43.3/2), and then argued that 'made' here must have the sense of 'create' because there was another verse (6.1) where this word 'made' clearly had the sense of 'create': 'Praise be to God who created (*khalaqa*) the heavens and the earth and made (*ja'ala*) the darkness and the light.[4] Even purely political disputes often led to interpretation and counter-interpretation of Traditions, with a complicating factor in the possibility of inventing, adding to or modifying them. Such procedures greatly increased the amount of material with which Muslim scholars had to be familiar. There was now no lack of intellectual furniture.

As a result of all the developments described, it became necessary in course of time for the various disciplines in the 'religious' field to be distinguished from one another and organized, and for men to specialize in one or other branch of study. For long a commentary on the Qur'ān might be the work of a man who was primarily a grammarian, but with greater specialization such a combination of studies became difficult, though closely related disciplines were often practised by one man; aṭ-Ṭabarī (d. 923), for example, was in the first rank both as a Qur'ān commentator and as a general historian, besides founding a school of jurisprudence. The organizing and establishing of the various religious 'sciences' or disciplines may be said to have happened from the middle of the ninth century to the beginning of the tenth. The first great collections of 'sound' Traditions are those of al-Bukhārī (d. 870) and Muslim (d. 875). The vast Qur'ān commentary of aṭ-Ṭabarī contains nearly all the important material in this field prior to his own time, for the author does not merely give his own view, but also all the other views which have been held by scholars of note. Questions about the text of the Qur'ān, or 'Qur'ān-reading', reached a definitive position through the work of Ibn-Mujāhid (d. 935).

As the various disciplines became organized, a subordinate branch of study grew up, namely, 'knowledge of the men' (*'ilm ar-rijāl*), or biography. One of the earliest books of this kind was the *Ṭabaqāt* of Ibn-Sa'd (d. 845), containing brief biographical notices of many persons responsible for handing on material for the biography of Muḥammad. Such material was not carefully distinguished from the Traditions in general, though the chief interest in these was legal. It was in this field of Traditions that the interest in biography appeared first, since, according to the Arab conception of knowledge as contained in a verbal form derived from a man with more than ordinary wisdom, it was necessary to know something about the persons who had handed on this knowledge in verbal forms. Were they trustworthy, and did they hold sound opinions? Had they a good memory or did they sometimes make mistakes? Did they really meet the teachers from whom they alleged they had received the material, and the pupils to whom they were supposed to have passed it on? The study of biography, thus begun in connection with the Traditions, was eventually extended to most other disciplines cultivated in the Islamic world. In this way the intellectual world of the Muslim was extended back into the past intellectual history of his own community.

3. The expansion of the Arab secular heritage

The Arabic contribution to Islamic culture was not limited to religion, but also had linguistic or philological aspects. This doubtless goes back to another important feature of the life of the nomadic Arab, his love for poetry and his feeling for language. To understand how this can be so one must realize that the poets were mouthpieces of public opinion in much the same way as journalists are now. It was their function to sing the praises of their own tribe or family and to vilify opposing tribes, especially those against whom the poet's tribe was about to fight. A skilful turn of phrase in a poet's invective could be as effective as a daring raid. In a proper 'ode' (*qaṣīda*), however, only a small part was occupied with praise or satire; the rest followed a set pattern of themes. In the opening of the poem the poet was standing at a deserted encampment and was reminded of a lost love; this would be followed by a description of the swift steed on which he rode away or by a description of a wild animal to which the steed might be compared; and so on. Thus the skill of the poet was shown in his verbal dexterity and in his careful description of desert scenes. As time went on there came to be less fresh observation and the chief interest was in the novelty of expression for the set themes. Thus the chief aesthetic interest of the Arabs was in the skilful use of language.

The Arab's feeling for words and his pride in his language no doubt helped to bring about the wide acceptance of Arabic throughout the Islamic empire. This acceptance was not simply the result of conquest. Arabic was accepted by the Persian inhabitants of the empire to a much greater extent than Latin, for example, was accepted by the Greek-speaking inhabitants of the Roman empire. The Syriac language, which in the year 600 was important as the vehicle of a Christian Hellenistic culture, was in most spheres soon replaced by Arabic. With their language the Arabs carried their love of poetry, and it continued to be cultivated not only by the Arabs themselves but also by many of those who adopted the Arabic language. There is a well-known passage in the writings of a Christian bishop in Spain after the Arab conquest, where he complains that his Christian young men are fascinated by Arabic poetry and for this reason are learning that language instead of Latin. Immediately after the death of Muḥammad, however, poetry was for a time eclipsed, because of its connection with the old pagan outlook. During the Umayyad period, apart from one or two outstanding poets (notably Jarīr, Farazdaq and al-Akhṭal), the best poetry came from the sectaries and rebels known as Khārijites, who also seem to have been trying to re-create on an Islamic basis small groups comparable to the desert clans or extended families (cf. p. 117).

It was also during the Umayyad period that scholarly interest in language may be said to have first shown itself. There is much obscurity about the early history of the Arabic language, and in particular about the relation of the language of the Qur'ān and the pre-Islamic poems to the dialects then spoken. Whatever the truth about these matters, however, it is clear that by A.D. 700 neither the new non-Arab converts to Islam nor even the Arabs themselves could easily understand all the vocabulary of the Qur'ān. Where the interpretation of a word was obscure or uncertain, the scholars would turn to pre-Islamic poetry and try to find verses which established the meaning. Thus Qur'ānic scholarship united with the general love of poetry to revive interest in the work of the pre-Islamic poets. What was still remembered was collected and written down either in anthologies or as Dīwāns, each with the works of a single poet or group of poets. Among the famous early anthologies are the *Mu'allaqāt*, seven complete odes collected by Ḥammād ar-Rāwiya (d. 771), and the *Mufaḍḍaliyyāt*, so called after the collector al-Mufaḍḍal (d. 784?). There was much in these poems, of course, that was obscure. Apart from unusual and half-forgotten words, there were allusive references to persons and events of far-off days. So to understand the poems it became necessary to study the accounts of the 'days', that is, battles, of the Arabs and other matters of tribal lore. The first notable collector of such material was Abū-'Ubayda (d.c. 825), and his collections are included in *Kitāb al-Aghāni*, a vast encyclopaedia in twenty-one volumes compiled by a later scholar, Abū-l-Faraj al-Iṣfahānī (d. 967).

Interest in the interpretation of poetry and of the Qur'ān was almost inevitably combined with interest in grammar. The founders of Arabic grammatical science are usually reckoned to be al-Khalīl (d. 776–91) and his pupil Sībawayh (d. 793–809). They were the founders of the philological school of Basra, which soon had a rival school of Kufa, while another developed later at Baghdad. After jurisprudence grammar was perhaps the most prominent feature of Arabic intellectual life. Because the Arabic of the Qur'ān admits of many interpretations, it was necessary to be able to say which were grammatically possible and which not. Beyond this, however, the study of grammar was in line with the deep interest in language.

There is also something distinctive about the literary forms which were cultivated in Arabic. It is noteworthy that there was no interest in long connected stories. There were no epics, no plays, no novels; the only connected narratives were in historical writings. The stories of *The Thousand and One Nights*, which delight the modern world, were recounted orally among the common people and despised by the educated. Among prose writers there may be said to be a tendency towards the miscellany, a collection of anecdotes or short verse quotations loosely strung together. There may be some connection between this literary form and the atomism which is found in the philosophical theologians and which indeed characterizes various other aspects of Arabic thought.

The really distinctive Arabic literary form is undoubtedly the Maqāma or 'assembly'. The full-fledged form is the invention of Badī'-az-Zamān al-Hamadhānī (d. 1008), but its roots go far back into the past. It had apparently been normal in pre-Islamic times to use rhymed (or assonanced) prose in oratory. The earlier passages of the Qur'ān are in a form of this rhymed prose or *saj'*. Because of the use of rhymed prose in the Qur'ān it was abandoned for a time for secular purposes under Islam, but about the ninth century it came back into use in formal addresses or sermons in the mosques, and in the tenth century came to be used for epistles. It became normal practice to have something in rhymed prose as the exordium of a book. The invention of al-Hamadhānī consisted in applying this stylistic form to a series of dramatic anecdotes. These were loosely connected with one another by having the same central figure, a witty and unscrupulous vagabond. The story was secondary to showing off the author's virtuosity in the use of the Arabic language. The Maqāma was thus very much for the connoisseur of language, and could be unintelligible to even moderately well-educated people without a considerable amount of explanation. The Maqāma reached its zenith as a literary form in the work of al-Ḥarīrī (d. 1122). After all that has been said about the Arab feeling for language, it is seen to be appropriate that Arabic literature should reach its highest point of achievement in a form of this kind.

The development of historiography is an informative illustration of the process by which the Muslims expanded the secular Arab heritage, but, since various points have already been touched on, the matter may be dealt with briefly. By way of history the pre-Islamic Arabs had only a collection of anecdotes, mainly about battles, and genealogical material which provided a rough idea of chronology. Nothing much could be done with this, but it was carefully collected. The anecdotes in the Qur'ān from the Bible were arranged chronologically on the basis of biblical chronology and were expanded from other Jewish and Christian material. The purely Arabian genealogies were linked with the biblical genealogy of Ishmael. In such ways later historians were able to produce what they called 'universal history'. The main emphasis, however, was on the Islamic peoples and their antecedents. One important history, that of Ibn-al-Athīr (d. 1234) devotes more space to the story of Joseph—which is already told fairly fully in the Qur'ān—than to the whole of the Roman empire. In contrast to this neglect of the non-Muslim world early Persian legendary history is inserted into the biblical chronological scheme at appropriate points, doubtless because with the coming of the 'Abbāsid dynasty the Muslims took over much Persian statecraft with maxims based on the Persian past, whether historical or legendary.

Thus Arabic historiography is a very selective expansion of the Arab and Qur'ānic heritage in this field. For long, too, its method was typically Arab. Even the great history of aṭ-Ṭabarī (d. 923) looks at first glance (in respect of the Islamic period) like a mere collection of source material. It is only after a scholar has worked with aṭ-Ṭabarī at some depth that he realizes the skill and judgment that have gone into the selecting and arrangement of material and understands that aṭ-Ṭabarī has a fairly definite view of his own. Later Arabic historians usually abandoned this method and preferred to give a connected account of the events they described.

Altogether the expansion of Arabic literature in the first three centuries after the Hijra was phenomenal. The bare tent of nomadic Arab culture was transformed into a richly furnished dwelling where men could live in truly human fashion.

4. The replacement of Christian culture

Before the Arab conquests most of the intellectual culture of the Middle East wore a Christian dress; that is to say, most of the bearers of this culture were Christians, and the Greek element was inextricably mingled with specifically Christian ideas. There was indeed a school of non-Christian philosophers in Harran until at least the early tenth century; and there was probably also some Hellenistic culture among the Persians, that is, the descendants of Persian-speaking inhabitants of the Sasanian empire. On the whole, however, it was mainly Christians who ran the schools or colleges where Greek science and philosophy were taught. Medicine was much studied, and philosophical arguments were employed in the defence and exposition of Christian doctrine. In view of this state of affairs it is all the more remarkable that after four or five hundred years Christian higher education had largely disappeared and there had grown up in its place a new higher education which was specifically Islamic and used only the medium of Arabic.

The intellectual culture of the Greeks, as suggested above, came to the Muslims in two waves. The first reached its height about the beginning of the ninth century and is particularly associated with the caliphate of al-Ma'mūn (813–33). This caliph not merely set up an establishment for the translation of Greek scientific and philosophical works into Arabic, but encouraged a group of men, the Mu'tazilites, who made use of Greek ideas in the exposition and defence of Islamic theological doctrine. The Mu'tazilites were regarded as heretical by the main body of Sunnite Muslims, but about 912 al-Ash'arī, who had been trained as a Mu'tazilite, abandoned the doctrines branded as heretical and attached himself to the main body. Al-Ash'arī took with him, however, a knowledge of certain Hellenistic ideas and methods of argument, and is consequently regarded as the founder of the most prominent school of philosophical theology in Islam, the Ash'arite.

The result of this first wave of Hellenism, however, was nothing like a complete acceptance of Hellenistic thought. Somewhat apart from the main stream of Islamic life a few men cultivated Greek philosophy and other disciplines to a much higher degree. Two in particular, al-Fārābī (d. 950) and Avicenna or Ibn-Sīnā (d. 1037), produced original work of the first quality in the Neoplatonic tradition. Though they had no disciples of equal distinction, they had a certain following; and by the latter half of the eleventh century the Ash'arite theologians were becoming aware that their methods of argumentation were inferior technically to those of the two philosophers mentioned. The second wave of Hellenism may be said to have broken over the Muslims when the

Ash'arite theologian al-Ghazālī (d. 1111) thoroughly examined the Greek philosophical heritage and managed to have most of it accepted by at least one wing of the main body of the Muslim intellectuals—so far, that is to say, as it was compatible with Islamic doctrine. In this way, through the work of the Neoplatonizing Arabic philosophers and then of the philosophizing theologians, the highest scientific and philosophical thought of the time was incorporated into the Arabic and Islamic intellectual world.

This was no mere translation, but a radical transformation. A change of language means a whole change of intellectual environment. In this century the abandonment of the Arabic script by the Turks has cut them off from most of their Islamic intellectual heritage. In the early centuries of Islam the outstanding cultural event was the replacement by Arabic of the 'Christian' languages of Greek and Syriac. This whole process merits further study, but certain points are already clear. Before the appearance of Islam there had been many translations from Greek into Syriac, and these included the most important works of Greek science and philosophy. As Christians adopted Arabic as a language, they made a vast number of translations into Arabic of specifically Christian books—witness the great number of works described in the first volume of Georg Graf's *Geschichte der christlichen arabischen Literatur* (Vatican, 1944). Yet despite all these translations the Arabic-speaking Christians certainly did not live in the same intellectual world as the Christians who spoke Latin and Greek. In Arabic there is virtually nothing about the history of the Greek and Roman world, and there was not much in Syriac either. Did the Christians of the Orient not feel themselves part of the Graeco-Roman world even when they were included in the Roman empire? Certainly as the centuries passed the Christians in the Islamic world seem to have become more and more circumscribed in their outlook. They had some ideas of this wider Christian world outside Dār al-Islam, but more and more they came to be dominated by the Islamic intellectual environment, and to think chiefly of the passive defence of their small communities by concentration on their distinctive religious standpoint.

It has been said that Muḥammad 'was the answer of the East to the challenge of Alexander'.[5] The more one studies the Christian Orient before Islam, the more one realizes how profoundly it was resentful and even hostile towards the ruling circles of the Byzantine empire. It was already almost cut off emotionally from that

Greek world. It would almost seem to be true that the Islamic neglect of so much of the life of the Greek-speaking world, apart from its science and philosophy, was a continuation of the attitudes of Syriac-speaking and other oriental Christians. It was not simply the Muslims who were uninterested in Greek and Byzantine culture but also the Christians of Syria, Iraq and Egypt. The adoption of Arabic would be facilitated by the disaffection already felt towards everything Greek. The pride of the Arabs in their language and their nomadic and early Islamic heritage—the factors leading to the expansion of that heritage—were not countered by any corresponding cultural pride in the Christians of the Islamic empire; such pride as they had was limited to a narrow 'religious' field. They acquiesced in the severance from Greek and Byzantine culture when Arabic became the dominant language of the Islamic empire. (There can be little doubt about the broad lines of the view just stated, though the details are worthy of much fuller investigation.)

There may also be said to have been studied neglect by Muslims of the Christian intellectual world, especially in its Greek forms. The Qur'ān spoke about the *taḥrīf* or 'corruption' of the Christian and Jewish scriptures. The Qur'ānic statements were elaborated in various ways by later Muslim scholars. The result was that the ordinary simple-minded Muslim had a ready answer to criticisms of his religion by Christians and Jews on the basis of allegedly superior knowledge; he could refuse to listen to their arguments on the ground that they were based on scriptures which were corrupt. In effect the Muslims were asserting that the Qur'ān was the standard and that other scriptures must be judged by their conformity with this standard. There could be no question of studying the Bible to gain religious insight. To begin with some Muslims might read the Bible in order to gain fuller versions of the stories referred to allusively in the Qur'ān; but as time went on they became less interested in this and, if they read the Bible at all, only did so in order to get arguments against the Christians.

In general the attitude of Muslims to alien cultures seems strange to modern occidentals. One side of this attitude is well illustrated in the great biographical dictionary of Ibn-Khallikān (d. 1282). In the article on a scribe who was a noted calligraphist[6] he has a discursive passage on the history of scripts. In the whole history of the world he only knows of twelve scripts, of which five he considers no longer extant, including the Greek. Of the remainder four are used in the Islamic countries, namely, Arabic, Persian, Hebrew and Syriac. The remaining three are the Roman (Byzantine?), Indian and Chinese, 'and there is no one in the Islamic lands who is familiar with these'. The last phrase could conceivably mean that no group of people in the Islamic world use these scripts, but it probably also means that there are no scholars acquainted with them. The occidental thinks it necessary just for efficiency that he should have some knowledge of the languages of the great foreign powers with which he is in contact, including a reading knowledge—the Muslims doubtless had some knowledge of the spoken language. Basically, however, they must have been so proud of their own culture that they neglected alien cultures and merely waited until these should be incorporated into Dār-al-Islām.

Finally it must be noted how Christian material was incorporated into the intellectual world of Islam without any acknowledgment of the source. Muslim scholars early realized that Traditions about the sayings of Muḥammad were being invented. The inventions were usually made to justify some political or theological viewpoint within the Islamic world; but Christian or general Middle East wisdom could also be brought into Islam in this way. Thus Muḥammad is made to recommend a prayer that largely coincides with the Lord's Prayer of the Christians.[7] Similarly Muḥammad was alleged to have said that 'God created Adam in his image', but great ingenuity was shown in avoiding the normal Christian and Jewish understanding of this statement, and in the end Islam may be said to have decided against it.[8]

In various ways, then, the Islamic world became a self-sufficient cultural entity, able to provide a satisfying intellectual environment for its intellectuals. It was also capable of spreading its culture into less-developed regions like East and West Africa; but it was not so successful in its relations with equally developed cultures, still less with Euramerican culture when that had become materially superior and was invading the Islamic world. The expansion of the Islamic world view to include the insights of modern science is still in process, and it remains to be seen how successful Islam will be here. There are great difficulties, but the task is by no means impossible. It is only one of several tasks, however, which confront Islam at the present time, and success in this may depend on a satisfactory outcome of the 'dialogue' between Islam and the other great religions.

Chapter 10

Islamic worship and piety

1. Worship and the vision

The aim of the present chapter is to describe something that is near the heart or centre of all that is being surveyed in this book, namely, worship and the personal religious life. To some readers what is about to be said may seem to omit all that is characteristic of worship, whether he calls it warmth or ecstasy or a sense of the numinous. In reply to this unvoiced criticism it may be said that this book is attempting to give an objective presentation and is not trying to rouse worshipful feelings. Its standpoint is that of the observer and not of the participant. The two standpoints are complementary and not opposed, and it is even good for the worshipper occasionally to stand back and look at his worship; but it is difficult both to participate and to observe at the same time.

It was suggested on page 12 that 'the purpose of worship' is 'the revival or renewal of vision'. The essential basis of worship includes a presentation of the 'dynamic images' present in the particular religion's vision. In the case of Christianity important 'dynamic images' are found in the life of Jesus, especially in his passion, crucifixion and resurrection. In Protestant worship this is mostly presented by words—by lessons from the Bible, by prayers and by sermons. Catholic worship consists much more of symbolic acts, as in the Mass, Eucharist or Liturgy. Whichever method of presentation is used, the worshipper contemplates the 'dynamic images', and in this contemplation finds that psychical energy is released in him which makes him able to overcome difficulties which would otherwise be insuperable, and not least to quieten and harmonize the anger, anxiety and other discordant impulses within himself.

The heart of Islamic worship is the *ṣalāt*, which means 'public worship' rather than what the word 'prayers' usually connotes in English. It consists of various actions, such as standing and bowing, accompanied by appropriate exclamations of praise; and its climax is when the worshippers touch the ground with their foreheads in acknowledgment of the supreme might and majesty of God. The *ṣalāt* must always be preceded by ablutions (though these may be performed with sand if one is in the desert); though primarily concerned with physical purity, the ablutions probably remind the worshipper of the need for purity in every respect when approaching God. When a number of Muslims perform the *ṣalāt* together, they arrange themselves in parallel rows behind an imam or prayer-leader, and stand, bow and prostrate themselves in time with the leader. The brotherhood of all Muslims is thus given tangible form; and it is further made explicit when, towards the close of the *ṣalāt*, each worshipper pronounces 'peace' on his brothers to right and to left. In the course of the *ṣalāt* the Fātiḥa and other passages from the Qur'ān are recited; and perhaps one might see in this—among other things—Islam's assertion of its place among the religions of the Book. In normal circumstances it is the duty of a Muslim to perform the *ṣalāt* after due ablutions at five prescribed times each day, namely, *fajr* or dawn, *ẓuhr* or midday, *'aṣr* or afternoon, *maghrib* or sunset, and *'ishā'* or evening. A Muslim should perform the *ṣalāt* alone if there are no other Muslims about.

An important part of Islamic worship is the *ḥajj* or pilgrimage to Mecca, which takes place each year in the twelfth month, *Dhū-l-Ḥijja* or 'pilgrimage month'. In this are incorporated many ancient ceremonies such as circumambulating the Ka'ba—a square building in the centre of the *ḥaram* or sanctuary at Mecca—kissing the Black Stone (set in a corner of the Ka'ba), running between two points, flinging pebbles at large blocks of stone, and sacrificing an animal. All these ceremonies doubtless had a meaning in pre-Islamic times, though the meaning may have been forgotten before Muḥammad began preaching. This meaning, however, was neglected by Islam, and the practices were simply accepted by the Muslims as things prescribed by God whose will in many respects was inscrutable. Thus the devout Muslim, in making the pilgrimage, considered that he was simply obeying the command of God. It is also possible that some of the ceremonies by their very nature exercised some unconscious influence on the participants. Certainly the pilgrimage has always increased the sense of brotherly solidarity among the Muslims. In recent times with greatly improved travel facilities many Muslims from distant regions take part; but crowds of the not so rich are still prepared to endure great hardships to reach Mecca by the more traditional methods.

The solidarity of Muslims is also fostered by the annual fast (*ṣawm*). For the whole of the month of Ramaḍān all Muslims who are in good health and not engaged on a journey are required to refrain from eating, drinking, smoking and sexual intercourse from half an hour before sunrise until half an hour after sunset. They may eat within the hours of darkness, but even so the fast is a great feat of endurance, especially when it occurs in summer. It tends to play havoc with the routine of a modern commercial or industrial community, since people's efficiency is greatly impaired. Yet the very effort of endurance promotes the solidarity of the community, for men know that they are in this together. The fast, like the pilgrimage, may also be said to help to extend the control of the Islamic vision over all the spheres of life, since both are undertaken out of a desire to obey God's commands.

One of the unusual features of Islam is its official acceptance of a lunar calendar of twelve lunar months or 354 days. This means that all the months, including those of the pilgrimage and the fast, become about eleven days earlier each year by solar reckoning. The pre-Islamic Arabs kept their lunar calendar in accord with the solar by inserting an intercalary month where necessary. This practice was forbidden by the Qur'ān, and occidental scholars have wondered how a great civilization could be satisfied by so clumsy a system of time-reckoning. Partly it goes back to the nomadic Arabs. Rain tends to be very irregular and erratic in the Arabian peninsula, so that the nomads are not accustomed to rely on the regularities of nature as peasants do. Besides this Mecca was a commercial city, and the great centres of Islamic life in later times were towns like Baghdad. For townsmen, then, like the Meccans, there is no great disadvantage in a lunar calendar. One should also notice, however, that Islam's adoption of the lunar calendar may be regarded as an expression of contempt for the whole life of the peasant—a sentiment natural to the nomad—and also of contempt for his religion. The lunar calendar does to a great extent[1] prevent Muslims from taking part in the seasonal observances of the nature religions of the peasants. Is this another aspect of Islam's neglect for whatever is alien to itself?

Another of the Five Pillars of Islam (after *ṣalāt*, fast and pilgrimage) which might be considered as worship is *zakāt* or almsgiving. This has meant different things at different periods. It has been a tax levied by governments, and it has also been voluntary alms-giving according to the individual conscience. Originally it was probably more like a tax, and was insisted on by Muḥammad. Yet essentially it seems to have been an adaptation of the custom observed in the nature religions of paying first-fruits from crops and herds to the deity. In Islam it is of course commanded by God and so no ground for it need be asked. Yet the detailed rules for *zakāt* and the discussion of it by Muslim scholars—for example, by al-Ghazālī (d. 1111) in Book 5 of the *Iḥyā'*—suggest some awareness of the link with the older practices, even though the reasons for it were different. (The last of the Five Pillars is the repetition of the Shahāda or confession of faith, namely, 'There is no god but God; Muḥammad is the messenger of God'; but this need not be considered here.)

Besides the forms of worship prescribed by the Sharī'a and accepted by all Sunnites (and to some extent by Shī'ites also), there were other devotional practices. There was a certain bareness and austerity about the *ṣalāt*, and this was doubtless felt as such by some who had come into Islam from other religions of the Middle East. Eventually the quest for mystical ecstasy was embarked on by Muslims. Those who did this took to wearing a special dress of wool (*ṣūf*) and are consequently known as *ṣūfīs*, while their practices are called collectively *taṣawwuf* or ṣūfism. In many cases they seem to have taken over or adapted Christian techniques, but they gave whatever they did a strictly Qur'ānic basis. In this way, also, then, the Islamic vision was extending its sway over spheres of human life which were originally independent, even if certain mystical features are to be found in Muḥammad himself.[2]

At first *ṣūfī* practice was largely an individual matter, though most *ṣūfīs* tended to associate with others, and younger men would go to older for instruction. Gradually, however, local groups began to have a more definite organization. Two main features may be mentioned. Firstly, there were developed certain forms of common worship. Such worship is known as *dhikr* (less correctly *zikr*). The word properly means 'mention' or 'remembrance', that is, of God, and has a prominent place in the Qur'ān. In the *dhikr* as it was developed there was often a long-continued repetition of the name of God—*Allāh*, *Allāh*, . . .—which might be accompanied by rhythmic movements such as a circling dance (as in the case of the so-called 'whirling dervishes'). The aim of all this was to induce a state of mystical ecstasy, and for those properly instructed it was effective. Secondly, the organized groups of *ṣūfīs* were given permanence as orders or *ṭarīqas*. This process began about the early thirteenth century, though there had been experiments in common living since the ninth century. By the nineteenth century it was normal for members of the urban proletariat to be adherents of a *ṭarīqa*. The position at the present time is obscure, but it seems certain that in many Islamic countries the influence of the orders has greatly decreased.

In the development of the dervish or mystical orders it is possible to see, as suggested above, an extension of the sway of the Islamic vision over various non-Arab religious practices of the Middle East. At the same time there was in some instances a danger that the Islamic element might be swamped by the non-Islamic element. The revulsion of feeling against the orders may be in part due to the abuse of their position and privileges by some of the leaders; by way of example one may quote Ṭāhā Ḥusayn's account in *An Egyptian Childhood* of how the chief of an order and his entourage descended on a poor village and expected to be feasted royally for several days. The revulsion of feeling is also in line with the tendency to return to Qur'ānic Islam and neglect later accretions. This tendency is itself a reassertion of the pure Islamic vision and so is a necessary part of the process of showing that Islam rightly understood enables man to deal satisfactorily with the contemporary situation.

2. Ethical and ascetic ideals

The relation of ethics or morality to religion is not altogether simple. Men naturally tend to suppose that there is a close connection, since we commonly speak of Buddhist ethics, Christian ethics and Islamic ethics. Yet a little reflection shows that ethics has always a certain autonomy. The same practice may be accepted (or rejected) in societies with different religious visions. A practice may be taken over by one society from another whose general outlook is completely different, apparently for no other reason than that it works in practice; much of early Christian ethics is said to be derived from Stoicism.

These points are worthy of fuller consideration. It would seem to be normal for a specific ethical outlook to be associated with a religion in its formative stages. In the Old Testament God gives commands to the Israelites about what are essentially ethical or moral matters. There is much moral teaching in the New Testament. Such teaching is apparently included because it is appropriate to the needs of the times. The moral teaching of Jesus is appropriate to a situation in which Jews were constantly having dealings with non-Jews, in particular with the agents of Rome the occupying power. To this situation the ethics of the Pharisees was inappropriate since it could only be carried out by religious men if there were sufficient 'irreligious' Jews to have the necessary daily contacts with the Romans. So early Christian ethics has a distinctive colouring that makes it appropriate to people with no political rights and in danger of persecution. This 'distinctive colouring' or particularization of the ethical ideal is accepted on the basis of the general criterion that in practice it produces a satisfactory life for the whole society.

In most situations what people adjudge satisfactory in practice will be the same, whatever their beliefs about the nature of the universe and of human life in it. Yet in some cases such beliefs will affect the judgment of what is satisfactory, and through this moral belief. Thus for the Buddhist who believes in reincarnation it may be a laudable thing to end his present life by burning himself in order to make a conspicuous protest against some wrong. Again, whether we believe in the brotherhood of all men of whatever race, or in special privileges for the white race, may depend in part on whether we believe that God created all men equal or made some constitutionally superior. The more a man believes in a future life the more ready will he be to sacrifice his life for some cause. In particular it would seem that the beliefs associated with a religion give some support to the ethical practice of the religious community, so that there is a danger of morality collapsing in some respects when the system of beliefs collapses. This may be because the life of the community as a whole is dependent on the system of beliefs.[3]

The primary ethical need in Mecca and Medina when Muḥammad was preaching was for a code of conduct appropriate to an urban and increasingly individualistic population. The old morality of the nomadic Arabs had been suited to desert conditions and presupposed a large measure of tribal solidarity. In Muḥammad's time, so far as the taking of life and the inflicting of personal injury was concerned, tribal and clan solidarity continued to function. In Mecca, however, there was serious neglect of the duties of clan chiefs to look after the poor and unprotected members of the clan;

most of the rich merchants were clan chiefs, but were so interested in money-making that they were not prepared to spend any of their wealth on widows, orphans and other poor persons. The Qur'ānic doctrine of the Last Day—if they believed in it—was a sanction to encourage these persons to perform their traditional duties. In general we may say that the ethics of the Qur'ān is an adaptation of the ideals of human excellence worked out in the desert where life is exceptionally difficult for men—an adaptation which aims at making these ideals relevant to urban man.

This view is opposed to that of Ignaz Goldziher in the first chapter of his *Muhammedanische Studien* (Halle, 1888), where he contrasts the *muruwwa* or 'manliness' of the pre-Islamic Arab with the *dīn* or 'religion' taught by the Qur'ān. Now there was admittedly a contrast between the Muslim's sense of dependence on God and the pagan's presumptuous self-reliance. On the strictly ethical level, however, Goldziher overstates his case. He speaks of Muḥammad preaching forgiveness as against the nomadic duty of revenge, and of the Islamic limitations on personal freedom as regards wine and women. In reply to this it is to be noted that the Qur'ānic commands to forgive apply to the faults of close relatives (24.22 as traditionally interpreted) or to those of other Muslims (3.134/128). In cases of killing or personal injury it was accepted that the family or clan of the injured party still had the duty of revenge (42.40/38 f.), but they were encouraged to take a payment of camels or money instead (cf. 4.92/94).[4] The Qur'ān undoubtedly places restrictions on wine and women, but in this respect it has to be asked how far these restrictions were due to the new religious outlook and how far to the development of an urban and more individualistic society; in general it would seem that the Qur'ān was not innovating in this respect but simply accepting the positions towards which the better elements in society were moving as a result of recent social changes. The chief weakness of Goldziher's thesis, however, is that he does not mention that there are many aspects of the ideal of *muruwwa* which are reaffirmed by the Qur'ān, such as endurance of hardship or patience (*ṣabr*) and generosity. It has also to be remembered that when the nomadic Arab became a Muslim many of the laudable attitudes towards his tribe which he held were attached instead to the Islamic community as a whole, and came to be adopted also by non-Arab Muslims. Thus at the ethical as distinct from the religious level there is a high degree of continuity between pre-Islamic and Islamic ideals.

While there is a considerable ethical element in the Qur'ān, the Qur'ān is not the sole or complete expression of the ethical ideal of Islam. To the Qur'ān must be added the Traditions (about the sayings and doings of Muḥammad), for these constitute a secondary form of revelation, which amplifies and extends the primary revelational material in the Qur'ān. From the point of view of modern scholarship a few Traditions may be genuine, many may be tendentially shaped modifications of something genuine, and many again sheer inventions; the older Muslim scholars recognized that there were inventions, but cannot be said to have distinguished the second of the above categories from the first. This question of precise scholarship is fortunately not relevant to the present discussion, since even invented Traditions are evidence for the ethical outlook of early Islam. In some respects it is not the origin of the Tradition which one needs to know but the extent to which it was quoted in the time of the Būyids or the Seljūqs. An ethical ideal expressed in material such as the Traditions has great variety and richness, and this makes it difficult for the present-day student to know what the contemporary emphasis was. Yet through all the bewildering process what may be called the 'mind of Islam' was being formed and made more definite. Views held by non-Arabs before they became Muslims could be justified by Traditions and be given a certain place in Islamic thinking; but whether such views would eventually commend themselves to the main body of Muslims had to be discovered slowly over centuries.

Partly through the Qur'ān and still more through the Traditions Islam absorbed much of the ethics of Judaism and Christianity and also the traditional wisdom of the Middle East. Before Muḥammad's mission the more enlightened men in Mecca and Medina were familar with biblical ideas. Qur'ānic passages addressed to such persons, while perhaps modifying the ideas, also strengthened their hold and led to their wider dissemination. Again, points of morality currently practised in the lands conquered by the Arabs could be incorporated in a Tradition and thus given *droit de cité* in the Islamic world.

An interesting example of how this might be treated is in connection with the punishment of stoning for adultery. This punishment is prescribed in the Bible (*Deuteronomy*, 22.22; cf. *John*, 8.5), and may have been practised in some settled communities. From what we know of the marital practices of the nomadic Arabs it is unthinkable in the desert. When the Muslims came in contact with communities which practised stoning for adultery, or perhaps merely raised the point to criticize the Qur'ān, some Muslims tried to deal with the problem by supposing that there had once been a 'verse of stoning' in the Qur'ān in which the punishment was prescribed; and a story was told about the caliph 'Umar saying how they had once recited this verse.[5] It is virtually certain that this is invention and that there never was such a verse in the Qur'ān. Nevertheless it came to be accepted by Islamic jurists that the punishment of stoning for adultery was recognized in Islam, though at the same time they made such stringent conditions—four adult males must have witnessed the act in full physical detail—that the stoning could never legally be carried out. In this way the harsh Deuteronomic law was accepted, but was so hedged in with restrictions that more lenient treatment became permissible or indeed obligatory.

Finally it may be noted that certain forms of ethical striving came to be associated with mysticism. From time to time there have been Muslim ascetics who practised celibacy, though on the whole the view has been that there is no 'monkery' in Islam (*lā rahbāniyya fī 'l-Islām*)—a Tradition for which there is a variant 'no celibacy' (*lā ṣarūra*).[6] Certainly the impression is given that Muslim ascetics and mystics have been above all concerned with poverty of worldly goods and with simplicity of food and clothing. Thus the Islamic vision was stretched out over this great area of human life, and practices which may first have been seen in other cultures were given a place at the heart of Islamic mysticism.

Chapter 11

Islam in a competitive world

1. The growth and decay of religions

There are many correspondences between the history of a religion and that of an individual. In the growth to maturity of one of the great religions we can normally find a series of crises. At each of these the religious community has been confronted with a fresh challenge, and it is in its response to these challenges that it has reached its maturity. Had it not responded in the way it did, its religion would not have become one of the great world religions. Nowadays there are numerous new religions seeking a 'place in the sun', and their position in the future history of mankind will depend on how their adherents respond to the successive challenges which they have begun to meet and will continue to meet.

To those familiar with Islamic history the challenges by which the community of Muslims grew to maturity can easily be discerned. The first serious challenge was the opposition shown by many of the leading men of Mecca to this new movement led by Muḥammad, and then their active persecution of members of their own clans. A part of this was the opposition to Muḥammad within his own clan of Hāshim, especially after Abū-Lahab became chief of the clan. The Hijra or migration to Medina was part of the response to this first challenge; but it in its turn brought fresh challenges. An adequate source of livelihood had to be found for the Emigrants. When they brought back booty from the raid to Nakhla, many of the inhabitants of Medina were afraid, chiefly of Meccan vengeance, it would seem; and their fears had to be set at rest. Peace had to be kept within Medina, and those who did not wholeheartedly support Muḥammad had to be rendered harmless. The military threat from Mecca had to be met at Badr or some such place. The despondency of the Muslims after the battle of Uḥud had to be replaced by confidence. The Meccans had to be defeated but not, if possible, turned into irreconcilable opponents. An outlet had to be found for the energies which as Muslims the Arabs could not expend in raiding one another. Then on Muḥammad's death the embryonic state had to be held together. Unity had to be restored after the civil wars following the death of ʿUthmān in 656. In the later Umayyad period the grievances of the non-Arab Muslims had to be met. Under the early ʿAbbāsids Persian and Greek influences had to be prevented from destroying the essential core of Islam. So we might go on for long.

By the way in which Muslims met these various situations as they arose, the religious community of Muslims as a whole was growing to maturity and becoming more definite in the process. In the more important of these challenges the community of Muslims may be said to have come to some fundamental decisions which shaped Islam for all its future. The decision on the day of Muḥammad's death that he was to be succeeded by Abū-Bakr included a decision that the head of the community was to be a Meccan of Quraysh and not one of the *Anṣār*. Later there was the decision that made the community predominantly Sunnite and not Shīʿite, namely, that the divinely revealed law as contained in the Qur'ān (and, later, also in the Traditions) was to be above the imam and not the imam above the law. Linked with this latter point was the doctrinal assertion that the Qur'ān was the uncreated Word or Speech of God. Through these and many other decisions first of all the community of Muslims as a body politic received a definite shape, and secondly the beliefs and practices of Muslims also attained definiteness.

This increase of definiteness does not imply the appearance of a monolithic uniformity. In respect of many of the decisions there were dissidents, and many groups of dissidents continued for long to exist as groups. Some, like the Shīʿites and even the Khārijites, still exist. From one point of view such sects make Islam not one but many; and yet they also express facets of the Islamic vision which are insufficiently expressed by the main body of Sunnites. They also indicate to us later observers false or unsatisfactory roads which the main body of Muslims might have taken, but fortunately did not. The process of confrontation by challenges and response to them continues at the present time. It may be specially difficult for the new religions to meet the challenges. In their maturity and their definiteness the older religions have an advantage; they are established, and they have a momentum which will carry them through several decades at least. Nevertheless in being definite they have acquired a rigidity which makes it difficult to respond adequately to the rapidly changing conditions of the present age.

While historical changes give a religious community opportunities for growing and maturing, it must not be forgotten that there are also opportunities for decay. Failure to respond adequately to a challenge is to that extent failure to grow; and that is tantamount to decay. The individual also grows by responding to the various challenges presented by his environment from infancy onwards; but he may fail to respond or may respond inadequately. In such cases there is usually a neurosis present; or rather a neurosis develops after the failure or inadequacy. When, as a result of failures to respond adequately, unsatisfactory attitudes develop in the members of a religious community, these are comparable in some ways to the neuroses of individuals, though the parallelism is not exact. In what follows I propose to consider false attitudes under the three heads of: isolationist, inflationary and fixational. These closely resemble certain neurotic attitudes, but the resemblance need only be mentioned incidentally here, since it has been treated more fully elsewhere.[1]

Many of these neurotic attitudes become manifest or explicit in the relation of the religious community to other groups. It is for this reason that the present chapter has been entitled 'Islam in a competitive world', that is, in a world in which it is in competition with other religions. From its beginnings Islam was in some respects a rival of Judaism and Christianity. The rivalry became more intense after the surge of Arab expansion into Syria, Egypt and Iraq. In course of time, however, the situation changed, for Islam became the dominant religion in the area subject to the caliphs and other Muslim rulers. It thereby came to be geographically cut off from the other great religions. Any inhabitants of Islamic lands who belonged to 'religions of the book' received the status of protected persons (*dhimmīs*) and could have business relations with their Muslim fellow-citizens. Yet, sometimes through being required to wear distinctive clothing, often in more subtle ways, these non-Muslims were as effectively cut off from personal friendship with Muslims as if they had lived in a different geographical region. In so far as this was the case competition between Islam and other religions had ceased. The nineteenth and twentieth centuries and the increasing ease of communications, however, have produced a new situation in which the great religions have much closer and more frequent contacts with one another and also with new upstart rivals.

All the great religions have had similar experiences in the course of their history. They have had to struggle with other religions; they have found a *modus vivendi* (not always entirely satisfactory) with those who shared the same geographical area; and they are now plunged into the maelstrom of the modern world. In its formative period each religion adopted certain attitudes towards its rivals, and these were linked with its conception of its own identity. It is in these attitudes and in this idea of self-identity that the neurotic trends become apparent. In the great religions, of course, which are only 'great' because they have somehow met the spiritual needs of millions of men over centuries, the element of neurosis is slight. Yet neurotic tendencies, which, while the religions remained in partial isolation, had no ill effects, may be a serious disadvantage in the contemporary situation of interreligious competition. Similar neurotic attitudes to the three discussed here can also be found in the relations of sects within a religion, but this is not the primary concern in this study. It is, however, relevant to note that the neurotic tendency in a religion may be found chiefly or solely in one section of the adherents of that religion.

By an *isolationist* attitude is to be understood that of a religious group which is content to shut itself up, as it were, in a private world and to have the minimum of relations and contacts with the rest of the world. In many parts of Christendom there has been a tendency, especially since the middle of the nineteenth century, to shut oneself off from the dominant intellectual culture of the day because it was difficult to harmonize various scientific discoveries with the traditional understanding of the Bible, or rather with the traditional understanding of the epistemological status of the biblical record. This tendency is commonly described as fundamentalism. It may also be combined with more specific beliefs and practices. We then have such bodies as Jehovah's Witnesses and the Closed Brethren. In extreme cases the whole intellectual and social life of the members of the group is within the group. Such a body is properly called a sect because, by shutting itself off from the rest of the world, it is accepting a permanent minority status. The great religions, on the other hand, necessarily seek to become *the* religion of the whole cultural or political unit. This means further that the great religions want to propagate their beliefs in every social and intellectual milieu. The 'sects' may also have missionary zeal, but their successes would rather be described as 'proselytization'. That is to say, it is not the extension of a religious vision into the whole life of a community, but the removal of individuals from the general life of the community to bring them into the life of the separated group. The religion of a whole community must be capable of becoming the religion of its political and intellectual leaders.

Another common weakness is an *inflationary* attitude. This occurs when a group exaggerates its own importance in comparison with other groups. Groups with an isolationist attitude always tend to exaggerate their own importance and to feel superior to everyone else; but they usually keep this belief mainly to themselves. The inflationary attitude as here understood is not hidden in this way but involves making public claims of one's superior status. Nearly all religious bodies have at least a little of this inflationary attitude. Those who claim to be 'orthodox' are *ipso facto* claiming that they alone have the true doctrines and are thus superior to others. The statement *extra ecclesiam nulla salus* ('outside the Church there is no salvation') is, at least as popularly understood, inflationary. Because the religious group referred to by the term *ecclesia* is alone salvation-giving it is thereby thought of as superior to other groups, and this is indeed claimed for it publicly. It may be objected that such claims are sometimes—or at least in one case—true. To this objection I would reply that most religious groups make a claim of this kind, and there would appear to be no objective criterion for judging between the claims. It is right, of course, that a man should attach himself to a particular religious group and bear positive witness to the fact that he and his friends have found salvation within this group. This positive assertion is fully justified; but there is little justification for the negative assertion that so often accompanies the positive, or is implied by it, namely, that other persons cannot find salvation within other religious groups. The failure to admit that we cannot *know* that this is not so is the heart of the inflationary attitude.

Lastly, there is the *fixational* attitude. This consists in maintaining religious attitudes, beliefs and practices after the conditions to which they were appropriate have disappeared. It is right that there should be continuity in religious matters as in many others, and it is indeed one of the functions of religion to be conservative of all that is good. There are also times, however, when fundamental changes sweep over a whole society. Such changes are not usually in any way deliberately willed, but have simply to be accepted by those experiencing them as given facts. Such acceptance of what cannot be changed by human effort naturally leads to attempts to achieve readjustment. Where readjustment is not attempted we have the fixational attitude. A well-known example is that of the Pharisees in the New Testament. Their code of conduct with its elaborate rules for avoiding sullying contacts with non-Jews and non-practising Jews was appropriate—we may allow—in the second century before Christ when the religion of Judaism was threatened with assimilation to Hellenism; but it had ceased to be relevant in the Roman empire of the first century A.D. when many old religions were ceasing to be effective and when countless men and women in the cities of the empire were seeking something like the faith of the Jews (as we learn from the fact that groups of 'those who feared God' had grown up round the synagogues). The present age is one in which farreaching readjustments are needed by all religions and in which all are to some extent showing the fixational attitude.

This list of the neurotic attitudes affecting communities does not claim to be complete though it seems to include most of the weaknesses affecting communities as communities. There are also, of course, the numerous faults of the individual members of the various communities or even of whole sections of the communities, such as the clerical class. What is distinctive of the attitudes here criticized is that they are attitudes of the community as a body and are usually included in its official teaching about itself. This makes them more serious. Ultimately, however, neurotic attitudes in a community are no more hopeless than neurotic attitudes in an individual. There appear to be forces working in the hearts of men singly and collectively which make for the healing of neurosis. Just because of the difficulties of the present world situation such forces are gathering strength in men's hearts, and we may look to the future with much hope.

The three following sections deal with some illustrations in the Islamic world of the three attitudes described. I hope it will be clear to Muslim readers that these are the criticisms of a friend, intended to help towards the overcoming of weaknesses. What has been said in this section will show that I make similar criticism of Christianity and other religions, while it will be clear, I hope, from the final chapter of this book that I have a high positive appreciation of Islam. With this word of caution I set about an exposition of certain aspects of Islam without which any account of 'What is Islam?' would be incomplete.

2. The isolationist attitude in Islam

In its early stages Islam was non-isolationist. Islam originated in Mecca where there was some slight contact with Judaism and Christianity, and it accepted these religions as valid for their adherents. Indeed it regarded Muḥammad as bringing in Arabic to the Arabs of the Hejaz and elsewhere a message similar to that of Judaism and Christianity or even identical with it. One of the stories about the early days of Islam is that, just after Muḥammad had received the first revelation, his wife Khadīja went to a Christian kinsman of hers, Waraqa, and told him about Muḥammad's experience; he thereupon said 'This is the *nāmūs*', and the word *nāmūs* is often taken to be a form of *nomos* (Greek for 'law') and to refer to the Old Testament or to the Bible generally. Whether the story is true or not, the fact that it gained currency shows that the Muslims attached some importance to approval and acceptance from 'the people of the book'. The Muslims also seem to have been on good terms for a number of years with the Christian rulers of Ethiopia.

A reversal of Islam's attitude to the older religions was brought about by the behaviour of the Jews of Medina. Before he went to Medina Muḥammad seems to have thought that he would be accepted as a prophet by the Jews there. When instead they rejected and criticized him, the experience must have been traumatic. Jewish criticism, however, was also dangerous. The Qur'ān claimed to refer to events recorded in the Bible, and that made it possible for the Jews to argue: 'What comes in the Qur'ān does not tally with what we have in the Bible, and therefore Muḥammad cannot be a prophet.' If such an argument, supported by numerous bits of evidence, was not quickly countered, it would soon erode away the whole foundation of the religious movement led by Muḥammad.

Islam also had difficulties with Christians in the last two or three years of Muḥammad's life. As the power of the Muslims grew they came into contact with Christian tribes on the borders of Syria, and these tribes—no doubt for reasons that were mainly political—were not prepared to abandon their alliances with the Byzantines and go over to Muḥammad. A little later, especially during the reign of the caliph 'Umar (634–44), the situation changed rapidly, and the Muslims found themselves masters of Syria, Egypt and Iraq—the two former predominantly Christian and the last nearly half Christian. In many cases the local Christians had welcomed the Muslims as liberators, so that to begin with relations were good. In course of time, however, there were difficulties because of the superior education of the Christians and their ability to use arguments which threatened the foundation of Islam. (From a certain standpoint there may be said to be something of a fixational attitude in the inability of the Jews and Christians to respond appropriately to the new situation created by the advent of Muḥammad.)

In attempting to overcome these difficulties Islam worked out a new conception of its own identity. The Muslims came to think of the Jews as the religious community of those who accepted the revelation given to Moses, or perhaps as the physical descendants of Jacob. In either case Abraham was not a Jew, since he lived long before Moses and was the grandfather of Jacob. They probably also thought of his son Ishmael as an ancestor of the Arabs, though the final linking-up of traditional Arab genealogies with biblical genealogies presumably did not come till later. Certainly, near the beginning of the Medinan period, the Qur'ān made the claim that it was presenting the pure religion of Abraham, from which Jews and Christians had deviated. It pointed to many cases of disobedience, to the concealment of passages in the Bible foretelling Muḥammad, and to the 'corruption' of passages in the Bible. So far as the Qur'ān itself is concerned the references to 'corruption' seem to mean no more than that the Jews engaged in various forms of play on words to make fun of Islam and the Muslims.[2] After the first wave of conquests, however, something more was needed to give the ordinary Arab a defence against the arguments of Jews and Christians. This was found in the elaboration of the doctrine of 'corruption'. The extended doctrine was never precisely formulated, since there were advantages in a degree of indefiniteness—when one formulation of 'corruption' proved unsatisfactory one could shift to another.

The point to be emphasized at the moment is that the net effect of this doctrine is isolationist. The most usual forms of the doctrine are that the Bible as a whole is textually corrupt, that the Jewish and Christian interpretation of the Bible is corrupt, and that sections of the text have been removed. Whichever form or combination of forms is chosen, the final result is that Muslims, though accepting Christianity (and Judaism) in theory, refuse to accept its concrete manifestations in the present. In particular they remove what might have been a common basis of discussion when they refuse to accept the actual text of the Bible. In other words the Muslims have refused to enter the intellectual world of the Christians. They were not prepared to argue with Christians on the basis of the Bible and what Christians believed about it. A few Muslim scholars in the early centuries did indeed make some use of the Bible, but it was chiefly to find verses which might be considered as foretelling Muḥammad or to point to weaknesses in the Christian case. Such arguments involved assumptions which were unacceptable or even meaningless to the Christians; but there was no further exploration of these assumptions, and no real 'dialogue'. The effect of all this on the ordinary Muslim must have been to confirm him in his belief that there was no point in trying to argue with Christians.

The doctrine of 'corruption' did not by itself completely isolate Muslims from Christians and others in the religious sphere. A few intellectuals found common ground for discussion of theology in their studies of Greek philosophy. For a time in Baghdad in the tenth century A.D. the interest in philosophy overcame confessional differences. Muslims studied philosophy under Christians such as Abū-Bishr Mattā (d. 940) and Yaḥyā ibn-'Adī (d. 974),[3] and Christians studied under Muslims like al-Fārābī (d. 950). Yet the discussions which took place in this milieu had only very limited repercussions among Muslims in general, perhaps because Muslims like al-Fārābī were themselves outside the main stream of Islamic thought and life. Common ground might also have been found in the Qur'ān, and a few Christians knew something about it. Had Muslims been prepared to give an eirenic interpretation of the passages in the Qur'ān which Christians found difficult, an advance towards 'dialogue' might have been possible; but more and more the Muslims came to accept as the standard interpretation of such passages the one which emphasized most their differences from the Christians. This is indeed a further manifestation of the isolationist attitude.

Fortunately there are signs at the present day that Muslims are realizing that, even if this attitude was adequate where Islam was dominant, it is unsatisfactory in the contemporary world where Islam finds itself one world religion among several. In the English-speaking world the best-known example of this new approach to

Christianity by Muslims is the imaginative reconstruction of the events leading up to Good Friday in *City of Wrong* ('*Al-Qarya aẓ-Ẓālima*') by M. Kamel Hussein.[4] One or two other works of a similar kind have been published, however,[5] and more will doubtless follow. Conversations with educated Muslims in many of the great Islamic cities indicate the beginnings of a feeling that Islam and Christianity are ultimately on the same side in the spiritual struggles that lie before humanity, even if they are sometimes still on opposite sides politically. This is, then, a slight indication that Islam is abandoning its isolationist attitude with regard to Christianity.

3. The inflationary attitude in Islam

Inflation of one's own importance is an almost universal human phenomenon. There may be some exceptions among individuals, but there are very few indeed among groups of whatever type, from local football teams to worldwide religious communities. The poetry of the pre-Islamic desert tribes of Arabia is said to belong to two categories, namely, 'praise' (*fakhr*, *mafākhir*) and 'satire' (*hijā'*, *mathālib*). In the former the poet sang the praises of his own tribe, its prowess in battle, its generosity, and so forth; in the latter he flung all the taunts he could think of at an enemy tribe. There was naturally a tendency to exaggerate the merits of one's own party and likewise the demerits of the other side.

When one comes to ask whether there is some inflation of this kind in the Islamic religion, it is difficult to be completely objective. A certain latitude has therefore to be left in any judgments on these matters. Thus it might be thought that there was some inflation in Muḥammad's claim to be the Messenger of God to a relatively small community near the west coast of Arabia. In much the same way it might be thought that there was inflation in the claim of a small hill-community in Palestine in the first half of the first millennium B.C. to be in a special covenant relation with the God who had created the whole earth. Yet later history has shown that the hill-community has achieved something on behalf of all mankind; and the existence today of between 500 and 600 million Muslims rather supports the claim of Muḥammad. Thus the claim of Muḥammad is, at least in some respects, to be allowed; he has brought spiritual guidance to a large section of the human race, and may yet give something to the whole of it.

There is more justification for thinking that there is exaggeration in respect of the claim that the Qur'ān is a source of historical knowledge parallel with the usual sources of historical knowledge and even superior to them, for example, in respect of the crucifixion of Jesus. Whether this claim is in fact made in the Qur'ān may be disputed, for the verses that seem to make it may be interpreted to mean that the novel contribution of the Qur'ān is to point the moral or lesson to be learned from stories of past events. Undoubtedly, however, later Muslims have claimed that the Qur'ān was a source of historical knowledge; and this is a claim which to the modern scholar seems to be exaggerated and so inflationary.

In other ways also the possible instances of inflationary attitudes raise the question of what may be properly known by revelation. A popular view is that a prophet is a man who can foretell the future because things not known to ordinary men are revealed to him. But does a prophet have in this way a detailed knowledge of future events, or does not he rather have a knowledge of the ways in which God usually deals with men? This point is relevant to the understanding of a passage in the book of *Deuteronomy* (18.15–18) which Muslims claim foretells the coming of Muḥammad. In the passage the people of God are told that God will raise up for them one of their own number, similar to Moses, and that this man will bring them guidance. Must this be taken as a precise prediction, referring—for Christians—to Jesus? Or is it a statement of how God may be expected to work, namely, by sending such men when required? Jesus could then be regarded as the supreme exemplar; but Muḥammad could not be wholly excluded. If an argument along these lines is possible, then the Muslim claim that Muḥammad is foretold in this passage is not inflationary.

There is yet another set of claims which might be considered inflationary, namely, that Islam supersedes and corrects Christianity, and that Muḥammad is the supreme prophet and the bearer of a message to all mankind. There are grounds for thinking—though this is not the place to expound them—that the advance of Islam in the Middle East is not unconnected with certain flaws and weaknesses in the Christendom of the area, above all, the unsympathetic treatment of Nestorians and Monophysites (whose primary languages were Syriac and Coptic) by the Christians who spoke Greek and Latin. Christians who, because of their Syriac or Coptic background, were unable to feel themselves at home in the Great Church (dominated by Greek-speakers) were made more fully at home in the community of Islam. In this particular matter Islam may claim to have done something which Christianity had tried to do and failed; so there is some justification for the first part of the set of claims now being considered. The idea that Muḥammad is the supreme prophet is sometimes based on the Qur'ānic phrase 'seal of the prophets' (*khātam an-nabiyyīn*; 33.40); but this is to press, perhaps unduly, one connotation of the word 'seal'. With regard to the more general question of the universality of Muḥammad's message, there is support for this in the fact that Islam has spread to some 600 million people of many different races and social classes. On the other hand, the adoption by Muslims of an isolationist attitude with regard to Christians and Jews seems to show that those at least who adopted this attitude were not fully persuaded of the universality of their religion. In this matter, then, the situation is not altogether clear; one would have to define more exactly the sense in which it is claimed that Muḥammad is universal.

There is also an element of inflation in the attitude of the Arabs to the non-Arabs within the Islamic community. For a time only Arabs could be Muslims, and any non-Arabs who wanted to become Muslims had first to become quasi-Arabs by incorporation into an Arab tribe as 'clients' (*mawālī*). Under the 'Abbāsids, when the ruling institution of the caliphate and various other aspects of its culture showed strong Persian influence, the demand was dropped that non-Arabs should become 'clients', but there was no full admission of the extent to which contemporary culture was indebted to the Persians or other previous inhabitants of Iraq. This failure to admit indebtedness was particularly noticeable in respect of those elements of intellectual culture where the previous bearers had been Christians, for this was the case with most of the philosophy and science. In this sphere Muslims cannot be acquitted of the charge of having an inflationary attitude, though one may allow that it is cultural rather than religious.

4. The fixational attitude in Islam

The attitude of clinging to the past and of following exactly all past precedents was deeply rooted in the Arabs. Probably without such an attitude men would have had insufficient confidence to meet the hardships and accidents of desert life. They thought of this as following the *sunna*, the path which had been trodden, and so beaten and made evident, by their forefathers. To deviate from this path was *bid'a* or innovation. One can see that there is much justification for this attitude in the conditions of desert life, which are in essentials unchanging. Even the metaphor of the path is suggestive. Paths in the desert are not always very evident; but, if one can keep to a well-beaten track, one has some assurance of reaching one's destination safely and not dying of thirst and exposure.

Something of this attitude of the desert Arab was taken over by Islam. Here also there was justification for it, since Islam, like all other religions, requires to maintain continuity with its original vision. The conservative attitude becomes unjustified and fixational, however, when it is insisted on to an extent which makes more difficult any adjustment to changing circumstances. Most religions have at some periods been over-conservative. It is natural to man in many situations to cling to the familiar and to avoid the novel; and this is particularly so at times when because of deep changes in the fabric of society men feel insecure. In Islam, because of its desert heritage, a fundamental place came to be held by the conceptions of following the beaten path (*sunna*) and avoiding innovation (*bid'a*).

This is to be seen above all in the process by which the practice of Muḥammad came to be accepted as normative for the community. Something has already been said about this process, so the briefest description will suffice here. The practice of Muḥammad as reflected in his actions and words was given verbal form in the anecdotes which are technically known as Traditions. After the time of the great jurist ash-Shāfi'ī (d. 820) it was held to be necessary, except in the few cases where there was a clear Qur'ānic rule, to support a legal opinion by reference to one or more Traditions. Muslim scholars realized that it was comparatively easy to invent Traditions, and soon after 850 there appeared the first of the collections of 'sound' Traditions, that is, of Traditions which have been scrutinized and adjudged 'sound' or genuine. Occidental scholars in the last century have continued the earlier Muslim scholars' critique of Traditions and have taken the view that even among the 'sound' Traditions are many which were either inventions or had been considerably modified from genuine stories.

The point to be made in the present context is that, whether one sides with the older Muslim scholars or with the occidentals, one is admitting some invention of anecdotes about Muḥammad, and this admission is sufficient to show that the conception of following a beaten path made it difficult for Muslims to effect adjustments in their social norms. When Muḥammad died the Islamic state was a federation of nomadic Arab tribes which included a few groups living in small towns like Medina. By 850 the Muslims had a huge empire and many of them lived in vast cities such as Basra and Baghdad, or cultivated lands which were much more productive than those of Arabian oases. While the basic principles of a satisfactory human society may be allowed to be the same everywhere, there must have been many differences between conditions in Iraq in 850 and those in Medina in 632. Yet the Arab urge to follow a *sunna* was so imperious that it was necessary to invent Traditions in order to assure people that their present practices (modified to suit the new conditions) were in accordance with the original Islamic vision. (What is said here must be taken in conjunction with an argument to be advanced in the next chapter to the effect that even sheer invention is not always unjustified.)

It would be interesting to trace the history of this conception of following the *sunna* or beaten path (from which the main body of Islam has received the name of Sunnites), but there is only space for one or two points. One is that Muslim jurists have taken advantage of the preference for the unchanging to protect themselves (according to a likely hypothesis) against the encroachment by rulers on the sphere of justice. This was done by the theory that 'the gate of *ijtihād* had been closed'. It was long recognized that the principles expressed in the words of Muḥammad in the Traditions required some interpretation before they could be applied to the decision of concrete legal cases. The word *ijtihād*, though it primarily means 'effort', came to be used for this work of interpretation by an individual; and the closing of the gate of *ijtihād* means that a jurist or judge must follow some interpretation current in his rite or school and must not base his decision on an individual interpretation. This limitation must have been of value to men who were under pressure from a strong ruler to vary the interpretation of the law in his favour. Things have changed radically in the last century for it has become necessary to introduce farreaching modifications of earlier practice, and reformers have been seriously hampered by popular insistence that they must adhere to the *sunna* of Muḥammad. The *sunna* apparently permitted a girl to be married at the age of nine, and countenanced claims for alimony based on allegations that pregnancies had lasted for four years.

The jurists were put to many shifts to achieve reforms in these and similar matters.

It cannot be emphasized sufficiently that the present age is an exceptional one, in which all the great religions are faced with the need for a more radical readjustment than any they have made since they reached a degree of maturity. If modern apologists for Islam allege that its unchangeableness is a virtue, they are merely showing their ignorance of history. All living religions are *ipso facto* growing and therefore changing. It is natural, however, that in periods of specially rapid or radical change men should seek security in the familiar past. There are Christians who maintain that what we need in the present age is a strong reaffirmation of the basic unchanging dogmas of their religion. Now dogmatic formulations, whether in Islam or Christianity, are attempts to provide a framework within which the ordinary worshipper may have an opportunity to re-experience something of the original vision of his religion. In many parts of the Christian world the existing formulations are proving no longer effective in introducing the worshipper to the experience; and the same would seem to be true—though still on a lesser scale—in parts of the Islamic world.

In the crisis of our time merely to hold on doggedly to old formulations is this fixational attitude, which is neurotic. The more balanced and mature attitude which is required today is one which realizes the need for continuity with the original vision, but understands that such continuity in respect of the vision cannot be identified with any continuity of doctrinal (dogmatic) formulations in words. To put it differently, we need to revise radically our forms of words and even some of our ways of thinking, and yet at the same time we must preserve some obvious continuity with the past. The next chapter will indicate a possible line of advance.

Chapter 12

Islamic values today

1. The contribution of Islam to the 'one world'

The question 'What is Islam?' does not simply refer to the past but is also relevant to the present and the future. Because of its past Islam is a force to be reckoned with in the present; and as for what it may contribute to the future of the 'one world', that, as the Muslims say, God knows best. There are possibilities of contributions in the political sphere. The Islamic powers might even come to constitute a third bloc in world politics, over against the Atlantic and Russian blocs. Such a development is problematic, but at the regional level—for instance, in East Africa[1]—there is a fair likelihood of Islam growing rapidly in political importance. A book like the present, however, is not the place for such prognostications which necessarily have a large speculative element. Rather let us turn again to the abiding religious values of Islam, and try to see how these are relevant to the lives of individuals today. A religion only has influence in world affairs in proportion to the devotion of its adherents; and therefore neither Islam nor any other religion will have much influence on the course of history unless it can show the ordinary man that it meets his personal needs in his life from day to day.

Human nature appears to have changed not at all in its essentials through all the centuries of recorded history; but within the last hundred years there have been cataclysmic changes in the world in which men have to live. Because of this, even though the basic needs of men remain the same, the form of these needs has changed; and therefore fresh efforts—both in thinking and in living—are required to show men how the old religious values are relevant to their needs in the form in which they now experience these needs. Before anything is said about the values, then, we must look again at this contemporary world.

In the first place it is 'one world' in a superficial sense. It has been unified by modern technology. By the improvement of communications men and goods move all over the world much more easily than they moved from one province to another in the days of the 'Abbāsid caliphate. Technology has led to mass-producing industry, which is more profitable the more goods it produces, and which sees the whole world as its market. I have been into a grocer's shop in the old 'stone city' of Zanzibar and found not merely that the commodities he stocked were almost the same as those in my grocer's in Edinburgh, but that in not a few cases he stocked the same brands in the same tins or wrappings. The motor-car has become ubiquitous. The differences in clothing in cities all over the world is very slight, though here and there some item of clothing has become a symbol of a separate national identity. Yet besides the increase in the homogeneity of mankind in externals, there is also an increase in the causes of friction and the extent of the repercussions of any trouble. The world has become, as it were, a single large pool; if a stone is flung in at any point the ripples from it spread over the whole pool. In this 'one world' the ordinary man feels more insecure, because what happens ten thousand miles away may seriously affect his livelihood.

Secondly this is a world in which the adherents of the different religions are mingling with one another on a scale unprecedented in history except perhaps in the Roman empire in the first three centuries of our era. With the religions are to be reckoned the quasi-religions of humanism and Marxist communism. It is not impossible that as the years pass the world religions will become more and more relevant to world politics. There is a case—though this is not the place to advocate it—for thinking that, while the big and little waves of day-to-day politics are produced by many local causes, the ebb and flow of the great tides of political affairs are the consequence chiefly of religious movements. It may be, for example, that in East Africa, where there is something of an ideological vacuum, the real political struggle will be not between merely political ideas but between Islam and the religious element in Marxism. Be that as it may, it is already clear that the adherents of all the great religions will have to learn to rub shoulders with adherents of other religions; for the bare fact of meeting with those who hold another faith brings a slight loss in security. This is particularly so when (as was noted in the previous chapter) the old defences against other religions are proving out-of-date and ineffectual. All religions now require to reformulate their attitude to other religions in the light of the present situation, and in many cases there will have to be radical rethinking. This will not be a one-way traffic. Islam will have to rethink its attitudes in the ways already indicated, but it will also contribute, for example, to the rethinking by Christians of their attitude to other religions and even to their own faith. Contacts with Muslims will force them to take more seriously the belief they already possess in the oneness of God and to reformulate their doctrines of how this oneness or unicity is combined with a certain threefoldness.

Thirdly, the world in which we now live is one with a relatively new intellectual outlook. What might be called the first wave of scientific advance in Europe, from the fifteenth century to the early nineteenth, produced considerable changes in the general outlook. The new discoveries were chiefly in astronomy, physics and chemistry, and by the middle of the nineteenth century these had been incorporated into the general intellectual outlook. Subsequent discoveries in these fields have been numerous, but they have been of points of detail rather than matters of principle (with the exception of the theory of relativity), and thus, again with the same exception, they have not disturbed the intellectual outlook. The same is not true of the discoveries associated with Darwin and Freud. The theory of evolution brings about a radical reassessment of man's place in the universe. The Freudian concept of the unconscious and still more the Jungian concept of the collective unconscious have opened the way to new dimensions of thought. Associated with these at certain points have been new ideas in sociology, especially that of unconscious motivation. Men now realize that what appear to be objective statements may be affected in various ways by subjective interests. One of the chief criticisms of religion today is that it is the opiate of the people; the people are unaware that religion is adversely affecting their interests and promoting those of the ruling class, and in some cases the ruling class may also be acting unconsciously. In other ways also interests may have a farreaching influence on ideas. Ultimately it is the same conception which underlies the assertion that God is a projection—the second main criticism of religion in our day. All these strands combine to produce a radically new orientation in human thought.

Another way of stating this is to say that man is no longer accepting language naïvely at its face value, but realizes in a sophisticated way that the relation of language to reality is complex. He does not simply think about reality, but is often at the same time aware of himself thinking about reality and aware in part of the nature of the linguistic tools he uses. This outlook is reflected in the linguistic philosophy of today. Such philosophy, however, is concerned with only one aspect of the general outlook, and the universe of discourse in which Islamic values have to be expressed is thus much wider than that provided by linguistic philosophy. In the present context it will suffice to insist on the need for a sophisticated attitude to language and to religious ideas and to state and employ a simple distinction in our use of language, namely, between the factual or materialistic use of language and its suggestive or pregnant use.

The factual, materialistic use of language is that in which language refers to or indicates things (in the widest possible sense) and relations between things. This is the normal scientific way of using language. From this I am here distinguishing the suggestive or pregnant use which is characteristic of the poet. The poet's language can often be translated into prose, that is, into factual language, but in so doing much of what the poet is trying to convey to his audience is lost. Literary critics may go to great lengths to expound the message of such and such a poet; some of their expositions may come near giving the essence of his message, but on the whole we find that we understand the message better if we read the poems themselves. This is because the poet uses the sound and rhythm of words to communicate something beyond their factual meaning, and also their associations in the past history of the language. His words also may in the first place convey concrete imagery which is itself suggestive and pregnant. That is to say, the poet's images may at the same time be 'symbols' in the sense in which a symbol has the ability to evoke responses—notably emotional—in men beyond what may be expected from its purely factual content. I have elsewhere used the term 'dynamic image' for the symbol in this sense, but without specially noticing the pregnant character of the image.[2]

The distinction just made is complicated by the question of metaphor. It is difficult at the present day to use the term 'metaphorical' without bringing in the connotation that there is something unreal about what is metaphorically described. To avoid this connotation I have sometimes used the term 'diagrammatic',[3] since a good diagram truly and validly conveys the limited aspect of reality which it is designed to convey. In theology, as also in metaphysics and indeed also in sociology and psychology, many metaphors are used, because the topics dealt with are other than simple objects of sense and of daily life. In such cases metaphorical or diagrammatic language is the only way of referring to the realities discussed. Diagrammatic language is specially frequent in theology, but this alone does not mark theology off from the other disciplines. The distinguishing feature is rather that the diagrammatic language of theology and religion is closely connected with the dynamic images, that is, with language in its pregnant use. A somewhat similar account can be given of the word 'myth' as used in contemporary thought.

To speak of language as being used in a poetic way has, of course, also the connotation of unreality, and this is the chief reason for speaking of the suggestive or pregnant use of language. It must be insisted that what such language conveys to its audience beyond the factual, materialistic meaning, is true and valid, at least in the best instances. There is certainly bad poetry, and it is pointless to ask whether it is 'true but worthless' or in some sense 'false'. The words of would-be prophets and men of religion may likewise also be trivial or even misleading. This is perhaps not because they are absolutely false, but because they are expressive of an individual or merely sectional attitude, whereas true prophecy is valid for large numbers of men, and perhaps for all mankind. From this standpoint all the great religions are true and valid at least for a large segment of mankind. Apart from all other considerations the fact that they are great religions and have many adherents shows that they have ministered to human needs over a wide area. In this way the extent of their 'fruits' or good results shows that they must have a high degree of truth and validity. We proceed, then, on the assumption that this is so, and that there can be no genuinely human life without this pregnant use of language.

Apart from these linguistic points, on which there is not yet any wide agreement, the general position adopted in the following pages is that the agreed results of science are to be accepted within their proper sphere. This is the only possible attitude in a world dominated by science as ours is, unless indeed we want to shut ourselves off as 'isolationists' from the great number of contemporary intellectuals who control and advance scientific and technological development.

It will be noticed that what follows is largely an exposition of ideas common to the three Abrahamic religions, but care has been taken to deal with them always in their specifically Islamic dress.

2. Islamic doctrines of what transcends man

A. THE RECOGNITION OF MAN'S FINITUDE AND DEPENDENCE

In the liberal climate of opinion surrounding the occidental scholars of Islam in the late nineteenth and early twentieth centuries there could be little sympathy shown for Islamic beliefs in predestination and similar matters. That Muslims held such views was a fact that was simply accepted and usually also regretted; preference was expressed for the views of the Mu'tazilites on this question. There was no appreciation of the religious values implicit in the beliefs of Muslims. The common statement on this matter that 'what reaches you could not possibly have missed you, and what misses you could not possibly have reached you' was regarded as showing a failure to understand the freedom of the human will.

It is indeed strange that occidental man, despite the advance of the sciences, should be so little aware of his own finitude. What the sciences have been making ever clearer is that human life is subject to cosmic laws. The development of physics and chemistry up to the later nineteenth century showed that man's body was subject to the laws of matter, but it appeared to leave his soul or spirit largely independent of all such laws. Subsequent progress in psychology and sociology has extended scientific determinism or the rule of natural law to every aspect of man's inner life. Freud worked from the assumption that all mental phenomena, however apparently spontaneous or random, were produced according to laws of cause and effect; and further exploration of the unconscious by Freud and others has tended to confirm the assumption. Thus the general scientific view is that man is subject to physical, chemical, biological, psychological and sociological laws, or, in other words, that entities obeying these laws make the course of man's life what it is.

It is important at this point to distinguish between the assured results of science and the 'metascientific' speculations of scientists themselves and still more of amateurs of science. Two points may be made. Firstly, it is necessary to look at the epistemological status of the belief that laws of cause and effect are universally applicable. Strictly speaking, this is an assumption, though there are also strong grounds for holding it. It has not yet been applied to all phenomena, but there is no class of phenomena to which it can be shown to be inapplicable. Perhaps it should be regarded as a necessary 'regulative principle' in the Kantian sense or as a 'projection' with the psychologists. There is thus a slight chink in the coat-of-mail of determinism, but my personal view is that it is pointless to try to make use of this chink in order to maintain some view of human responsibility. What is needed is rather further investigation of the epistemological questions bound up with the belief that laws of cause and effect are universal in application. Is there any necessary contradiction between freedom and determinism? It at least is possible to feel free when in fact we are determined. Again, does the process of abstraction necessarily involved in science somehow vitiate the results when we try to make a grand synthesis? Or is there some point at which concrete reality refuses to yield further to scientific abstraction?

The second point is that there has so far been only an inadequate tie-up between the earlier results of science and the new conceptions of sociology and the Jungian conception of the collective unconscious. Here I can only state very briefly the results of my own 'metascientific' speculations as an amateur, though I am encouraged by the fact that others appear to be moving in a similar direction. The existence of the unconscious shows that there is a life in each of us that transcends our consciousness and is in some sense greater than our conscious life. The life that is in me is also in some sense one with the life that is in you and the life that is in my dog and in the rose growing outside. There is thus a certain unity of life. From this life in man's unconscious emerge the ideas and images which guide man in his efforts to attain higher forms of civilization. This life may also influence the direction of evolution—though this is a point which requires to be carefully formulated—since the fitness of a species to survive is connected with the life in it. Personally, then, I hold that there is a unity underlying all living things, and that, even if it does not transcend space-time, it transcends its actual manifestations in that it contains in itself the potentiality of something nobler than anything already living. I further hold that we may properly think of this unity as a single entity called Life (distinguished by a capital letter), and that we may learn more about its nature and laws (if that term applies) by studying societies and individuals.

This piece of 'metascientific' speculation is contrary to another view, which is just as much 'metascientific' speculation, namely, that human life is completely determined by forces which act according to *impersonal* laws. Yet, though something like this is widely held at the intellectual level, it has so far had little influence on the general outlook of occidental man (except perhaps in penal questions, and there the influence has come chiefly from psychology). The primary effect of science on modern man has been to inflate his pride and give him an exaggerated idea of what can be achieved by human intellectual efforts. Can he not send men into space? Will he not soon be able to control all the thoughts and emotions of the masses?

This is the context in which it is to be asserted that one of the abiding values of Islam is its insistence on a certain inevitability in events and on man's inability to control them, that is to say, its recognition that man is a dependent and finite being. This is thoroughly in accord with modern science; but in its place within Islamic thought this idea has religious overtones which are missing in the conception of scientific determinism. The affirmations of the Qur'ān on this point were made against the Meccan merchants' pride in their own achievements, and are thereby all the more relevant to the contemporary situation. The early Muslims did not, of course, deny the place of human thought and effort, and admitted a man's responsibility in some sense for his actions; but they realized that, however hard a man may work, both in planning and in executing, his efforts may be overridden by the forces operative in the world. This is still true despite all the modern techniques of control both of human beings and of inanimate things. Contrary to expectations there can appear in masses of ordinary men a great upsurge of feeling so powerful that it sweeps away all the dams carefully built by politicians and other would-be controllers. Something of this kind happened in the movement for African independence from about 1955 onwards. The wiser among the statesmen have always recognized the limitations to what they can achieve. In a sense the famous *Muqaddima* or *Introduction* to the History of Ibn-Khaldūn (d. 1406) is the product of his reflection on the overriding forces that shape the ends of human history, rough-hew them how the politicians may.

An emphasis on the inevitability of many events and on the limitations of human power is specially useful in the present age when man is tempted to exaggerate the extent of his power. Such exaggeration leads to frustration and anxiety, and should be countered by learning to accept the element of inevitability in human life, including the inevitability of death. For those who fully accept life with its inevitabilities anxiety disappears. It is like being in a large passenger aircraft; once it has taken off there is nothing the average passenger can do to promote a safe landing (though he might hinder it by criminal acts)—it is entirely in the hands of the pilot and those in the 'plane and on the ground who cooperate with him, and all the passenger can do is to trust them.

B. HUMAN VALUES IN THE UNIVERSE

Acceptance of the inevitabilities of human life cannot, of course, be the whole of religion. There is always the possibility that an individual may meet complete frustration and failure. It is even conceivable that a whole community may meet this fate. In such a case is there not a justification for struggling against adverse circumstances and not simply accepting them? In part this question is based on confused thinking, since, if a thing is inevitable, there is no use struggling against it. It is true that sometimes we cannot be absolutely certain that a thing is inevitable until we have struggled against it and failed. This question of when one is justified in struggling, however, is a secondary one; the primary one is whether the universe is such that complete failure and frustration is possible. The Islamic answer to this question is partly contained in the doctrines that there is no deity but God and that God is merciful and compassionate (*ar-Raḥmān ar-Raḥīm*).

The first of these doctrines may be taken as asserting in the context of modern thought that the totality of forces determining human life is a unity and not a multiplicity. The practical implication of this is that, even if some forces seem to be pushing men in one way and some in another, the two sets of forces are not to be thought of as in any way rivals. So far as the sciences dealing with inanimate nature are concerned, there is no great difficulty about this assertion of unity. There are also grounds—as has been indicated in the previous section—for thinking of Life as a unity, and indeed as a unity which somehow includes inanimate matter. The chief difficulty is perhaps in psychology. Apart from cases of the type of Dr Jekyll and Mr Hyde, there is a lack of unity in the lives of many people. Then, too, there is the multiplicity of the dynamic images to which a man responds—and this multiplicity is probably connected with the belief in many gods. It is clearly impossible to discuss these questions adequately here. Let it suffice to say that there seems to be no insuperable objection from the standpoint of modern science to the assertion that the forces determining human life and the course of the universe are in some important sense a unity; and that this is in accordance with the Islamic doctrine of 'no deity but God'. Occidental readers should remember at this point that the Islamic emphasis has not been on God's initiation of the cosmic process in the distant past, but on his continuing operation in every moment of our lives; and this is closer to scientific conceptions.

On the other hand, it must be admitted that Islam has traditionally belittled the relative autonomy of the various items that constitute spatio-temporal existence, and has tended to ascribe all process to the (apparently) direct action of God. This may go back to the lack of regularity in nature in the experience of the Arabian nomad. Modern science must certainly insist on the relative autonomy of natural processes, since this autonomy is the source of the laws which are studied in physics, chemistry and other sciences. Perhaps just because modern science is absorbed in its study of the elements of the universe and their laws, it is the more necessary nowadays to proclaim that 'there is no deity but God', while giving this doctrine a sense that is not incompatible with the existence of scientific laws.

The second doctrine—that God is merciful and compassionate—becomes relevant at this point. The admission that the universe is unitary need not imply that this one universe is a satisfying one. It might go on its way regardless of man and his interests. To say, however, that the central all-controlling principle of the universe is merciful and compassionate—in other words, loving—implies that the forces in the universe as a totality favour human life. Muslims have generally held that God's favour is in fact shown in success that is manifest and visible to all. Some writers argued that the military conquests of the Muslims in the century after Muḥammad's death were a sign of God's favour and confirmed his prophethood.[4] He himself certainly saw the achievements of his own lifetime as a mark that God was with him. From a military point of view the battle of Uḥud may be said to have been drawn, but in the hearts of the Muslims their failure to win a clear victory raised serious doubts whether God was continuing to support them. Even the celebrated verse (4.157/156) usually interpreted as a denial of the crucifixion of Jesus is primarily a denial that the Jews were victorious over Jesus; and the underlying thought is that it is impossible that God should allow a prophet sent by him to fail.

Islam admits, of course, that it is possible for human beings to fail. They may be said to be in the state of *ḍalāl* or being astray. There may even be talk of God's abandonment of them (*khidhlān*). Some theologians attempted to show that God's abandonment of men followed on sinful actions of their own; but there were always cases where this could not be shown in detail. For a time some Mu'tazilites tried to argue that God acted according to his foreknowledge of the sins they would commit; but this did not take them very far. The main body of Sunnites realistically clung to the view that there was an element of inscrutability in God's dealings with men. This means that a good Muslim will never give up the belief that whatever happens to him and his friends is in accordance with God's mercy. He may not be able to understand how this is so, but he accepts the situation and does not doubt God's mercy. This brings us, however, to the next point.

C. THE TRANSCENDENT VALUE OF HUMAN LIFE

One of the fundamental assertions of Islam is that there is a Day of Judgment at the end of the world and that on this day God will judge men and assign them to Paradise (Heaven) or Hell. In the Qur'ān the basis of God's judgment is sometimes the individual's conduct and sometimes the attitude of his whole community, especially their attitude towards God and his messengers. In later Islam the emphasis came to be more and more on the community; and the most widespread view was that the man who had remained a good Muslim (by not falling into *shirk* or polytheism) would always eventually enter Paradise, though he would also be punished for his sins and this punishment might be by a temporary sojourn in Hell. Such a view makes allowance for a judgment on both individual conduct and community attitude, though regarding the latter as fundamental and the former as subordinate to it. The traditional expression of these doctrines is in pictorial or 'diagrammatic' form, but the truths so expressed are still valid and relevant in the modern scientific world.

The first point to be made is that the dimension of transcendence exists. It is difficult, of course, to find adequate language for this. To say that this is 'something transcending space and time' is mainly negative. A more positive account would be to say that it is the dimension or sphere of 'ultimate value'; and this might be further defined as the value which we intuit to be unimpaired by spatio-temporal transience, that is, the transience of the events in which the value is manifested. The sphere of transcendence might further be described as 'where God is', since God is transcendent. These assertions raise many problems which cannot be adequately discussed here.

The most serious question is whether this is not all a projection. Are we perhaps saying that there is a Being transcending space-time simply because of our inner experience of something in us transcending our ego-consciousness? In this way we would be asserting that what is really in us is in some way external to us. Personally I am inclined to accept the view that there is an element of projection, but I would then add that in matters such as those being considered projection is not necessarily an invalid process but may sometimes be valid.[5] In considering this question about the sphere of transcendence we may begin from the position that there is in each human being a life which transcends his ego-consciousness and his individual life, and that this life in the individual is included in a single Life transcending individuals but not transcending space-time. This life in a man appears to aim at 'ultimate value'. If this is so, is it not conceivable that the life in a man is not purely immanent? May it not be the case that a man's spatio-temporal activity is linked with 'ultimate value' which transcends space-time? Islam affirms that there is such a link. Science based on observation is not in a position either to affirm or deny, and yet the question seems to be a proper question. It is an existential question, however. In a sense it is answered by experiment, but the experiment is the commitment to a certain course of action. In other words, the question can only be answered in living.

A subordinate question is how a man's conduct and attitudes in his spatio-temporal life affect his 'eternal destiny', that is, his link with 'ultimate value' and the dimension of transcendence. Traditionally this has been done by the conception of Heaven and Hell, which make use of language which is not merely 'diagrammatic' but also 'pregnant' in the sense given above. Fun has sometimes been poked in Europe at the Islamic idea of the dark-eyed houris who are allotted to the faithful in Heaven; but it is worth remarking that if one is to use 'pregnant' language, it ought to be capable of conveying what it is intended to convey. This Islamic language certainly conveys to simple-minded people—and even to the more sophisticated—that Heaven is supremely desirable; and this can hardly be said to be done by the Christian image of harp-playing, which the simple-minded man thinks would be incredibly boring. It should perhaps be added that the wives of the Muslims also go to Heaven, according to the Qur'ān (43.70), but to ask about their relation to the houris would be to press 'diagrammatic' language beyond the point it is intended to convey, and this is an illegitimate procedure.

The houris, however, are far from expressing the whole of the Islamic conception of Heaven, nor is it circumscribed by the idea of a garden (or paradise). A prominent place is given to being where God is and to seeing him. The vision of God is spoken of in the Qur'ān (75.22 f.), and has been accepted as an article of faith by the main body of Sunnites. To modern man the conception of the vision of God has probably less appeal than it had previously, since he tends to think of the universe as constituted not by relatively stable objects but by process. He might then be more inclined to emphasize as an important part of the vision of God a vision of God's purposes in the spatio-temporal world. This would involve regarding Life as an agent of God or demiurge, and the spatio-temporal purposes of Life as grounded in transcendent Being. The individual man who had consciously tried to realize these purposes in his life might be conceived as reaching a point of vision at which he could at least glimpse the transcendent purpose underlying all process and could have some appreciation of his own share in the realization of that purpose. Once the 'pregnant' character of eschatological language is understood, it will be found that traditional Islamic views are close to what is suggested here. To be in Hell will correspondingly be to be cut off from God and from such a vision, while having some awareness of the possibility of these things.

D. MAN'S KNOWLEDGE OF THE TRANSCENDENT

Another Islamic assertion that is important in the present age is that men have knowledge of the sphere of transcendence. This knowledge is technically known as 'revelation' (*waḥy*, *tanzīl*), and the persons through whom it is mediated are called 'messengers' or 'prophets' (*rusul*, *anbiyā'*). Such knowledge comes in the first place to these special persons, but from them it may be transmitted to all believers. The more naïve view was that the ordinary man simply heard and understood; but a sophisticated writer like al-Ghazālī held that the process was more complex and that those who advanced in religion eventually 'entered into' or came to appreciate the revealed truth in an experience that was at least analogous to that of the messenger. This last point is worth keeping in mind in that it shows that within Islam there were different ways of formulating and elaborating the doctrine of revelation. Our primary concern, however, is with the doctrine that human communities may receive by revelation some knowledge of the sphere of the transcendent, and that this knowledge is mediated by persons whom we shall normally call prophets.

Modern man finds some difficulties in the traditional Islamic account of revelation. By the phrase 'traditional account' one is here referring to the rational formulations of the doctrine by the theologians, which are indeed an interpretation of the words of the Qur'ān, but not identical with these. Thus it should be possible to criticize the 'traditional account' without denying the fundamental truth of the Qur'ānic words. In particular a modern man would be inclined to say that there was an element of projection in the ordinary Muslim's conception of revelation. This may well be so, but, as was argued in a previous discussion of projection, the existence of projection need not imply that the conception is invalid. Instead of criticizing the 'traditional account' in detail, however, it will be more satisfactory to show how the essential points on which the Qur'ān insists can be included in a modern account of revelation.

A modern view of revelation would regard it as, in the first place, the work of the collective unconscious. It is not the product of the prophet's consciousness, nor even of his personal unconscious. The fact that the revelation has an appeal for vast numbers of people shows that it must come from an area of life which is common to large numbers of people. The words 'in the first place' are to be emphasized, since according to views outlined above what comes from the collective unconscious comes from the Life that has been postulated and then ultimately from the transcendent Being in which that Life is grounded. Thus the assertion that revelation is from God is maintained, but some attention is paid to the secondary or intermediate causes. This view of revelation admits some similarities between it and works of man's creative imagination such as drama and poetry. Both the dramatist and the poet, in so far as they have a wide appeal, are producing material from the collective unconscious. A good drama gives the spectators in a concrete form, stimulating the imagination, something which touches and makes them partly aware of unconscious elements in themselves. An outstanding example here is the Oedipus story, especially as it was used in the *Oedipus Rex* of Sophocles, for it dealt with unconscious contents which the researches of Freud and others have shown to be almost universal in the human race.

The difference between the work of the prophet and that of the dramatist is that the prophet presents in essentials a complete world view, whereas the dramatist at least ostensibly is concerned with a relatively limited aspect of human life. This distinction is not obliterated by the fact that a dramatist may present a relatively complete world view, for, when the dramatist does so, he is always assuming the truth of something like the current world view. The prophet, on the other hand, is much more explicit in his presentation of a world view. He may largely accept contemporary ethics, history and cosmology, but he also goes beyond the latter into the sphere of the transcendent—into what might be called 'metacosmology'.[6] The Islamic assertions being considered in this section of this chapter are metacosmological in this sense. They might also be called 'dogmatic', but that word is unpopular at the present time. The emphasis here on the completeness of the prophet's world view should not be taken to mean that each prophet stands entirely by himself and has not been influenced by others. Those prophets of the Israelites whose writings are in the Old Testament supplemented one another and were conscious of doing this. Even Muḥammad was aware that the conceptions of God and revelation had been held by Jews and Christians before him.

This account of prophetic revelation does not rule out the possibility that the prophet may allow purely personal considerations to weigh with him at some point, and the Qur'ān indeed allows that Satan may alter the revelation in accordance with the prophet's (personal) desire (22.52/51). It is assumed in Islam that all such Satanic alterations in the Qur'ān have been discovered and corrected (notably the so-called 'satanic verses' about the idols); but this assumption cannot be proved from the Qur'ān itself.

It would therefore seem to be a possibility that some verses still found in the Qur'ān have come not from the collective unconscious but, for example, from some element of pride in Muḥammad's personal unconscious. On the other hand, it is virtually impossible to prove that this possibility has been realized, since one can usually find an interpretation of the words or verses which is in harmony with the general interpretation of the corpus of prophetic revelation; and it should normally be taken as a principle of exegesis that the corpus of revelation is to be interpreted as a harmonious whole.

It is worth while to look a little more closely at the relation of the corpus of revelation to the continuing life of the religious community. In the case of Islam the primary revelation is the Qur'ān, and this alone will be considered here, though there is a sense in which the Traditions are secondary revelation. Because a corpus of revelation like the Qur'ān is largely in 'pregnant' language, there are many possibilities of interpretation; and thus the conceptions in the revealed scriptures may be adapted to the needs of the adherents of the religion in many different situations. In course of time, however, it is found that different sections of the community begin to move in different directions, and this is reflected in differing interpretations of the scripture. In most communities there are centripetal forces which encourage attempts to overcome such differences. This has been especially so in Sunnite Islam. To remove differences which are linked with different interpretations it is necessary for the parties to reach an agreement to accept certain interpretations and to reject others. In this way there is a passage from the pregnant language of the revealed scriptures to the more rational language of theological doctrine, and this may be described as giving increased definition to the revelation.

In Sunnite Islam two main trends may be distinguished in this work of the theologians. One trend may be described as fundamentalist, and is represented chiefly by the Ḥanbalites. This group recognized the pregnant character of Qur'ānic language in its conception of *balkafiyya*, an abstract term derived from the phrase *bi-lā kayf*, 'without (specifying) how', and perhaps to be translated by 'amodality'. They therefore refused to go beyond the words of scripture in their formulation of dogma, though by this procedure they cut themselves off from contemporary science and philosophy, or forced men to keep these in a separate compartment from religious dogma. The other trend was the intellectual or rationalistic, and its best-known representatives are the Ash'arites. From small beginnings they more and more fully reduced the pregnant language of the Qur'ān to something more factual and materialistic, and it was thus possible for them to link up theological doctrine with a form of contemporary philosophy (mainly Aristotelian cosmology with some Neoplatonic elements). When this trend had reached its zenith, Islam possessed a world view containing both religious and scientific elements and possessing a high degree of intellectual harmony. After Islam came into closer contact with Europe in the nineteenth century it made the unfortunate discovery that its science and philosophy were out-of-date. It also became clear that the rationally formulated doctrines of the Ash'arites had less power to evoke responses in ordinary men than the pregnant language of the Qur'ān itself. Many Muslims have turned back to the Qur'ān and to doctrinal formulations of a Ḥanbalite type.

It is against this background that one must look at a possible objection. Someone may admit that the Qur'ān gave the men of the seventh century knowledge of the sphere of the transcendent in a form suited to contemporary needs, but may assert that what was suited to seventh-century needs is not well suited to twentieth-century needs. In particular it may be said that the Qur'ān itself presupposes an out-of-date cosmology. In reply to such an objection the first point to be made is that the religious affirmations of the Qur'ān (which were later expressed in theological doctrines and dogmas) are primarily about the relations of man to the transcendent source of his being and are therefore not affected by detailed differences between the cosmology of the seventh century and that of today. What may be admitted, however, is that today we stand at the beginning of a new process of giving a rational, intellectual formulation to the essentials of the religious message contained in the Qur'ān. This will not be a mere restatement of the doctrines of, say, the tenth century in any automatic or mechanical fashion; but it will go hand in hand with a fresh estimate of the relative importance of different points of Qur'ānic teaching. The relative emphasis on the various matters will thus be something new, though the words of the Qur'ān itself will still be in the centre. The supposed objector may now retort that this is merely a plan, and that he has seen little evidence that it is being carried out. There is perhaps more evidence than he allows, but it is certainly the task of those Muslims who believe that their faith can be stated in modern terms to work for the realization of such a programme.

3. Islamic values in individual and communal life

The previous section has dealt with man's relation to the transcendent source of his being, and it is in such matters that the affirmations of Islam and other religions are most important for modern man. Yet in the relationships of men to one another there are points on which the religions have important affirmations to make. The view adopted in this book is that ethics has a certain autonomy or, in other words, that ethical principles cannot be deduced from religious dogma. This has the further implication that the Islamic ethical ideal is not very different from the ethical ideals of the other religions. It is indeed obvious that virtues such as honesty or respect for property, truthfulness, respect for life, respect for marriage, endurance of hardship, and concern for the weak and needy, must have a place in any great civilization. Yet it is worth considering how such ideals in their specifically Islamic dress are relevant to the modern world.

A. THE TRANSCENDENTAL ORIGIN OF ETHICAL NORMS

A point that is well made by Islam is that ethical norms are beyond man's will, even beyond the collective will of all mankind. The ethical norms of Islam are constituted by the Sharī'a or 'revealed law' which is contained in the Qur'ān and Traditions. Because their source is thus in revelation they cannot be altered by man, and this is important in ages when powerful rulers, without explicitly asserting that might is right, try to get measures and even principles accepted that favour the strong against the weak. This is a state of affairs that is by no means impossible in some of the new states of Africa, and it remains to be seen whether Islam will be strong enough to oppose this trend effectively.

The modern intellectual is chiefly conscious of the relation of ethical norms and ideals to man's nature, especially his nature as a social being. It is roughly true to say that the ethical norms and ideals which are generally accepted are those which have been shown in practice to produce a satisfactory society. It is unfortunately the case that in the ethical field there can be no experimenting with alternative principles in order to discover which works better in practice. Yet occasionally historical conditions occur which approximate to the experimental situation. Thus Russia may be said to have experimented with freedom in sexual relations in the period after 1917, but the experiment resulted in such a vast social problem in the shape of children without proper families that the rulers gave their fullest support to the ideal of monogamy. This would seem to show that human nature is such that monogamy works better in practice than any other system so far devised. The acceptance of monogamy as an ideal by many Muslims nowadays might be regarded as further evidence in the same direction. All this goes to confirm the modern intellectual's view that ethical norms and ideals are rooted in human nature.

Ultimately there need be no contradiction between this view and the Islamic affirmation that the source of ethical norms is transcendent, but superficially there might seem to be some incompatibility. The important point to insist on is that to say that ethical norms and ideals are rooted in human nature must not be understood as giving man any choice in respect of them. The norms and ideals are rooted in human nature simply because they are norms and ideals for men. In this it is also implied that there is a certain fixity or definiteness in human nature which places it beyond man's conscious control. In religious terms human nature is 'created'; and men have simply to accept this fact that they are created, that they are what they are, and that they cannot make themselves essentially different from what they are. There is a place for conscious thought and perhaps experiment in the details, but in essentials man cannot change himself. In the light of what has been said above, we can proceed to think of this fixity as coming from the Life that is in man, and beyond that from the transcendental source of being. There is nothing here to contradict the assertion that ethical norms and ideals are rooted in human nature; but the Islamic affirmations imply not merely a certain fixity in human nature but also that a complete account of that nature must include its relation to the transcendent.

Islam, however, in accordance with the view of the nomadic Arabs that innovation is always bad, has tended to exaggerate the fixity of ethical norms. In particular Muslims have tended to attach universal validity to practices that were primarily appropriate to the cultural context of the heartlands of the Islamic world (Arabia, Iraq, Syria and Egypt). This is a point that may be troublesome in the present period of adjustment to the contemporary world situation. Is the permission for a man to have four wives an essential part of Islam? Is the Islamic system of inheritance appropriate in all cultures? It would seem that it must be made possible for certain changes to take place; and this implies a distinction between basic and fundamental principles and the particular applications of these in varying circumstances. It will be difficult to state these principles in such a way as to win general approval, but if Muslims tackle these problems piecemeal, something will eventually be achieved. There is already in Islam in the conception of abrogation a recognition of the need for some changes to meet changed circumstances; this is usually referred to under the heading *nāsikh wa-mansūkh*, 'abrogating and abrogated'. Certain verses of the Qur'ān were held to abrogate certain other verses prescribing acts for which the need had passed. Thus the command, appropriate at Mecca, to spend a large part of the night in devotions was abrogated at Medina where the Muslims, especially Muḥammad himself, had responsible work to do during the day; but the abrogated verses were allowed to remain in the Qur'ān (*sūra* 73. 1–4; abrogated in v. 20).

B. MUḤAMMAD AS EXEMPLAR

So much moral abuse has been hurled at Muḥammad in Europe over many centuries that it is difficult, if not impossible, for any occidental to think of him as a moral exemplar. Yet even in the fact that Islam makes Muḥammad its great exemplar there may be something of value for the world as a whole. There are certainly questions here sufficiently important to justify a brief glance at them.

The first point to notice is that Islam has given its ethical ideal a concrete embodiment in Muḥammad. This has been done by the general picture of him in his *Sīra* or biography, but still more by the highlighting of particular traits of character in the vast collections of Traditions about him. Occidental scholarship has been much concerned with the question of the historicity of the Traditions, and has tended to conclude that a large proportion of them are unauthentic. At the same time it has failed to consider adequately the prior question of the relevance of the criterion of historicity to the treating of Muḥammad as a moral exemplar. This point may be put more concretely. It must be allowed that

Muḥammad is the paradigmatic embodiment *par excellence* of the Islamic vision in a human life in so far as we consider the relation of the human to the divine. Is it then unjustifiable to attach to him stories showing his freedom from annoyance when a baby wet him or his concern for a bitch with puppies?[7] Some Muslim must have put these stories into circulation, and, if challenged, would presumably have said, 'This is the way in which one would have expected Muḥammad to have acted.' Is not such an argument used to defend some of the stories about Jesus in the Gospels?—'Even if Jesus did not act in this way (say, towards the woman taken in adultery), this is how his followers must have thought he would have acted.'

To attribute to a specific person one's ideals or expectations in respect of conduct is really a form of projection. The view has been put forward in this book that projection is a justifiable epistemological procedure in theological matters. May it not be also in the ethical sphere? Certainly it is widely agreed that in setting an ethical ideal before men abstract language is far less effective than concrete examples. It may be objected that concrete examples are more effective when one knows that they are stories from real life and not inventions; and there is some truth in this. Yet a novel about purely imaginary people may convey truth; this is because the novelist has based the story on his vision of the heights and depths of human life. One may even go on to say that, despite the fact that characters are 'imaginary', the novel as a whole is not unreal, because it is based on and expresses the reality of the novelist's experience, and in this way has an element of historicity. In the same way the fact that certain Muslims circulated stories about Muḥammad, whether Muḥammad acted in the way described or not, has this element of historicity and 'reality' that these Muslims believed that the acts described were in accordance with the basic ethical ideal of Islam. In the case of stories about Jesus in the Gospels there is, in the acceptance of these by later Christians, an element of historicity that is usually neglected.

A slightly different topic may be mentioned at this point, namely, the fivefold scheme of ethical categories commonly used by Islam. There are many advantages in this in contrast to the twofold scheme used by occidental moralists. The latter is the division of acts into right and wrong, and sometimes also into good and bad, and virtuous and vicious; the latter pairs are often assumed to be identical with the first. In Islam, on the other hand, it is normal to classify acts according to five categories: obligatory or commanded; approved or commended; neutral; disapproved; prohibited. Such a scheme is closer to the phenomena of the moral life, even in Europe and America, than the rigid right-wrong disjunction which so often monopolizes the discussions of moral philosophers.

C. THE ACCEPTANCE OF SEXUALITY

The favourite occidental critique of Islam has been its laxity in sexual matters, and it is perhaps paradoxical to speak of its attitude to sex as a value. On the other hand, psychology teaches that men often project their own faults on to other people, and criticize other men for what is really a more serious fault in themselves; and something of this kind may have happened here. Whatever the rights and wrongs of these criticisms of the past, the time has surely come to admit that the occident has not the final word in this sphere, but rather is bewildered by contemporary sexual problems. The world is passing through a period of rapid change in this as in other respects, and so it is important to look at the possible contributions of the various cultures. In contrast to Europe and America the Islamic world is characterized by its frank acceptance of sexuality and its belief that the exercise of sexuality should be a normal part of the life of every human being. For better or for worse Christianity has had as its exemplar a celibate man; and it has also been deeply influenced by the contempt for the body found in the Greek dualistic conception of man. The result has been confusion both in thought and conduct, ending in the present state of affairs where to find due forms for the expression of sexuality is one of the great problems for occidental culture.

The Islamic acceptance of sexuality is perhaps most noticeable in some of the conceptions of Paradise. Some form of sexual delight is included in eternal bliss, and there is nothing of the Greek conception which makes Paradise a place where man has escaped from his body and is thankful for the escape. The permission for a man to have four wives and slave concubines in addition could be taken as evidence pointing in a similar direction, but its interpretation is more complex. The permission is to be understood against the background of a society where collective ways of life were being replaced by a measure of individualism. Associated with the collective ways of life was a matrilineal system of kinship whereby a woman seems to have been valued chiefly for ability to bear children for the group, while the precise paternity of any child was relatively unimportant. This system offered possibilities of abuse, especially when the ratio of males to females was upset, as happened to the Muslims at Medina after the battle of Uḥud in 625. The chief danger was that the males who dominated a kinship group (though the kinship was reckoned through the females) would force most of the women under their care to live as prostitutes, more or less, so as to increase their own wealth and perhaps also power. The injunction to Muslim men to marry two, three or four wives was designed to give Muslim women a more satisfactory marital status, by ensuring that they had marital relations with only one man at a time. By the further provision that women whose husbands died or who were divorced were to wait three months and ten days before remarrying, the paternity of any child was made certain; and this doubtless gave some satisfaction to the growing individualism of the men. In the rules for inheritance also, women were treated as individuals and not part of a collectivity.

The net result of this Islamic system of marriage relationships is to be looked for in the condition of Islamic society. Over many centuries, and often through great political upheavals, it has been remarkably stable; and to this stability the system of marriage and the family must have contributed. One might argue that with a different system for marriage and the family some of the weaknesses of Islamic society might have been avoided; but unless worked out in considerable detail this argument carries little weight. The broadly satisfactory nature of society is impressive, and cannot have been built on wholly unsatisfactory families. Another piece of evidence tending to confirm what has just been asserted is the apparent absence of any serious problem of sexuality in Islamic spiritual and mystical writers. One can be certain that, if sexuality had been a spiritual problem for them (as it is for so many occidentals at the present time) they would not have hesitated to write about it. A brief survey of spiritual writings, however, suggests that gluttony and, more generally, the proper use of material things, were much more serious problems for these men. So we come back to the comparative success of Islam in its handling of sexuality, and the possibility that the occident has something to learn here.

D. THE ACCEPTANCE (IN PART) OF HUMAN IMPERFECTION

In the Abrahamic religions, and perhaps also in others, there is a danger of excessive moralism—of an exaggeration of the place in human life of avoiding what is absolutely wrong in social relations. This is linked with the idea of a judgment with eternal consequences, since good acts are eternally rewarded and bad acts eternally punished. This belief is found in both Christianity and Islam. In the latter it is most prominent in Muḥammad's Meccan period, but much later, in 1095, we find al-Ghazālī saying that his motive in leaving Baghdad was fear of Hell. There is also another strain in most religions, which holds that sins do not matter overmuch and do not necessarily disturb man's right relation to the powers that control his destiny. There is a deep religious conviction underlying this, a conviction which finds a Christian expression in the idea of 'justification by faith', which asserts that a man enters into a right relation to God merely by believing in God's love and mercy, though it is expected that this right relationship will normally express itself in good works. In practice, however, at least in some varieties of Christianity, the element of moralism has crept back again, and emphasis is placed on man's efforts to avoid sins and obey the commandments of God.

Islam obtains a balance between moralism and laxity by its doctrine that all Muslims will eventually go to Heaven or Paradise, but that those who have sinned will first suffer some punishment. In this way men are given a basic confidence in life, but are also made to feel that sins matter. The one sin which brings a man to Hell is *shirk*, 'associating', that is, treating as divine certain beings other than God. This sin makes a man cease to be a Muslim or believer, and he then forfeits the privileges of believers. So long as he remains a member of the Islamic community, however, he is assured of Paradise in the end, whatever he does; but his sins matter to the extent that he will have to undergo a punishment commensurate with them, unless God remits this. As mentioned at an earlier point in this study, the punishment may be in this world, or it may be for a limited period in Hell. The final attainment of Paradise is sometimes linked with the intercession of Muḥammad with God on behalf of members of his community.

With these doctrines there is by implication an acceptance of the mystery of human imperfection, for it is assumed that man is normally incapable of living a perfect life. This also is something which mankind in this present age requires to appreciate. Islam speaks of some men being in a state of *ḍalāl*, 'being astray', or *khidhlān*, 'abandonment', in contrast to others who have received *hudā*, 'guidance'. Attempts were sometimes made by theologians to justify God's differential treatment of men, but on the whole these attempts were unsatisfactory and instead his inscrutability was acknowledged. Similarly attempts to show that he was obliged to do what is best for men had to be given up, and, while his goodness and mercy was maintained, it was agreed that these were above human conceptions of good and bad. It was even allowed by some theologians that God might impose on men duties *fawq aṭ-ṭāqa*, 'beyond their power to perform'—yet another way of admitting that man is incapable of achieving perfection. Thus Islam has in various ways a deep realization of the fundamental imperfection in human nature, which leads most men into greater or lesser sins. This realization of imperfection is complementary to the realization that man is a created being, and it requires to be kept constantly in mind in this age when mankind is in grave danger of succumbing to pride in the vastness of its achievements in the control of nature and of other human beings.

E. MEMBERSHIP OF AN INTEGRATED COMMUNITY

Undoubtedly one of the outstanding successes of Islam has been its creation of a great community of many races, in which there has been a genuine sense of brotherhood. The brotherhood of different races may never have been perfect, for there are occasional traces of race consciousness in medieval writings; but there was certainly never any of the racial animosity which is found in occidental countries in the present century. The dislocation of the traditional social structure as the result of the impact of Europe in recent times has weakened the sense of brotherhood in various ways. Perhaps the chief of these has been the break-up of the community of scholars in Islam, and its replacement in part by occidentally educated intellectuals who tend to live within their separate nationalisms. Arabic-speaking Muslims, for example, generally show little interest in their fellow Muslims of East Africa or Indonesia. The pressures of world politics, however, are likely to bring them more together in the future, and it is not impossible that there will be a renewal of the sense of worldwide brotherhood in Islam at both the personal and the political level.

The basis of this integration of communal life and the sense of brotherhood is the deeply rooted belief of Muslims that their community or *umma* is a charismatic one, in virtue of its being divinely founded and having a divinely given law—or in more modern terms, in virtue of its being a bearer of values. When the religious community is thought of in this way, it takes over some of the functions formerly performed by a nomadic Arab tribe for its members—it gives them an identity (as members) of which they are intensely proud, and with this a confidence to meet the various trials of life. Often the spread of Islam has been largely due to the intense belief of Muslims in themselves and in their religious community. On the whole this is an excellent thing, even if it sometimes blinds Muslims to the merits of members of other religious communities.

In the occident there are traces of a similar attitude towards the national or religious community, especially among Catholic Christians, though on the whole individualism is stronger in occidentals. Yet belief in a charismatic community is of the utmost importance for the whole world at the present time. No one is going to make costly sacrifices just for the totality of mankind. Men are looking for a charismatic or value-bearing community, capable of embracing all mankind, and only a community with a religious basis fulfils this requirement. It is difficult to imagine Islam superseding or somehow incorporating into itself the other great world religions. Yet mankind needs a religious community which is charismatic, and Islam more than any other great religion has realized in actual life the idea of the charismatic community.

With these thoughts we complete our answer to the question 'What is Islam?'. We have looked long at certain aspects of its past, for the past has done much to constitute the present. Finally we have tried to isolate some of its chief values in the present, for the religion of Islam is the soul of a living community of great power which has important contributions to make to the world of the future. It is my hope that this book will enable occidentals to understand better this living and powerful community which is both their partner and their rival, and also that it will show Muslims how a sympathetic occidental sees them and will thus bring them to appreciate another facet of their own identity.

Epilogue (1979)

In the twelve years or so since this book was written Islam has not remained static. Even at the statistical level the number of Muslims in the world has reached about 600 millions, chiefly through natural increase. Muslims have continued to respond to the challenges arising from 'the impact of Europe and America' (pp. 142 ff.) in all its various aspects—economic, political, technological, intellectual and social; and some of the trends beginning to be visible twelve years ago have now more definite lineaments. In these years also I have personally become more familiar with the contemporary Islamic scene, largely through contacts with individuals; but further opportunity for reflection does not suggest that the presentation of Islam in the book requires to be modified. Since there was a unity of conception in that presentation, it would be inadvisable to make a number of small adjustments; and so it has seemed preferable to bring together in an epilogue some updating observations.

The resurgence of Islam referred to once or twice (pp. 148, 168) may be said to have continued. It is a complex phenomenon and means something different in different groups of people. In most cases, however, it can be described as a reaffirmation of Islamic identity by those who feel threatened by the impact of the West and by the consequent internal changes. Sometimes, especially in young people, this reaffirmation may arise primarily from genuine religious belief. Sometimes it may be no more than a 'secular patriotic attachment to Islam as a cultural community' (p. 147). Frequently, however, there is also an explicit demand for a return to a true Islam, to the Islam of Muḥammad himself and his four rightly-guided successors. Among those prominent in making this demand in various countries are many of the *ulema* or members of the religious institution; and these have normally had the support of the masses of the people. As a class the *ulema* are aware that their power and influence have declined since the early nineteenth century through the appearance, first in penal matters and commerce, then in other spheres, of legal codes which were not based on the Sharī'a and which therefore required lawyers with a non-traditional training. A return to something like the Sharī'a as traditionally understood would certainly be in the interests of the *ulema*; but it is vigorously resisted by most of the statesmen responsible for efficient government of a modern type. The statesmen are aware that, though 'Back to the Sharī'a' is a fine-sounding war-cry, it is essentially negative—a protest against 'innovations' like giving interest on loans, not a positive programme enabling Islamic states to function as efficient modern states. It is not a serious attempt to deal with the contemporary problems of Islamic society, but a device to allay the anxieties of those disturbed by the rapid changes of recent years. These anxieties are certainly a problem, but it is unfortunate, perhaps disastrous, if in dealing with this problem the solution of other problems is made more difficult.

In the reaffirmation of Islamic identity by the conservative *ulema* and their vast following among the masses three ideas appear to be especially emphasized: the finality of Islam, its self-sufficiency, and its superiority to Western thought. In a sense these ideas are giving precision to the isolationist, inflationary and fixational attitudes described in Chapter 11, but they are worthy of being considered also as ideas.

The idea that Islam is the final religion, which will eventually become the religion of all mankind, unless there is some global disaster (due to man's unbelief), is linked with the idea that Muḥammad is 'the seal of the prophets' (cf. pp. 89, 205). For the first hearers this probably meant no more than that the revelation to Muḥammad confirmed revelations to previous prophets such as Moses and Jesus; but today almost all Muslims understand it to mean that Muḥammad is 'the last of the prophets'. This interpretation implies that the Islamic revelation contains all the guidance necessary for the whole of mankind from now to the end of time. This guidance, of course, is not all explicit; but the essential principles are already present in the Qur'ān and the example of Muḥammad, and from these principles suitably qualified scholars can work out the correct rules to follow in whatever novel circumstances or situations have arisen or may arise in the future. It may be noted that the belief that Muḥammad is the final prophet is the basis of the recent decision of the government of Pakistan that the Aḥmadiyya sect is outside the Islamic community because of their belief that their founder Mirza Ghulam Ahmad was a prophet (cf. p. 153). The Qur'ānic teaching that Judaism and Christianity were in essentials the same as Islam is set aside by the dogma that later Jews and Christians have deviated from the original purity of their message (pp. 183 f.). Thus on Islam and Islam alone, it is held, rests the salvation of mankind.

Secondly, the belief that Islam is self-sufficient, and owes nothing to Judaism or Christianity or any previous system of thought, is based on the doctrine that in essentials all truth is contained in the Qur'ān together with the 'wisdom' given to Muḥammad and expressed in the Traditions. Since the Qur'ān and this 'wisdom' came to Muḥammad directly from God (according to Muslim belief), and since God cannot be subject to human influences, it follows that Islam owes nothing to earlier religions and philosophies and is entirely self-sufficient. No attention is paid to the fact that the human beings to whom the Qur'ān was first addressed had been influenced by Jewish and Christian ideas, and that the Qur'ān, as an 'Arabic Qur'ān', was adapted to the mentality of the Arabs to whom it was addressed.

The implications of this idea of self-sufficiency are well expressed in a story about the Arab conquest of Alexandria in the seventh century (told by Edward Gibbon, among others, in his *Decline and Fall*). The story is probably apocryphal, but this does not affect its symbolic value. After entering the city and finding a great library of Greek books, the general is said to have written to the Caliph 'Umar I asking for instructions about the disposal of the books. He got the reply: 'If these writings of the Greeks agree with the Book of God, they are superfluous, and need not be preserved; if they disagree, they are pernicious, and ought to be destroyed.' In accordance with the attitude expressed here, conservative Muslim scholars are still reluctant to study anything non-Islamic; and this is an aspect of isolationism.

Thirdly, Islam is held to be superior to all forms of Western thought. Though in Muslim eyes Judaism and Christianity were originally true, later generations have somehow corrupted the scriptures and deviated from that truth (as has been frequently mentioned). Thus nowadays these religions are inferior to Islam. For conservative Muslims the moral and spiritual crisis they see in Western society is a not unexpected outcome of this deviation from the truth.

Evidence of the strength of these three ideas may be found, for example, in the recommendations of the First World Conference on Muslim Education, held at Mecca in April 1977 (as reported in *New Horizon*, London, April 16–29, 1977). Though there were some liberal-minded Muslims at the conference, the recommendations reflect the outlook of the conservative majority. They call for a research institute to develop plans and programmes for a genuinely Islamic education 'based on the Islamic outlook, and that derives its principles from Islamic sources'. There is no mention of the need for Muslims to study Western subjects such as philosophy. Instead there is a demand that the (Western) empirical sciences 'should be reformulated in such a manner that will attach them to the Islamic faith and deepen the religious sentiments of students'. There are other similar phrases in the recommendations and in the prospectus for a series of books planned as a follow-up to the conference. Those who drew up these documents appear to believe that all sciences, natural and social, can be reformulated on the basis of 'Islamic concepts', and also that this will remove the tension between religion and science. To the occidental observer it is obvious that such persons have no understanding of modern science and philosophy. They fail to realize the extent to which they are isolating themselves from the modern world and making themselves incapable of entering the universe of discourse of Western scholars and thinkers.

Fortunately there is also in Islam a small but increasingly influential number of liberal-minded men, who combine their Islamic faith with an awareness of contemporary thought. Some of these have the courage to make their voices heard even in conferences dominated by conservatives. They also participate and make helpful contributions in the movement for 'dialogue' between Muslims and Christians which has grown rapidly in the last twelve years. 'Dialogue' in one form or another has become so fashionable that there is a periodical devoted to it called *Islamochristiana* (published in Rome). One of the more notable occasions was the Seminar of Islamo–Christian Dialogue held in Tripoli, Libya, in February 1976. Though the primary participants were limited to teams of a dozen or so chosen by the Libyan government and the Vatican, there were also about five hundred observers from over fifty different countries – all as guests of the Libyan government. An important part of the significance of this Seminar was that the initiative had come from Muslims, and that Christians were in a sense on the defensive. It was also significant that, although Colonel Qadhafi would be reckoned religiously conservative, he was prepared in this way to move away from isolation.

The desire to abandon isolationism would also seem to have

motivated the organizers of the International Congress of Seerat in Pakistan in March 1976. 'Seerat' (Arabic *sīra*) is the life of the Prophet, and the congress was above all an opportunity for Muslims to take counsel together on the contemporary challenges to their religion and religious community. Several of the leading religious figures in Islam were present, such as the Imam of the Ka'ba in Mecca and the Shaykh of al-Azhar university in Cairo. Although the Congress was thus entirely concerned with Islamic religious questions, Christians were invited to give two out of seven plenary addresses, and others were present as guests and had the opportunity to speak more briefly. These happenings may be small straws in the wind, yet they show that the liberalizing tendency in Islam is gaining strength. If Islam is to make its full potential contribution to the welfare of mankind as a whole, that can only come about through a further growth of this liberalizing tendency.

Finally, mention must be made of a demographic factor which has come to be of major importance only during the last twelve years, namely, the immigration of Muslims into Western countries, especially into Western Europe. The European Muslims referred to above (p. 142) are the three and a half millions in Eastern Europe who have been there for centuries. In 1977, however, it was reckoned that there were also about five million Muslims in Western Europe, such as Algerians in France, Turks in West Germany and elsewhere, Pakistanis in Great Britain, and Indonesians and others in the Netherlands. Some of these had from the first intended to be permanent residents; others had come as temporary labourers, but had shown a tendency to remain. This Muslim presence in Western Europe may be part of the stimulus to 'dialogue'. It is also a great challenge to the Muslims themselves. How in this non-Islamic environment are they to practise a religion which is also a whole way of life? Can they, for example, maintain traditional Islamic ideas of the relation between the sexes and of family life, if their daughters go to co-educational schools? Are they to acquiesce in their religion becoming largely a private matter for them, or are they to insist on cultural practices which isolate them from their non-Muslim fellow-citizens in a kind of ghetto? Some of the positions of leadership in the associations of Muslim immigrants seem to be in the hands of conservatives, who want to maintain their culture even at the cost of some isolation, but there is a chance that many of the younger generation will challenge such leadership. In Canada and the United States the problems of Muslim immigrants seem to be less acute, perhaps because in these countries there are also other immigrant communities.

While for the masses the resurgence of Islam is essentially a reaffirmation of Islamic identity, for the conservative *ulema* it is also a chance to recover the influence in the community which they have lost during the last century. Because of their deficient information about the modern world this attempt, even if for a time successful, is bound to end in failure. A modern state cannot be run on the basis of mediaeval ideas. The masses, and the *ulema* themselves, need the services and conveniences of modern technology in the framework of a modern state. What exactly will happen will depend on the extent to which the liberalizing trend produces capable individuals to take over the positions of leadership in this struggle between liberals and conservatives. As for the outcome of the struggle, God knows best.

Notes

Full details of the authorities cited are given in the Bibliography, p. 246.

Introduction

1 Thomas Carlyle, *Heroes and Hero-worship*, 1890 edition, p. 52.
2 For example, Daniel, *Islam and the West*.
3 Dean Humphrey Prideaux in *The True Nature of Imposture fully displayed in the Life of Mahomet*.
4 Carlyle, *op. cit.*, p. 40; the following quotation is from p. 41.
5 This phrase is used of Durkheim by Morris Ginsberg, p. 231.
6 Further justification for some of the statements here about religion will be found in my books, *Islam and the Integration of Society* and *Truth in the Religions*.
7 Carlyle, *op. cit.*, p. 52.

Chapter 1

1 Cf. Watt (vi), p. 14.
2 *Ibid.*, pp. 126–7.
3 Durkheim, pp. 416 f.
4 A justification for these assertions will be found in my books, *Muhammad at Mecca*, and *Islam and the Integration of Society*.
5 Cf. Bell (ii), p. 12.
6 Andrae, p. 63, asserted that 'he arrived at this daring conception of the unbounded majesty and omnipotence of God without being influenced, as far as I can see, either by Judaism or by Christianity'.
7 Cf. Watt (ii), p. 55.
8 Bell (ii), pp. 30–4.
9 Carlyle, *op. cit.*, pp. 42, 43, 50.
10 Arberry, p. xii.

Chapter 2

1 Al-Bukhārī, *Qadar*, 1b; cf. Wensinck, 54; Watt (i), p. 18.
2 Lyall, *Mufaḍḍalīyāt*, no. cxx. 34; quoted by Ringgren, p. 68.
3 For this war of Basūs, as it is called, cf. Nicholson, pp. 55–61.
4 Quoted from *Aghānī* by Wellhausen, p. 222.
5 'Amr b. Qamī'a, *Dīwān*, vi. 7–10; quoted from Ringgren, p. 64.
6 Cf. Wellhausen, p. 29. From comparative religion we learn that the mother-goddess has an aspect of inexorability. Cf. Suttie, p. 104, etc. One might speculate that the nomads, through their poets, have

emphasized this aspect of inexorability in an agricultural, providing mother-goddess.

7 Cf. Nicholson, p. 105.

8 Wellhausen, pp. 59 f.; cf. Ibn-Hishām, p. 53.

9 Cf. Watt (ii), p. 24; the modifications suggested by Ringgren, pp. 59 f., are taken account of in the rest of this paragraph.

10 Nicholson, p. 100.

11 Abū-Tammām, *Hamāsa*, no. 168, lines 12 f., p. 248; cf. 'Amr ibn-Qamī'a (ap. Ringgren, p. 63), 'my hurrying away a day earlier will not help me to outstrip death'.

12 Suwayd ibn-'Āmir, quoted by Ringgren, p. 53.

13 Al-Ḥārith ibn-Ḥilliza, *Mu'allaqa*, lines 25 f.; tr. Lyall (iii), p. 22 (modified); quoted by Ringgren, p. 53.

14 Cf. Watt (i), pp. 19–29; Ringgren, pp. 125 f.

15 The word is now held to be of Iranian origin, though Arabized before Muḥammad's time (Jeffery (i), s.v.). Despite a remark of Jeffery, the word is not frequent in pre-Islamic poetry. The form *ruziqat* in Labīd, *Mu'allaqa*, line 4 seems to mean 'was rained upon'.

16 On 3.156/150; the word is *ḍaraba.*

17 Al-Bukhārī, *Adab*, 101, etc. for references to other forms of the Tradition, see EI(2), art. 'Dahr'; also Watt (i), pp. 31, n. 23.

18 Cf. Goldziher (iii), pp. 153 f.

19 Notably Richard Bell; cf. Bell (ii), pp. 115–19.

20 Cf. az-Zamakhsharī on 16.15.

21 Cf. Barthold, 'Der Koran und das Meer'.

22 Cf. Watt (iii), pp. 313.

23 For the story cf. Watt (ii), pp. 102 f. The words rendered 'high-soaring ones', *al-gharānīq al-'ūlā*, probably refer to high-flying Numidian cranes, but the idea seems to be that because of their high flight they were suitable as intercessors with God (cf. Lane, s.v.).

24 Cf. 2.34/32, 36/34; the same change from Iblīs to *ash-Shayṭān* is found in 7.11/10–25/24 and 20.115/114 ff. and this makes 'the demon' seem a more likely translation than 'Satan'.

25 Cf. Jeffery, s.v.

26 Cf. Wellhausen, pp. 148–59.

27 *Shayṭān* appears to be an Arabic word meaning serpent, but later to have been applied to the Evil One (or in the plural to evil spirits) and to have acquired Jewish and Christian connotations. The Qur'ānic conception (like that of angels) appears to contain a fusion of Arabian and Judaeo-Christian elements.

Chapter 3

1 Cf. *Genesis* 46. 26: 'All the souls that came with Jacob into Egypt . . . were threescore and six'.

2 The verses are 3.169/163 f.; 40.11,45/48 f. (Gardet, 86). For the topic see Wensinck, pp. 117–19.
3 Cf. Bell (ii), p. 156.
4 Cf. Wensinck, pp. 232 f.; The word occurs in 36.66 and 37.23 f., but in neither place does it necessarily mean this type of ordeal.
5 Andrae, 87 f., notes that the description of Paradise, including the maidens, is anticipated in Syrian Christianity.
6 For a further justification of these statements cf. Watt (ii), pp. 69–71, and (iv), pp. 31–3.
7 Cf. 16.104/106–107/109; 10.95; etc.
8 Al-Ḥārith ibn-Ḥilliza, *Mu'allaqa*, 25 f., translated by Lyall (iii), p. 22 (modified).
9. Cf. 13.26; 28.60; 57.20/19; 87.16 f.

Chapter 4

1 Cf. Goldziher (i), i. 17–20; cf. idem (ii), i. 44 f.
2 Cf. Ibn-Hishām, p. 293, line 5 (from Goldziher).
3 *Genesis* 27. 33; *Numbers* 22–4.
4 Cf. Schacht (ii), p. 7 f.
5 Blachère, trad. i. 91 f. places this passage a little later but has references to 'judgment' (*dīn*) in 107.1 (p. 19) and 95.7 (p. 23).
6 Horovitz, pp. 47–51.
7 Similarly in 89.5/6–13/14 'Ād, Thamūd and Pharaoh are destroyed because they are proud and act corruptly.
8 Cf. 69.4–12, destruction of Thamūd, 'Ād, Pharaoh and the Subverted Cities; they denied the Last Day, or 'committed error' and 'rebelled against the Messenger'. Also 25.35/37–40/42; people of Moses, people of Noah, 'Ād, Thamūd, men of ar-Rass were destroyed because they rejected the message.
9 There are also groups of stories about messengers or of references to them in other *sūras*; e.g. 19, 21, 23, 27, 37, 38. These have different points, however, and in each group the stories vary.
10 Cf. 44.19/18–33/32; 26.52–68.
11 For example 53.36/7, 'pages of Moses'; 37.114–22; 28.43; 41.42/45, Book leading to differences; 2.51/48–53/50, Book and Furqān. Cf. Bell (ii), pp. 134–6.
12 A translation will be found in Watt (iii), pp. 221–5.
13 Rudi Paret, art. 'Umma' in EI(1); cf. Buhl, p. 277; Bell (i), ii. 492 n. 4. The remarks in Watt (iii), pp. 240 f., require some modification in the light of what is said here.
14 Horovitz, p. 52, and Jeffery (i), s.v., also indicate other possible sources of foreign influence; but the importance of the Arabic root should not be minimized.
15 Cf. 16.63/65; 29.18/17; 40.5.
16 Jeffery (ii), p. 32; cf. Watt (vii), pp. 360 f.

Chapter 5

1 Cf. 5.77/81, which might refer to former generations of Jews and Christians, but speaks of them as *qawm qad ḍallū min qabl.*
2 Cf. 19.37/38; 43.65; 23.52/54 ff. Jesus is certainly sent to the Children of Israel; 43.59; 5.72/76; etc.
3 The word *qawm* is used for 'community'.
4 Farrukh, p. 128, etc.; cf. Watt (iii), p. 143.
5 Cf. Faris and Glidden, conclusion; and EI(2), art. 'Ḥanīf'.
6 Cf. 2.140/134.
7 Cf. Watt (iii), pp. 205–7.

Chapter 6

1 The account is based on my books on Muḥammad, Watt (ii, iii, iv); detailed references are therefore omitted.

Chapter 7

1 Cf. Schacht (i).
2 Cf. Watt (viii).
3 Cf. Watt (v), pp. 126–39.

Chapter 8

1 I have attempted a fuller treatment of it in *Islam and the Integration of Society* and *Truth in the Religions.*

Chapter 9

1 Cf. Watt (vii), pp. 361–4.
2 Goldziher (iv), esp. pp. 1–64.
3 Cf. Watt (ix), pp. 23–34.
4 Cf. Patton, p. 58.
5 Dawson, p. 107.
6 Ibn-al-Bawwāb; tr. de Slane, ii, pp. 284 f.
7 Cf. Goldziher (ii), ii. 386; also Massignon (ii).
8 Cf. Watt (x).

Chapter 10

1 It is worth noting that the Festival of Nabi Musa (near Jerusalem) takes place about the same time as the Christian Easter and thus follows the solar calendar.
2 Cf. Archer.
3 Cf. Watt (vi), pp. 91–5; also Macbeath, pp. 291–327, etc.
4 Cf. Watt (ii), p. 82, (iii), pp. 267-70.
5 Cf. art. 'Zinā' in EI(1) by J. Schacht; also Ibn-Khallikān, iv, pp. 255–8.
6 Cf. Massignon (i), pp. 145–53.

Chapter 11

1 Watt (vi), esp. pp. 51–5.
2 Cf. Watt (xi), esp. §1; also (v), pp. 260–7, and pp. 171, 183 above.
3 Cf. Graf, ii, pp. 153 f., 233–49.
4 Tr. by Kenneth Cragg, London n.d. (1960?).
5 Cf. the list (including some more polemical works) given by Nolin, pp. 243 f.

Chapter 12

1 Cf. Watt (xii).
2 Cf. Watt (xi), esp. §1 pp. 110–17.
3 Ibid., pp. 127 f.
4 For example ʻAlī aṭ-Ṭabarī, *Kitāb ad-Dīn wa-d-Dawla.*
5 See further Watt (vi), index, s.v. ʻprojectionʼ.
6 See Watt (vi), pp. 105–10.
7 Watt (iii), p. 323.

Bibliography

ABŪ-TAMMĀM. *Hamāsa*, ed. G. S. Freytag, Bonn 1828–47.

ANDRAE, TOR. *Mohammed the Man and his Faith*, second ed. New York, 1955

ARBERRY, A. J. *The Koran Interpreted*, 'Introduction', Oxford University Press, (World's Classics), 1964 (Original edition: London, Allen & Unwin, 1955)

ARCHER, J. C. *Mystical Elements in Mohammed*, New Haven, 1924

BARTHOLD, W. W. 'Der Koran und das Meer', *Zeitschrift der deutschen morgenländischen Gesellschaft*, 83 (1929), 37–43

BELL, RICHARD. (I) *Translation of the Qur'ān*, Edinburgh, T. and T. Clark, 1937–39

(II) *Introduction to the Qur'ān*, Edinburgh University Press, 1953

BLACHÈRE, RÉGIS. *Le Coran*, Paris 1949

BUHL, FRANTS. *Das Leben Muhammeds*, Leipzig, 1930

AL-BUKHĀRĪ. *Ṣaḥīḥ*, ed. Krehl and Juynboll, Leiden, 1862–1908

CARLYLE, THOMAS. 'The Hero as Prophet', *On Heroes and Hero-worship*, London (stereotype edition), 1890, pp. 39–71

DANIEL, NORMAN. *Islam and the West, the Making of an Image*, Edinburgh University Press, 1960

DAWSON, CHRISTOPHER. *The Making of Europe*, London, Sheed and Ward, 1932

DURKHEIM, EMILE. *Elementary Forms of the Religious Life*, London, Allen and Unwin, 1915

Encyclopaedia of Islam, 1st edn., Leiden, 1913–42; 2nd edn., Leiden, Brill, and London, Luzac, 1954, continuing

FARIS, N.A. and GLIDDEN, H.W. 'The Development of the Meaning of the Koranic Ḥanīf', *Journal of the Palestine Oriental Society*, 19 (1939), 1–13

FARRUKH, O. A. *Das Bild des Frühislam in der arabischen Dichtung*, Leipzig, 1937

GARDET, LOUIS. *De Islam*, Roermund, 1964

GINSBERG, MORRIS. *On the Diversity of Morals*, London, Heinemann, 1958

GOLDZIHER, IGNAZ. (I) *Abhandlungen zur arabischen Philologie*, Leiden, 1896–9

(II) *Muhammedanische Studien*, Halle, 1888–90

(III) *Die Ẓâhiriten*, Leipzig, 1884

(IV) *Die Richtungen der islamischen Koranauslegung*, Leiden, 1920

GRAF, GEORG. *Geschichte der christlichen arabischen Literatur*, vol. ii, Rome, 1947

HOROVITZ, JOSEF. *Koranische Untersuchungen*, Berlin, 1926

HUSSEIN, KAMEL. *City of Wrong*, tr. Kenneth Cragg, London, Bles (n.d., ? 1960)

IBN-AL-ATHĪR, *Kāmil*, Cairo, 1348 (1929), etc.

IBN-HISHĀM, *Sīra*, ed. Wüstenfeld, Göttingen, 1858–60

IBN-KHALLIKĀN, tr. by Baron McGuckin de Slane, Paris, 1843–71

JEFFERY, ARTHUR. (I) *Foreign Vocabulary of the Qur'ān*, Baroda, 1938

(II) *Materials for the History of the Text of the Qur'ān*, Leiden, 1937

LYALL, CHARLES JAMES, ed. (I) *Mufaḍḍalīyāt*, Oxford University Press, 1918

(II) *Mu'allaqāt*, Calcutta, 1891–4

(III) *Ancient Arabic Poetry*, London, Williams and Norgate, 1930

MACBEATH, A. *Experiments in Living*, London, Macmillan, 1952

MASSIGNON, LOUIS. (I) *Essai sur les origines du lexique technique de la mystique musulmane*, 2nd edn., Paris 1954

(II) 'Le "Hadith al-ruqya" musulman, première version arabe du "Pater" ', *Revue de l'histoire des religions*, 133 (1941), 57–62; reprinted in *Scripta Minora*, Beirut, 1963, vol. i, pp. 92–6

MU'ALLAQĀT. See Lyall (II).

NICHOLSON, REYNOLD A. *Literary History of the Arabs*, London, T. Fisher Unwin, 1907

NOLIN, KENNETH. 'Truth: Christian-Muslim', *The Muslim World*, 55 (1965), 237–45

PATTON, W.M. *Aḥmed ibn Ḥanbal and the Miḥna*, Leiden, 1897

PRIDEAUX, HUMPHREY. *The True nature of Imposture fully displayed in the Life of Mahomet*, London, 1697

RINGGREN, HELMER. *Studies in Arabian Fatalism*, Uppsala, 1955

SCHACHT, JOSEPH. (I) *The Origins of Muhammadan Jurisprudence*, Oxford University Press, 1950

(II) *An Introduction to Islamic Law*, Oxford University Press, 1964

SUTTIE, IAN D. *The Origins of Love and Hate*, Harmondsworth, Penguin Books, 1960

'ALĪ AṬ-ṬABARĪ, *Kitāb ad-Dīn wa-d-Dawla*, ed. Mingana, Manchester, 1922

WATT, W. MONTGOMERY. (I) *Free Will and Predestination in Early Islam*, London, Luzac, 1948

(II) *Muhammad at Mecca*, Oxford University Press, 1953

(III) *Muhammad at Medina*, Oxford University Press, 1956

(IV) *Muhammad Prophet and Statesman*, Oxford University Press, 1961

(V) *Islam and the Integration of Society*, London, Routledge, 1961

(VI) *Truth in the Religions*, Edinburgh University Press, 1963
(VII) 'Two interesting Christian-Arabic Usages', *Journal of Semitic Studies*, 2 (1957), 360–5
(VIII) 'The Decline of the Almohads . . .', *History of Religions*, 4 (1964), 23–29
(IX) 'The Materials used by Ibn Isḥāq', in *Historians of the Middle East*, ed. B. Lewis and P. M. Holt, Oxford University Press, 1962, pp. 23–34
(X) 'Created in his Image', *Transactions of the Glasgow University Oriental Society*, 18 (1961), 38–49
(XI) 'The Early Development of the Muslim Attitude to the Bible', *Transactions of the Glasgow University Oriental Society*, 16 (1957), 50–62
(XII) 'The Political Relevance of Islam in East Africa', *International Affairs*, 42 (1966), 35–44

WELLHAUSEN, JULIUS. *Reste arabischen Heidentums*, 2nd edn., Leipzig, 1926

WENSINCK, ARENT JAN. *The Muslim Creed*, Cambridge University Press, 1932

AZ-ZAMAKHSHARĪ. *Kashshāf*, Bulaq, 1318–19 (1900–01)

Abbreviation

EI: *Encyclopaedia of Islam*

Index of Topics

Index of Proper Names and Arabic Words

(The Arabic article, al-, ash-, etc., is neglected in the alphabetical order)